WHAT IS HISTORY REALLY ABOUT?
A HISTORIAN REFLECTS ON
THEORY AND PRACTICE

Two other volumes currently available by Peter Burke from EER:

Secret History and Historical Consciousness.
From the Renaissance to Romanticism.

"Burke characteristically mixes seemingly opposing approaches – historical truth and fiction, oral and print sources, elite and folk tastes, mega- and micro history, symbolic and literal readings, private and public knowledge – to reveal their coexistence and interaction. He revisits received views with neglected or newly discovered sources and aperçus, not to overturn but to enlighten and amplify. Burke makes arcane topics of daunting complexity relevant and readily accessible in remarkable feats of translation from past to present. Familiarity with an extraordinary range of multilingual sources is couched in graceful and self-effacing prose, consistently instructive and entertaining."
– **David Lowenthal**, *Times Literary Supplement*, 7 April 2017.

"*Secret History* is a timely collection in which Peter's Burke's many strengths as a cultural historian are all on display: intellectual independence, restless curiosity, a willingness to seek out questions others have ignored, and a mastery of the early modern period and its legacy. It's also beautifully written. Anyone interested in intellectual history or the making of modern Europe will find this a deeply rewarding read."
– **James Shapiro**, Professor of English at Columbia University, and author of *1606: Shakespeare and the Year of Lear.*

"His erudition is enviable, and his lucid, effortless presentation exemplary."
– **John Pemble**, joint winner of the *Wolfson Prize* for *The Mediterranean Passion.*

Identity, Culture & Communications in the Early Modern World.
AND ALSO FORTHCOMING...
Myths, Memories and The Representation of Identities.

WHAT IS HISTORY REALLY ABOUT? A HISTORIAN REFLECTS ON THEORY AND PRACTICE

Peter Burke
*Emeritus Professor of Cultural History,
Emmanuel College, Cambridge.*

EER
Edward Everett Root, Publishers, Brighton, 2018.

EER

Edward Everett Root Publishers, Co. Ltd.,
30 New Road, Brighton, Sussex, BN1 1BN, England.
www.eerpublishing.com

edwardeverettroot@yahoo.co.uk

What Is History Really About? A Historian Reflects on Theory and Practice
Peter Burke

First published in England in 2018.
© Peter Burke 2018.
This edition © Edward Everett Root Publishers 2018.

ISBN: 978-1-912224-12-8 Paperback.
ISBN: 978-1-912224-11-1 Hardcover.
ISBN: 978-1-912224-74-6 Ebook.

Peter Burke has asserted his right to be identified as the author of this Work in accordance with the Copyright, Designs and Patents Act 1988 as the owner of this Work.

All rights reserved. No part of this publication may be reproduced, stored in a retrieval system or transmitted in any form or by any means, electronic, mechanical, photocopying, recording or otherwise, without the prior permission of the copyright owner.

Cover designed by Pageset Limited, High Wycombe, Buckinghamshire.
Printed and bound in England by Lightning Source UK, Milton Keynes.

Contents

Acknowledgements vii
Introduction ix

A. *Theory*
1. The Art of Re-Interpretation: Michel de Certeau 1
2. Performing History: the Importance of Occasions 13
3. Translating Knowledge: Translating Cultures 43
4. The History and Theory of Reception 55

B. *Practice*
5. Images as Evidence in Seventeenth-Century Europe 75
6. Reflections on the Cultural History of Time 101
7. The Cultural History of Intellectual Practices: an
    overview 117
8. The Invention of Micro-history 139
9. A Short History of Distance 155
10. Detachment and Involvement in Historical Writing 175
11. Exemplarity and Anti-Exemplarity in Early Modern
    Europe 185
12. Historical Discourse in Renaissance Italy 201

Acknowledgements

The author and the publishers gratefully acknowledge the permission of those publications in which the original chapters previously appeared in books or in journals, as follows: 'The Art of Re-Interpretation: Michel de Certeau', *Theoria* 100 (2002), 27–37; 'Performing History: the Importance of Occasions', *Rethinking History* 9, no.1 (2005), 35–52; 'The History and Theory of Reception', in Howell A. Lloyd (ed.) *The Reception of Bodin*, Leiden, Brill, 2013, 21–38; 'Images as Evidence in Seventeenth-Century Europe', *Journal of the History of Ideas* 64 (2003) 273–96; 'Reflections on the Cultural History of Time', *Viator* 35 (2004), 1–10; 'The Cultural History of Intellectual Practices: an overview', in J. Fernández Sebastián (ed.) *Political Concepts and Time*, Santander, Cantabria UP, 2011, 103–27; A Short History of Distance', in Mark S. Phillips, Barbara Caine and Julia A. Thomas (eds.) *Rethinking Historical Distance*, Basingstoke: Palgrave Macmillan, 2013, 21–33; 'Remembering and Reconstructing the Past in Brazil', in Marjet Derks et al. (eds.) *The Lieux de Mémoire of Europe beyond Europe*, Nijmegen, Vantilt, 2015, 133–9; L'età barocca', in Storia Moderna, Rome, Donzelli, 1998, 229–48; and [in Japanese translation], in *Shooting History: Linguistic turn, Cultural History, Public History and National History*, ed. Michihiro Okamoto, Tokyo, 2015 [not published in English, until included in the present book].

INTRODUCTION

This volume brings together some of my essays on the theory and the practice of history. In the first part, the main theme is the way in which some concepts borrowed from social and cultural theory may encourage historians to ask new questions about the past or help them to answer old ones. From the beginning of my career as a historian I have been interested in what historians can learn from neighbouring disciplines, beginning with sociology and anthropology.

Teaching at the University of Sussex when it was committed to interdisciplinarity encouraged this interest in the neighbours, and a short book that I published in 1980, *Sociology and History*, was commissioned by a colleague at Sussex, Tom Bottomore. Soon afterwards, an anthropologist friend, Alan Macfarlane, remarked that the book might equally well have been entitled 'Anthropology and History'. In its second edition, *Sociology and History* was transformed into *History and Social Theory* (1992), including a wider range of disciplines, not only anthropology but also economics, politics and geography.

If I were writing the essays in this book today, I would replace 'social theory' by 'cultural theory', as the first four essays collected here suggest. Each of these focuses on a key concept – 're-employment', 'performance', 'cultural translation' and 'creative reception' – and the uses of that concept in thinking and writing about cultural history.

The first essay is concerned with the work of the French Jesuit

Michel de Certeau, a remarkable polymath who is perhaps best known for his book *L'invention du quotidien* (1980, translated as *The Practice of Everyday Life*, 1984), in which he launched the concept of the 're-employment' of ideas or techniques for purposes other than the original one. This first essay, assisted by my own education at a Jesuit school in the 1950s, attempts to show that Certeau practised re-employment as well as writing about it and that his cultural theory drew on the theology of Jerome and Augustine.

The second essay takes up the notion of 'performance', a concept that has itself played an increasingly important role in the work of historians and their colleagues in neighbouring disciplines in the last two or three decades, although the pioneering studies in this domain – by Kenneth Burke (no relation) and Erving Goffman – go back to the 1940s and 1950s. Goffman was a sociologist but Burke was essentially a literary critic, although, like Certeau, he may be described as a polymath. For cultural historians, their colleagues in literature and philosophy play an important role, alongside the sociologists and anthropologists.

The third essay explores the idea of 'cultural translation' and the advantages of this concept over rivals such as 'cultural transfer' and 'cultural exchange' for understanding the ways in which individuals from one culture not only 'borrow' or 'appropriate' ideas, practices and objects from other cultures but also adapt or transform them, consciously or unconsciously, to make them fit for purpose in their new home. The same basic idea is regarded from another angle in the fourth essay, on the concept of 'reception', viewed not as passive but on the contrary, as an active and creative process. Once again we see how colleagues in departments of literature, in this case two Germans, Hans-Robert Jauss and Wolfgang Iser, have inspired work by cultural historians who are concerned with the reception of ideas and images no less than the reception of texts.

Certeau, like his compatriot Pierre Bourdieu, was a theorist who helped inspire the so-called 'practice turn' in sociology, history (including the history of science) and other disciplines. I had both of them very much in mind when writing the essays on histori-

Introduction

cal practice collected in the second part of this book. I have long been interested in the history of historiography, indeed I must confess that my dissertation for a D.Phil. at Oxford was entitled 'New Trends in Historical Writing, 1500-1700'. Unsurprisingly, it was never completed, partly because of an extension of my interests from the work of major historians such as Francesco Guicciardini, Paolo Sarpi and Jacob Burckhardt to what might be called a more general 'sense of the past' that was expressed in images as well as in texts.

Today, many historians are aware of the value of images as historical sources, as evidence to be used alongside the documents found in archives. At Cambridge in the 1980s, I used to teach a course for first-year students on this topic, alongside the late Bob Scribner, who made a perceptive use of sixteenth-century graphic art in his work on the German Reformation. Out of this course came the idea for a book, *Eyewitnessing* (2001) which attempted to provide guidelines for a critical use of images. The essay reprinted here, by contrast, traces part of the long history of the employment of images as evidence, focussing on European antiquaries of the sixteenth and seventeenth centuries, the intellectual ancestors of the professionals now known as 'archaeologists'.

In the 1990s, Yale University Press invited me to write a cultural history of time, a response to the famous *Brief History of Time* by Stephen Hawking (1992). The hope of the Press was that the book could be published in the year 2000 and so linked to interest in the millennium. I must confess once again to a mission not accomplished, although I have been reading and thinking about the topic for more than two decades since the original invitation. The sixth essay reprinted in this volume offers a kind of introduction to the unwritten book, comparing three approaches to the social or cultural history of time. The first approach is concerned with the view of time dominant in a given society, the second privileges contrasts between the views of time of different groups in the same society, and the third emphasizes different notions of time employed by the same individuals and underlying their practices in different domains of everyday life. The notion of 'practice', implicit in the sixth essay, becomes explicit in the seventh, concerned with an approach to history midway between intellectual history and cultural history, an approach that I call 'the cultural history of intellectual practices'.

Micro-history is a historical practice that became prominent in the 1970s, with the near-simultaneous publication of two books that immediately became famous, *Montaillou* (1975), a study of a medieval French village by Emmanuel Le Roy Ladurie, and *Il formaggio e i vermi* ('The Cheese and the Worms', 1976) by Carlo Ginzburg, reconstructing the world view of a miller from North-East Italy on the basis of his interrogations by the Inquisition. As in the case of images as evidence, I became interested in the earlier history of this practice, which is discussed in the eighth essay.

Most of our intellectual practices are conscious, but the attitudes underlying them are not. The feeling of proximity to the past (by some people, in some periods) or of distance from the past (by other people, on other occasions) is not something that we can choose or control. These feelings have rarely been explored, with the exception of two important studies, both written, as it happens, by friends of mine, *The Past is a Foreign Country* (1985) by David Lowenthal and *On Historical Distance* (2013) by Mark Phillips. Mark organized a conference on the topic and invited me to give a paper that turned into the ninth essay reprinted here. It is complemented by the tenth essay, which following the lead of Norbert Elias – another cultural theorist from whom I have learned much – combines a discussion of distance or detachment with its opposite, personal involvement with the past.

The last two essays in this volume are concerned with historical thought and writing in early modern Europe. The essay on exemplarity, once again the fruit of an invitation to a conference, is a dialogue with the work of two historians I much admire, the German Reinhart Koselleck and the Frenchman François Hartog, both of them concerned with the history of the idea that history is 'philosophy teaching by example'. The final essay, on 'discourse', deals not, as readers might expect, with the concept of discourse in the writings of the cultural theorist Michel Foucault, but with the use of invented speeches in Renaissance historians such as Guicciardini. I hope that these essays, together with some contribu-

Introduction

tions not reprinted here, go some way towards compensating for paths not taken, missions not accomplished and promises not yet fulfilled.[1]

---

[1] The Popularity of Ancient Historians 1450-1700', *History and Theory* 5 (1966), 135-52; 'The Idea of Decline from Bruni to Gibbon', *Daedalus* (1976), 137-52; 'The Politics of Reformation History: Burnet and Brandt', in *Clio's Mirror,* ed. Alasdair Duke and Coen Tamse (De Walburg Pers, 1985), 73-85; 'European Views of World History from Giovio to Voltaire', *History of European Ideas* 6 (1985), 237-51; 'Structural History in the 16th and 17th Centuries', *Storia della Storiografia* 10 (1986), 71-6; 'Ranke the Reactionary', *Syracuse Scholar* 9 (1988), 25-30; 'Introduction', to J. Burckhardt, *The Civilization of the Renaissance in Italy* (new edition, Harmondsworth, Penguin, 1990), 1-15; 'Some Seventeenth-Century Anatomists of Revolution', *Storia della Storiografia* 22 (1992), 23-35; 'The Myth of 1453: Notes and Reflections', *Querdenken: Dissens und Toleranz im Wandel der Geschichte: Festschrift Hans Guggisberg,* ed. Michael Erbe et al., Mannheim 1996, 23-30; 'The Rhetoric and Anti-Rhetoric of History in the Early Seventeenth Century', in *Anamorphosen der Rhetorik: Die Wahrheitspiel der Renaissance,* ed. Gerhard Schröder et al, Munich, Fink, 1997, 71-9; 'The Sense of Anachronism from Petrarch to Poussin', in *Time in the Medieval World,* ed. Chris Humphrey and W. M. Ormrod, York, York Medieval Press, 2001, 157-73; 'Sarpi storico', in Corrado Pin (ed.) *Ripensando Paolo Sarpi:* Atti del Convegno Internazionale di Studi nel 450 anniversario, Venice, Ateneo Veneto, 2006, 103-9; 'The New History of the Enlightenment: an Essay in the Social History of Social History', in Roberta Bivins and John V. Pickstone (eds.) *Medicine, Madness and Social History: Essays in Honour of Roy Porter,* Basingstoke, Palgrave Macmillan, 2007, 36-45; 'Popular History', in Joad Raymond (ed.) *Cheap Print in Britain and Ireland to 1660,* Oxford, OUP, 2011, 444-53; 'Lay History: official and unofficial representations,1800-1914', in S. Macintyre, J. Maiguashca and A. Pók (eds.) *Oxford History of Historical Writing* 4, Oxford, OUP, 2011, 115-32; 'Ernst Gombrich's Search for Cultural History', in Paul Taylor (ed.) *Meditations on a Heritage: papers on the work and legacy of Sir Ernst Gombrich,* London: Paul Holberton, 2014, 14-21.

1: THE ART OF RE-INTERPRETATION: MICHEL DE CERTEAU[1]

After a certain time-lag, the Jesuit Michel de Certeau (1925–86) has come to be recognized as one of the most creative cultural theorists of the late 20th century, in the same class as his more celebrated contemporaries Pierre Bourdieu and Michel Foucault.

The secondary literature on Certeau is increasing at a remarkable rate. A Certeau reader was published in 2000 and an intellectual biography in 2002.[2] A remarkable polymath, Certeau practised at least nine disciplines (history, theology, philosophy, sociology, anthropology, linguistics, literature, geography and psychoanalysis), and he has been discussed from many points of view. All the same, as this article will attempt to show, one of the various contexts in which his thought developed has been relatively neglected.

---

[1] What follows is the revised text of a lecture delivered at the University of Heidelberg on 2 July 2002. My thanks to the panel that discussed my ideas on that occasion, to Nick Dew and Wim Weymans for commenting on the manuscript and to Wim Weymans, again, for sending me xeroxes of material I would otherwise have missed.
[2] Graham Ward (ed) *The Certeau Reader* (Oxford, 2000); François Dosse, *Michel de Certeau: Le marcheur blessé* (Paris, 2002), a book to which I had access only at the last moment.

Certeau became widely known in France in thanks to his comments on the famous 'events' of that year. However, he had been writing steadily for a number of years before this. His publications on mysticism and ecclesiastical history go back to the end of the fifties.[3] Although his writings on theology and mysticism have not gone unappreciated, relatively little attention has been paid to the relation between these writings and his more famous sociological and anthropological theories.[4] Even more neglected are his articles on the problems of the Church and on Latin America, five of which were published in 1967, before the famous events of the following year.[5]

The explanation of this relative neglect is doubtless the remoteness of Catholicism, especially the French Catholicism of the 1950s and 1960s, from the interests of the scholars who write about him both in and for the English-speaking world. His *Fable mystique* was translated into English considerably later than his other major works, while his discussions of new trends in the Church in his time have not been reprinted, let alone translated.[6]

The aim of this article is therefore to replace Certeau in the ecclesiastical context in which his ideas developed, suggesting that his theory of practice was embedded in his own practices. It will approach his writings in the way in which he approached the writings of others, examining the place or places from which he was speaking and the way in which he re-employed old concepts to analyse new situations.

---

[3] These writings include Michel de Certeau, 'Le Père Maur', *Revue d'ascétique et de mystique* 35 (1959), 266–303; id, 'Surin', *The Month* 120 (1960), 340–53; id, 'De St-Cyran au Jansénisme', *Christus* 10 (1963), 399–417.
[4] For brief introductions, see the special issue of *New Blackfriars* 77 (1996), and Frederick Christian Bauerschmidt, 'The Abrahamic Voyage: Michel de Certeau and Theology', *Modern Theology* 12 (1996), 1–26.
[5] Michel de Certeau, 'La vie religieuse en Amérique Latine', *Etudes* 326 (1967), 108–13; id, 'Amérique latine: ancient ou nouveau monde? Notes de voyages', *Christus* 55 (1967), 338–51; id, 'Che Guevara et Régis Debray', *Etudes* 327 (1967), 624–9; id, 'La parole du croyant dans le langage de l'homme', *Esprit* 35 (1967), 455–73; id, 'L'injustice sociale dans le Nordeste', *La Croix* 21–22 May 1967;
[6] In any case, it is illuminating to read these articles in their original setting, flanked by discussions of Vatican II, poverty in Latin America, etc.

Certeau in his Time

To avoid possible misunderstandings, let me make it clear that I am not denying either similarities or relations between the ideas of Certeau and those of his contemporaries, his generation.[7] This generation includes Michel Foucault (born in 1926) and Pierre Bourdieu (born in 1930), theorists with whom he is in dialogue in the pages of *L'invention du quotidien*, as well as Jacques Derrida (born in 1930), whom he cites quite often. Certeau presents himself as turning Foucault on his head, asking questions which are at once 'analogues et contraires', using the idea of micro-politics, for instance, but focussing on 'antidiscipline'.[8] His concern with practice has much in common with that of Bourdieu, but he criticized Bourdieu's notion of 'habitus' for its implication that ordinary people are unconscious of their tactics.[9]

Again, Certeau's key notion of *ré-emploi* resembles the *bricolage* discussed by Claude Lévi-Strauss. If not exactly a structuralist, Certeau passed through structuralism and was marked by it. He makes frequent references to Vladimir Propp and Roman Jakobson and terms such as *repertoire* and *combinatoire* recur in his work. For example, he describes ordinary people as making selections from a cultural repertory, and combining what they select in new ways.[10] The linguistic metaphor or analogy is central in *L'invention*, and one might say that a major difference between his analysis of popular culture and that of those predecessors who assumed the passivity of consumers, is that they restricted themselves to *langue* while he, like Bourdieu, is also concerned with *parole*.

L'invention also owes something to the work of Henri Lefebvre on space and on everyday life, and there are occasional echoes of Jacques Lacan, whose seminars Certeau frequented from the six-

---

[7] Edward Said's essay on Foucault, reprinted in *Reflections on Exile* (London, 2001), 187–97, at 188, notes the importance of his generation, although Said makes no reference to Certeau as a member of that generation.

[8] *L'invention du quotidien* (Paris, 1980: English translation, The Practice of Everyday Life, Berkeley 1984) 14.

[9] L'invention, 123.

[10] L'invention, 75–94.

ties onwards.¹¹ More important for the central theme of this article, the term *ré-emploi* recalls the idea of 'appropriation' in the work of Paul Ricoeur.¹² Certeau also made use of the work of British and American theorists, from Austin to Goffman, and of German thinkers from Marx and Freud to Wittgenstein and Heidegger.

Placing Certeau

Certeau had a strong sense of place, literal and metaphorical. His way of doing the sociology of knowledge was to ask, Where do you speak from?[13] Where was Certeau speaking from? It is not an easy question to answer. In the first place he was a Catholic priest, a Jesuit who entered the order in 1950, at the age of 25. He was given the task of working on the history of the Jesuits and chose one individual from the sixteenth century, Pierre Fabre, and one from the seventeenth century, the mystic Jean-Joseph Surin. For a long time Certeau published his articles, including the comments on the events of May 1968 which made him famous in France, almost exclusively in Catholic journals and mainly in Jesuit journals such as *Christus*, the *Revue d'ascétique et de mystique,* and *Etudes*.[14]

Certeau's intellectual itinerary from a historian of mysticism to a sociologist of consumption is certainly an unusual one, as the historian Michelle Perrot has remarked.[15] It is important but not sufficient to note that he was radicalized or at least made conscious of his radical position by the events of May 68, *les événements*, which he compared in an article published that summer to the outbreak of the

---

[11] Emphasized (perhaps over-emphasized) by Ian Buchanan, *Michel de Certeau: Cultural Theorist* (London, 2000), 108–20.
[12] Paul Ricoeur, 'Appropriation', in his *Hermeneutics and the Human Sciences*, ed. John B. Thompson, Cambridge 1981, 182–93 (there is no reference to a French original).
[13] Michel de Certeau *L'écriture de l'histoire* (Paris, 1975), English translation *The Writing of History*, New York 1988, 58–64.
[14] According to the bibliography compiled by Luce Giard in *Le voyage mystique*, a special issue of *Recherches de science religieuse* 76 (1988), Certeau published 37 articles in *Etudes*, 26 in *Christus*, 15 in *Esprit*, 14 in the *Revue d'Ascetique et Mystique* and 12 in *Recherches de science religieuse*.
[15] Michelle Perrot, 'Mille manières de braconner', *Le Débat* 49 (1988), 117–21.

French Revolution and the beginning of a 'new culture' (he did not use the term 'cultural revolution', but it is likely that both he and his readers would have been thinking of Mao Zedong at this point).[16]

Certeau's decision to write about the events of 1968, like his support for the rebels was somewhat surprising. After all, he was a priest and a scholar, not a political activist, and forty-three years old at the time that Daniel Cohn-Bendit was telling the students not to trust anyone over thirty. To explain these paradoxes and understand Certeau's position, it is important to replace him in his ecclesiastical context. He was developing his ideas at a crucial moment in the history of the Church, in the age of French worker priests (suppressed by Rome in 1954) and, more generally, of Vatican II and liberation theology, developing in the sixties and especially visible after the publication of *The Theology of Liberation* by Gustavo Gutierrez in 1971. He was sympathetic to many of these new currents, including the critique of ecclesiastical bureaucracy put forward by Monsignor Ivan Illich, as he once was, a call for the withering away of the 'institutional Church'.[17]

Indeed, the intellectual itinerary of Illich from theologian to sociologist resembles that of Certeau in important respects, except that the latter continued to write about religion and indeed ended where he began with a study of mysticism. The two men belonged to the same generation (Illich was born in 1926). Illich became interested in Latin America a few years before Certeau, working in Puerto Rico before moving to Mexico in 1961. It seems that both men were made politically conscious – 'conscientized', as Paulo Freire would say – by their experience of poverty and oppression in this part of the world.[18]

The following section will therefore summarize what Certeau was saying about the Church in Latin America at this time, in order to prepare for the central argument of the article about the practice of re-employment in his later work.

---

[16] 'En Mai dernier, on a pris la parole comme on a pris la Bastille en 1789': Certeau, 'Pour une nouvelle culture: prendre la parole', *Etudes* 329, 29–42.

[17] Ivan Illich, 'The Vanishing Clergyman' (1967: reprinted in his *Celebration of Awareness*, 1971, 71–94); Michel de Certeau, 'Cuernavaca', *Etudes* 331 (1969), 436–40. On his reservations about liberation theology, Dosse, *Certeau*, 178.

[18] Cf. Dosse, *Certeau*, 181.

Certeau in the New World

Michel de Certeau first visited South America in 1966, when he was forty-one. It was a new world for him in more than one sense. He originally went there when he was commissioned by *Etudes* to observe a conference of Brazilian clergy in Rio de Janeiro, held in order to discuss the problems of the Church in Latin America.[19] One of the conclusions he drew from this meeting was the need for new theory, since old theoretical keys were unable to open new doors. Indeed, he ended by hoping for a '"nouveau monde" de l'Esprit'.[20]

A few months later, in December 1967, Certeau published his reflections on Che Guevara and Régis Debray, expressing respect and admiration for the guerrilla leader and drawing a moral for Christians from the link between the militant and the theorist.[21] This article was followed by a sympathetic if critical account of Illich and his centre at Cuernavaca, CIDOC, implying the need to keep him in the Church, and a still warmer appreciation of the campaign for social justice led by Dom Helder Camara, archbishop of Recife in North-Eastern Brazil, which ended with a call to action, '*faire* la vérité qu'il nous rappelle', in other words to get off the fence and support movements of resistance to oppression.[22] He later travelled to Venezuela, Chile, Argentina and Mexico as well as making a number of visits to Brazil, and continuing to write about the economic, social and political problems of Latin America.[23]

To sum up. I do not wish to deny the importance of the famous 'events' of 1968 in Certeau's intellectual development. This was the moment of Certeau's own 'prise de parole' in the sense that it was at this point that he began to write for readers outside the

---

[19] For details on his visits to Latin America and Brazil, Dosse, *Certeau*, 172-88.
[20] Certeau, 'La vie religieuse'.
[21] Certeau, 'Che Guevara', 624, 629.
[22] Certeau, 'Le prophète et les militaires: Dom Helder Camara', *Etudes* 333, 104-13. Cf. id, 'Les chrétiens et la dictature militaire au Brésil', *Politique d'aujourd'hui*, November 1969, 39-53.
[23] Certeau, 'Développement économique et sociale', *Masses ouvrières* 242 (1967), 49-57; id, 'Power against the People', *New Blackfriars* 51 (1970), 338-44; id, 'Le Chili après coup', Projet (December 1973); id, 'La longue marche indienne', *Le monde diplomatique* 273 (1976), 1-18.

Church. As a result, he became much better known in France. All the same, the decisive encounter that launched him on his career as an analyst of the secular world occurred in South America nearly two years earlier, preparing him for his stance in May'68.

The main purpose of this article, however, is to make a point not about Certeau's intellectual biography, which has now been reconstructed in detail, but about his theory, to show the religious origins of concepts which he adapted for use in the analysis of secular problems.

The Art of Re-Employment

To the question, Where did Certeau speak from? a possible response is that after 1966 he became increasingly bi-local, poised half way between the Church and the world, the seminary and the seminar, the theology seminar at the Institut Catholique de Paris and the anthropology seminar at Paris VII. He joined new networks, writing for secular journals such as *Annales* (the leading historical journal in France), and working for the Ministry of Culture and other secular institutions, though he did all this without breaking the links to his past and continued to contribute to *Etudes* until 1979. After the failure of an earlier attempt to join the Ecole des Hautes Etudes en Sciences Sociales, he was elected a *directeur d'études* in that institution in 1983, beginning work in 1984.[24]

In an important sense, Certeau was 'out of place' everywhere from the later sixties onwards. He lacked an official or at least a permanent position in the French academic system, though he had his seminars in Paris as well as his invitations to lecture in San Diego, São Paulo and elsewhere. His secular interests made it increasingly difficult for him to fit into the Society of Jesus, while his religious background made him unwelcome in some academic circles.[25] It might be argued that his marginal position was a good observation post, allowing him, for instance, to observe the practices

---

[24] Dosse, *Certeau*, 382–91, especially 390.
[25] Dosse, Certeau, 386.

of fellow-historians with an anthropological eye. Having absorbed the culture of a religious order, he was able to view what the clergy call 'the world' as an outsider, in a fresh and illuminating way.

Certeau may be described as bilingual as well as bi-local. He once described the bilingualism of contemporary Christians as a disadvantage, the result of a split between modern forms of consciousness and the socio-cultural language of faith.[26] However, it will be argued here not only that Certeau was a brilliant interpreter of these two languages and their different dialects (translating from the language of psychoanalysis, for instance, into that of theology) but also that his theoretical achievement can be usefully described in these terms. In commending Ivan Illich for realising that the first thing for a missionary to do was 'to learn the language of the other', Certeau was effectively describing himself.[27]

The analyst of the process of re-employment was himself a great master of the art. Certeau had a remarkable gift for analogical thinking. As he became increasingly interested in secular problems, he approached them by making use of concepts that had already been employed both by himself and by others in the religious domain and adapting them to new purposes. His conceptual apparatus, or in the historian Lucien Febvre's famous phrase his *outillage mental*, was taken from religion and translated into secular terms.

This point immediately becomes clear if one simply takes the trouble to read his work in chronological order, going back to the articles on theology, religion and the Church that he published in Catholic journals.[28] Religious concepts formulated in these contexts were later 'displaced' as Freud would say, or 'transposed', as the musicians say, and put to work in new settings.[29]

This process of secularization or translation is a key – if not the

---

[26] 'Un schisme entre les formes de la conscience moderne et le langage socioculturel de la foi': 'Apologie de la différence', *Etudes* 328 (1968), 81–106, at 87, 92.
[27] 'Evangéliser, c'est d'abord apprendre la langue de l'autre': 'Cuernavaca', 438.
[28] Michel de Certeau, 'Problèmes actuels du sacerdoce en Amérique Latine', *Recherches de Science Religieuse* 56 (1968), 591–601.
[29] Michel de Certeau uses the terms *déplacement* and *transposition* about the events of May 1968, *La prise de parole* (Paris, 1968), 45–6; English translation, *The Capture of Speech and Other Political Writings*, ed. Luce Giard, Minneapolis 1997), 20.

key – to understanding Certeau and especially the development of his thought.[30] A clear if relatively trivial example is Certeau's recurrent use of the metaphor of 'excommunication' to mean exclusion or eviction, as when he writes of the inhabitants of the *favelas* of Rio de Janeiro as excommunicated from the city.[31] In similar fashion, as we have just seen, when speaking of the split between modern forms of consciousness and the language of faith, he used the ecclesiastical term 'schism'.[32]

The last two examples might be dismissed as 'mere' metaphors, though revealing ones. A more central example of the process of re-employment comes from *L'invention du quotidien*. Certeau's emphasis on the creativity or inventiveness of ordinary people in their everyday lives, their individual selections of mass-produced objects, their combinations or re-arrangements of these objects, and the freedom with which the readers and viewers interpret what they read or see on the television screen – this emphasis can be read as a defence of free will against earlier sociologists who had stressed the passivity of consumers and their manipulation by the media. Certeau's voluntarism surely springs from Catholic theology. Indeed, remembering the controversy on grace within the Church at the beginning of the seventeenth century, in which the Jesuits argued for a greater degree of free will than the Dominicans would allow, it might be suggested that Certeau's position follows the traditions of his order.

Belief, *la croyance*, and the production of belief, *faire croire*, is another major theme in Certeau's work, the best-known example being the section in *L'invention* noting that the capacity to believe appears to be in retreat in the political domain. Once again we find him returning to a problem that he had confronted earlier in a religious context, in articles in Catholic journals such as *Etudes* and *Esprit*.[33] Certeau's

---

[30] Luce Giard, Dominique Julia and Jacques Le Brun are all obviously aware of this aspect of Certeau, although they have not chosen to discuss it in any detail. Cf. Graham Ward on the 'imprint' of the Jesuits on Certeau's writings: 'The Voice of the Other', *New Blackfriars* (1996), 518–28, at 525.
[31] Michel de Certeau, La culture au pluriel (Paris, 1974), 79, 106,121, 187; English translation *Culture in the Plural*, ed. Luce Giard, Minneapolis 1997, 33, 54, 67, 139.
[32] Above, note 20.
[33] Michel de Certeau *L'invention du quotidien* (Paris, 1980: English translation 1984), 299ff; *Etudes* 1967; *Esprit* 1969.

famous emphasis on place, asking where people are speaking from, echoes remarks he made earlier in his article on Helder Camara and the urgent need for political commitment.³⁴

Absence and related themes such as invisibility and silence play a central role in Certeau's political and social analyses: the significance of absence, the need to listen to silence, and so on. However, these themes emerged earlier in his studies of mysticism.³⁵ The negative theology of Dionysius (or Pseudo-Dionysius) was one major source of inspiration, while Certeau casually quoted the fifteenth-century theologian Nicholas Cusanus on 'learned ignorance' in a discussion of Bourdieu.³⁶ Certeau himself linked the concern with absence to the Christian motif of the empty tomb following Christ's Resurrection.³⁷

'Otherness' or *altérité* is another major theme in Certeau's work, most obviously in the posthumous collection *Heterologies* but also in *L'écriture de l'histoire* and elsewhere. This key concept is an adaptation to secular contexts, such as the colonial encounter, of a concept that Certeau had begun to use when studying religious experience in general and mysticism in particular, and continued to employ when he studied demonic possession, especially the devils of Loudun.³⁸ It is also linked to his defence of the foreigner, the outsider, the stranger (*l'étranger*), his argument that the Church is a stranger in the world and must be careful not

---

³⁴ 'L'urgence de parler de quelque part, d'ancrer la parole en un lieu défini par un choix': Certeau, 'Dom Helder', 111.
³⁵ 'ce que manque', *La culture au pluriel* 35; 'plages de silence', 'géographie de l'oublié', *La culture au pluriel* 63; 'entendre les silences', *La culture au pluriel* 69; walking as absence, *L'invention*, 188.
³⁶ *L'invention*, 108, using the phrase 'docte ignorance' in inverted commas but making no reference to Cusanus.
³⁷ Marian Füssel, 'Geschichtsschreibung als Wissenschaft vom Anderen: Michel de Certeau', *Storia della Storiografia* 39 (2001), 17–38, at 20. My thanks to Wim Weymans for drawing my attention to this passage.
³⁸ 'sous le masque de l'Autre' (*Guide spirituel*, 1963, 18, on Loudun). Cf. Certeau, *La possession de Loudun* (Paris,1970), English translation, *The Possession of Loudun*, Chicago 2000). On 'une société bâtie sur le silence et l'exclusion de l'autre', *La culture au pluriel* 63. On his treatment of the Loudun incident, see Wim Weymans, 'Der Tod Grandiers: Michel de Certeau und die Grenzen der historischen Repräsentation', *Historische Anthropologie* 11 (2003).

to exclude other strangers.³⁹ Again, Certeau's defence of cultural pluralism, articulated in *La culture au pluriel* (1974), developed out of his defence of Christian pluralism and what he called 'a theology of difference'.⁴⁰

By now there should be no surprise in noting that Certeau's emphasis on practices in both *L'écriture* and *L'invention*, something he obviously has in common with Bourdieu, was already a feature of his articles of the 1960s on religious topics, full of phrases such as *pratique sacramentelle, pratique chrétienne, pratique de l'amour*, and so on. These were traditional Catholic expressions, just as Certeau's recurrent emphasis on *faire* rather than *dire* (*faire croire, faire de l'histoire, arts de faire*, etc), is reminiscent of the traditional Catholic emphasis on the importance of 'works', an emphasis challenged by Luther. An article of 1970 marks the transition from theology to sociology by discussing the relation between 'Christian practice' and 'theological theory'.⁴¹

By 1970 we can already see Certeau combining the traditional Christian idea of *pratique* with the secular idea of *praxis* and putting the combination to new uses, in the history of reading, for instance. Even here though, it is worth noting that a text by the seventeenth-century Jesuit mystic Surin, a text which Certeau had edited, includes an explicit discussion of reading practices, *pratiques de lecture*. Surin asks, 'Quelle pratique faut-il tenir en lisant?' and he answers, 'avec poids et lentement'. 'Intensive' reading, as historians say nowadays.⁴²

Even the everyday was approached by Certeau via his concern with mystical experience, since the mystics found God 'caché dans le quotidien'.⁴³ His concern with ordinary people was linked not only to left-wing attitudes in general and to the radical wing of the French Church in particular, but also to a religious tradition. Surin,

---

³⁹ Michel de Certeau, 'L'Étranger', *Etudes* 330, 401–6.
⁴⁰ Michel de Certeau, 'Apologie', 95.
⁴¹ Michel de Certeau, 'Qu'est-ce qu'un congrès de théologie?' *Etudes* 333 (1970), 587–96, at 592.
⁴² Jean Joseph Surin, *Guide spirituel*, ed Michel de Certeau (Paris,1963), 175–83, at 183.
⁴³ Ibid., 37.

for example, declares that he learned a great deal from a conversation in a coach with an illiterate man with spiritual gifts, an 'illettré éclairé'.[44]

Finally, the idea of re-employment itself has religious origins. It is related to the idea of 'accommodation', which is to be found in many sixteenth- seventeenth-century Jesuits, including Matteo Ricci, the sixteenth-century missionary to China (a career that Certeau himself once wished to follow). For Ricci, accommodating Christianity to Chinese culture meant stripping it of its western accretions and emphasizing its compatibility with local traditions such as the cult of the ancestors.

The concept of re-employment is even more explicit in some of the Fathers of the Church, especially Augustine and Jerome, in the context of discussions of the relation between Christianity and classical culture. Augustine, for instance, quoting the Old Testament, compares the 'spoils of Egypt' taken by the Israelites at the Exodus. Augustine's metaphor of despoiling paganism was quoted by Ignatius Loyola in a letter of 1555 in the context of Jesuit education.[45]

Spolia might be translated as 'appropriations', or as 'conversion' to Christian purposes. Incidentally, IQ refers to this passage from Augustine (in passing and without a footnote as if the point was too obvious to emphasize).[46]

In other words, the social theorist drew on his intellectual reserves, his cultural capital, Catholic theology in general and Jesuit ideas in particular, gradually secularising and transmuting what he appropriated. This is the way in which human creativity works. What we call 'originality' is an unusually radical or successful adaptation. In any case, Certeau, who might be described as among other things a sociologist of creativity, was also one of the most creative of sociologists.

---

[44] My thanks to Nicholas Dew for this suggestion.
[45] 'Questi spogli d'Egitto', from a letter of 1555.
[46] Readers 'ravissant les biens d'Egypte pour en jouir' (L'invention, 292).

2: THE PERFORMATIVE TURN IN RECENT CULTURAL HISTORY[1]

In the last generation, an increasing concern with performance has become visible in a number of disciplines, among them anthropology, sociology, political science, psychology, art history, literature and folklore. The question that I should like to address here is the following: in what sense does this concern allow us to see the past in a new light? My attempt at an answer is divided into three parts. The first part concerns what might be called the theory of performance, the second part the response of historians to this body of theory, while the third part will focus on the future, on emerging possibilities – and problems.

I

The idea of life as theatre and the world as a stage on which we

---

[1] This essay draws on, but also attempts to go beyond, two earlier pieces, 'Performing History: The Importance of Occasions', *Rethinking History*, 9 (2005), 35–52; and 'Varieties of Performance in 17th-Century Italy', in *Performativity and Performance in Baroque Rome*, ed. by Peter Gillgren and Mårten Snickare (Farnham: Ashgate, 2012), pp. 15–23. It was first presented at the conference on 'Performance and Performers in the Eastern Mediterranean' (Boğaziçi University Istanbul, 2007); I am grateful to the participants for their comments.

all play our roles goes back at least as far as ancient Greece, where the theatre was of course part of everyday life. It was revived in Europe, together with the rise of the purpose-built theatre, in the late sixteenth century. In the last sixty years or so, this idea has enjoyed another revival, this time in the work of social and cultural theorists, four Anglophones in particular.

In the first place, chronologically speaking, came the critic Kenneth Burke, whose *Grammar of Motives* (1945) examined action – as classical rhetoricians used to do -in terms of what he called the 'dramatistic pentad', in other words five questions about act, agent, agency, scene and purpose. A few years later, the social anthropologist Victor Turner (whose mother, incidentally, was an actress) introduced the idea of what he called 'social drama' in order to discuss the life-cycle of crises in the collective life of the African community in which he had done his fieldwork. His model of drama distinguished four phases: breach, crisis, redressive action and reintegration.[2]

Not long after Turner's book on social drama was published, the sociologist Erving Goffman analysed what he called 'impression management' and the distinction between 'front' and 'back regions' in a study of the dramaturgy of everyday life.[3] Finally, another anthropologist, Clifford Geertz, regularly employed dramatic metaphors in his work on Bali, from his famous interpretation of the cockfight to the description of what he called the 'theatre state' in which pomp does not serve power but the other way round.[4]

Once surprising, or even disturbing, these ideas have had enormous appeal to scholars. The four mentioned above are among the most frequently cited, but there were other pioneers. A study by the French anthropologist Michel Leiris on dramatic aspects of possession cults appeared in 1958. The philosopher John Austin's

---

[2] Kenneth Burke, *The Grammar of Motives* (New York: Prentice-Hall, 1945); Victor Turner, *Schism and Continuity in an African Society: The Study of Ndembu Village Life* (Manchester: Manchester University Press, 1957); Victor Turner, *The Anthropology of Performance*, Performance Studies Series, 4 (New York: Performing Arts Journal Publications, 1988).
[3] Erving Goffman, *The Presentation of Self in Everyday Life* (New York: Doubleday, 1959).
[4] Clifford Geertz, *The Interpretation of Cultures* (New York: Basic, 1973); Clifford Geertz, *Negara: The Theatre State in Nineteenth-Century Bali* (Princeton: Princeton University Press, 1980).

analysis of what he called 'performative utterances' also goes back to the 1950s.⁵ The Russian semiologist Yuri Lotman discussed life as theatre in two important essays first published in the 1970s, describing the everyday behaviour of eighteenth-century Russian nobles as 'a ritualized play-acting of European life' and arguing that in Europe around the year 1800, 'the theatre invaded life and actively restructured everyday behaviour'.⁶

By the 1970s, the American folklorists Roger D. Abrahams and Richard Bauman, the anthropologists James Fernandez, Dell Hymes and Stanley Tambiah, and the political scientist Murray Edelman were all employing performance-centred approaches to ritual, to narrative, to gossip and other aspects of everyday life. Indeed, Hymes wrote of a 'breakthrough into performance' at this time.⁷

---

⁵ Michel Leiris, *La possession et ses aspects théâtraux chez les Éthiopiens de Gondar*, L'Homme; cahiers d'ethnologie, de géographie et de linguistique, n.s., 1 (Paris: Plon, 1958); John Austin, *How to Do Things With Words* (Oxford: Clarendon, 1962) (but given as lectures in 1955).

⁶ Yuri Lotman, 'The Theatre and Theatricality as Components of Early Nineteenth-Century Culture' (1973), trans. in Ju. M. Lotman and B. A. Uspenskij, *The Semiotics of Russian Culture*, ed. by Ann Shukman, Michigan Slavic Contributions, 11 (Ann Arbor: Dept of Slavic Languages and Literatures, University of Michigan, 1984), pp. 141–76 (p. 145); Yuri Lotman, 'The Poetics of Everyday Behaviour in Eighteenth-Century Russian Culture' (1977), trans. in Iurii M. Lotman, Lidiia Ia. Ginsburg, and Boris A. Uspenskij, *The Semiotics of Russian Cultural History: Essays*, ed. by Alexander D. Nakhimovsky and Alice Stone Nakhimovsky (Ithaca: Cornell University Press, 1985), pp. 67–94 (p. 70).

⁷ Roger D. Abrahams, 'A Performance-Centred Approach to Gossip', *Man*, 5 (1970), pp. 290–301, repr. in his *Man-of-Words in the West Indies: Performance and the Emergence of Creole Culture*, Johns Hopkins Studies in Atlantic History and Culture (Baltimore: Johns Hopkins University Press, 1983), and 'Toward an Enactment-Centered Theory of Folklore', in *Frontiers of Folklore*, ed. by William R. Bascom (Boulder: Westview Press for the American Association for the Advancement of Science, 1977), pp. 79–120; Richard D. Bauman, 'Verbal Art as Performance', *American Anthropologist*, 77 (1975), 290–306; James W. Fernandez, 'The Performance of Ritual Metaphors', in *The Social Use of Metaphor: Essays on the Anthropology of Rhetoric*, ed. by J. D. Sapir and J. C. Crocker (Ann Arbor: University of Michigan Books on Demand, 1977), pp. 100–31; Dell Hymes, 'Breakthrough into Performance', in *Folklore: Performance and Communication*, ed. by Dan Ben-Amos and Kenneth S. Goldstein, Approaches to Semiotics, 40 (The Hague: Mouton, 1975), pp. 1–73; Stanley Tambiah, 'A Performative Approach to Ritual', *Proceedings of the British Academy*, 65 (1979), 113–69; Murray Edelman, *Politics as Symbolic Action: Mass Arousal and Quiescence*, Institute for Research on Poverty Monograph Series (New York: Academic, 1971).

For her part, the linguist Anna Wierzbicka was analysing what she called psychological 'scenarios' and later, 'cultural scripts' such as 'the scripts of sincerity', 'the scripts of warmth' and 'the scripts of spontaneity'.[8] In the 1980s and 1990s, studies of performativity multiplied and were extended to new fields such as politics and gender.[9]

Of course, the dramaturgical metaphor is not a monopoly of cultural theorists. The idea is not even a monopoly of scholars. Artists, writers and playwrights from Marcel Duchamp and Antoine Artaud to Joseph Beuys and Yoko Ono, have also been thinking in these terms, trying to break down the wall between art and life from the other side. The idea of 'performance art' (a phrase first recorded in 1971) is now well established.[10]

These ideas have gradually come to be routinized, taken for granted. Thanks especially to the everyday practice of watching television, the equivalent of regular visits to the theatre by ancient Athenians or Elizabethan Londoners, more and more of us have come to view life in theatrical terms. Reflecting on events ranging from family quarrels to speeches by politicians, we often catch ourselves using words like 'role', 'scenario', 'repertoire' or 'script'.[11] Television dramas about the everyday lives of ordinary people particularly encourage the perception of the world in this way, as in the case of the Egyptian villager who told the anthropologist Lila Abu-Lughod that 'We are a soap opera!'[12]

The theorists mentioned above sometimes used the term 'per-

---

[8] Anna Wierzbicka, *Semantic Primitives*, trans. by Anna Wierzbicka and John Besemeres, Linguistiche Forschungen, 22 (Frankfurt am Main: Athenaum, 1972); Anna Wierzbicka, *Emotions across Languages and Cultures: Diversity and Universals* (Cambridge: Cambridge University Press, 1999).
[9] Robin Wagner-Pacifici, *The Moro Morality Play: Terrorism as Social Drama* (Chicago: University of Chicago Press, 1986); Judith Butler, *Gender Trouble: Feminism and the Subversion of Identity* (London: Routledge, 1990).
[10] RoseLee Goldberg, *Performance: Live Art 1909 to the Present* (London: Thames and Hudson, 1979).
[11] Wierzbicka, Emotions, pp. 14ff., 240ff.; cf. William M. Reddy, *The Navigation of Feeling: Framework for a History of Emotions* (Cambridge: Cambridge University Press, 2001).
[12] Lila Abu-Lughod, *Dramas of Nationhood: The Politics of Television in Egypt* (Chicago: University of Chicago Press, 2005), p. 124.

formance'. A chapter of Goffman's *Presentation of Self*, for instance, uses this title. All the same, it may be useful to employ the phrase 'performative turn' to mean something more precise.

Recent studies in anthropology, sociology and history all employ a notion of 'performance' or 'performativity' that subverts as well as continues the tradition to which I have just referred.

When earlier scholars compared life to theatre, they were suggesting that apparently spontaneous acts followed a kind of 'script', the rules of the culture or sub-culture. On the other hand, more recent studies of performance define it not against spontaneity but against scripts. Pierre Bourdieu introduced his central concept of the 'habitus', the principle of regulated improvisation, in the early 1970s, in reaction against the structuralist notion of culture as a system of rules, a notion he had come to regard as too rigid.[13] His work has an affinity with what we have come to think of as the distinctively post-modern emphasis on flexibility, fluidity and inventiveness, perhaps appropriate to our age of 'liquid modernity'.[14]

As a recent example of the performative turn in this second sense one might take a collective volume entitled *Social Performance: Symbolic Action, Cultural Pragmatics and Ritual*. The work of a group of sociologists in the USA and Germany, the volume represents a bold attempt to re-orient the social sciences in this direction. To this end the authors offer what are sometimes disturbing insights, notably the discussion of the events of 11 September as 'terror-performance.[15]

However, a sharp distinction between fixed and fluid, scripted and improvised or rehearsed or spontaneous is probably unhelpful. Like other binary oppositions, these concepts are useful at the

---

[13] Pierre Bourdieu, *Esquisse d'une théorie de la pratique: précédé de trois études d'ethnologie kabyle*, Travaux de droit, d'économie, de sociologie et de sciences politiques, 92 (Geneva: Droz, 1972).
[14] Zygmunt Bauman, *Liquid Modernity* (Cambridge: Polity Press, 2000).
[15] *Social Performance: Symbolic Action, Cultural Pragmatics, and Ritual*, ed. by Jeffrey C. Alexander, Bernhard Giesen, and Jason L. Mast (Cambridge: Cambridge University Press, 2006), especially pp. 91–114; cf. *Theatricality*, ed. by Tracy C. Davis and Thomas Postlewait, Theatre and Performance Theory (Cambridge: Cambridge University Press, 2003).

beginning of a study, but need to be abandoned or qualified as it progresses. In this article I shall follow the lead of some recent studies of ritual that refuse to treat it as a separate category of action. As Caroline Humphrey and James Laidlaw put it, 'the term "ritual" does not pick out a class of events or institutions in an analytically useful way'. Instead, these studies focus on the process of ritualization.[16] A binary opposition has been replaced by a spectrum of actions that are more or less deeply or thickly ritualized.

In similar fashion, I shall be discussing 'semi-performances', 'semi-rehearsal' and 'semi-improvisation' at different points along what is best regarded as a continuum between rehearsal and spontaneity, art and life. To explore this large frontier zone I should like to invoke the example of a study of popular narrative now nearly half a century old. The study is Albert Lord's *Singer of Tales*, published in 1960 but telling a story about research carried out in the 1930s, when the classicist Milman Parry and his assistant, Lord, went to Jugoslavia with a tape-recorder in order to test the theory that the Homeric poems were originally oral compositions by studying the performance of local 'singers of tales' (*guslari*).[17]

As the recordings showed, the *guslari* did not learn their stories by heart. They were able to sing for hours at a time in coffeehouses and at weddings, making their stories longer or shorter according to the occasion and the response of the audience. They were able to do this because their performances were not pure extemporization. The singers made use of what might be called 'prefabricated' elements, of which Parry and Lord distinguished two kinds.

At the micro-level there was the formula, a recurrent line or half-line such as *Vino pije/Kraljevici Marko*, 'Marko Kraljević was drinking wine' (or in Homer, 'wine-dark sea'). At the macro-level there was the theme, a recurrent episode such as a battle or the sending of a message, a theme to be found not only in Homer and the *guslari* but in medieval narrative poems such as *La chanson d'Antioche* or

---

[16] Catherine Bell, *Ritual Theory, Ritual Practice* (New York: Oxford University Press, 1992); Caroline Humphrey and James Laidlaw, *The Archetypal Actions of Ritual: A Theory of Ritual Illustrated by the Jain Rite of Worship* (Oxford: Clarendon Press, 1994), p. 3.
[17] Albert B. Lord, *The Singer of Tales*, Harvard Studies in Comparative Literature, 24 (Cambridge, MA: Harvard University Press, 1960).

in nineteenth-century ballads such as the Hungarian song about Lajos Kossuth in 1848: *Kossuth Lajos azt üzente, elfogyott a regimentje* ('Kossuth's message'). Thanks to these elements, which could be combined or adapted to fit new stories, the singer was able to take a 'rest on the way', with time to think about what to sing next.[18] In similar fashion, in the 1970s, Bourdieu would describe the habitus in terms of schemata.

II

As the world changes, we come to view the past from unfamiliar angles. Can today's postmodern performative turn illuminate the culture of earlier periods? The discipline or culture of professional historians is relatively conservative, especially the culture of 'plain' or 'general' historians as opposed to what might be called 'hyphenated historians' (art historians, literary historians, theatre historians and so on). This 'cultural lag', as sociologists call it, has some advantages, such as reluctance to be carried away by the latest fashion. It also has its price, a delay in the reception of illuminating new approaches.

In this case, I should like to suggest that historians have not yet taken unscripted or semi-scripted performances seriously enough, in the way that folklorists have done, for instance. Currently, the ideas of the original quartet – Burke, Turner, Goffman and Geertz – have been taken up and employed in historical analysis, but the newer performative turn in the strict sense has passed virtually unnoticed, despite the use of the word 'performance'.

Festivals, spectacles and other heavily or thickly ritualized actions have attracted a good deal of interest from historians. In the 1970s, for instance, Mona Ozouf and Michel Vovelle wrote on the festivals of the French Revolution.[19] In the 1980s, two well-known

---
[18] The phrase 'a rest on the way' comes from a preacher interviewed in Bruce A. Rosenberg, *The Art of the American Folk Preacher* (New York: Oxford University Press, 1970).
[19] Mona Ozouf, *La fête révolutionnaire, 1789–1799*, Bibliothèque des Histoires (Paris: Gallimard, 1976); Michel Vovelle, *Les métamorphoses de la fête en Provence de 1750 à 1820*, Bibliothèque d'ethnologie historique (Paris: Aubier/Flammarion, 1976).

collections of essays were concerned with 'Rites of Power and 'Rituals of Royalty', while other studies analysed the rituals of republics such as Renaissance Florence and Venice or modern France and the USA.[20] In the 1990s, the approach was extended to imperial rituals in Russia and Japan. The study of Russia emphasized what the author, Richard Wortman, called 'the performative character of Russian monarchy', the court as a stage. The 'individual modes of performance' of the tsars are described as 'scenarios' – the scenario of dynasty, enlightenment, happiness, reform and so on. In the eighteenth century the emphasis fell on scenarios of conquest, but in the nineteenth century Alexander I and Nicholas I were presented in a more demotic fashion, according to the scenarios of humility and domesticity.[21]

One of the best-known examples of the performance of monarchy concerns the court of Louis XIV at Versailles. Louis sometimes literally took the stage and danced in court ballets, but his principal role was to play himself, or rather the King of France. Contemporaries were well aware of the performative element in the 'fabrication of Louis XIV'. The metaphor of theatre was in constant use at the time, and came from the mouth of the king as well as from the pen of the Duc de St-Simon. Goffman's distinction between front and back regions was made by St-Simon (who wrote of *les derrières*) as well as in the design of the palace, with a private

---

[20] *Rites of Power: Symbolism, Ritual, and Politics since the Middle Ages*, ed. by Sean Wilentz (Philadelphia: University of Pennsylvania Press, 1985); *Rituals of Royalty: Power and Ceremonial in Traditional Societies*, ed. by David Cannadine and Simon Price, Past and Present Publications (Cambridge: Cambridge University Press, 1987); Richard Trexler, *Public Life in Renaissance Florence*, Studies in Social Discontinuity (New York: Academic, 1980); Edward Muir, *Civic Ritual in Renaissance Venice* (Princeton: Princeton University Press, 1981); Olivier Ihl, *La fête républicaine*, Bibliothèque des Histoires (Paris: Gallimard, 1996); David Waldstreicher, *In the Midst of Perpetual Fetes: The Making of American Nationalism, 1776–1820* (Chapel Hill: Omohundro Institute of Early American History and Culture, University of North Carolina Press, 1997).
[21] Takashi Fujitani, *Splendid Monarchy: Power and Pageantry in Modern Japan*, Twentieth-Century Japan, the Emergence of a World Power, 6 (Berkeley: University of California Press, 1996); Richard Wortman, *Scenarios of Power: Myth and Ceremony in Russian Monarchy*, Studies of the Harriman Institute, 2 vols (Princeton: Princeton University Press, 1995–2000), I, 139.

cabinet to which the king could retire.²² There is even a contemporary description of the king composing himself and looking more formal as he went through the door separating his private from his public sphere.²³

Many festivals may be regarded as 'performances of memory', re-activating what is coming to be called the 'cultural memory' in the sense of a repertoire of images and stories that influence the way in which individuals view and remember the past.²⁴ We might distinguish different kinds or genres of performance. At one extreme, we find historical plays and operas, in other words performances that are tightly organized, fully scripted and carefully rehearsed. At the other extreme, there are loosely organized, unscripted and unrehearsed attempts to re-enact past events in the sense of following past models. In between come commemorations, centenaries for instance, commemorating 1492, 1776, 1789 and so on, or anniversaries such as 14 July in France, in other words processions, pageants, or parades that mark the year or the day and evoke the memory of a historic event. They are rituals which 'canonize' particular events, in the sense of giving them a sacred or exemplary quality, making them 'historic' as well as historical.²⁵

In the case of events such as these, historians should surely think once again about the place of improvisation and semi-improvisation. In other words, they should look for what did not go according to plan – according, that is, to the 'script', whether this script was recorded in a book or existed only in the head of a master of ceremo-

---

[22] A similar distinction used to be made in other cultures, such as China and Japan, between the front or outer part of a house and the back or inner part (to which women were traditionally confined).

[23] Peter Burke, *The Fabrication of Louis XIV* (New Haven: Yale University Press, 1992); id., 'On the Margins of the Public and the Private: Louis XIV at Versailles', *International Political Anthropology* 2 (2009), pp.29–36.

[24] Peter Burke, 'Co-memorations: performing the past', in *Performing the Past: memory, history and identity in modern Europe*, ed.by Karin Tilmans, Frank van Vree and Jay Winter (Amsterdam: Amsterdam University Press, 2010), pp.105–18.

[25] Barry Schwarz, 'The Social Context of Commemoration', Social Forces, 61 (1982), 374–402; *Commemorations: The Politics of National Identity*, ed. by John R. Gillis (Princeton: Princeton University Press, 1994); Lyn Spillman, *Nation and Commemoration: Creating National Identities in the United States and Australia* (Cambridge: Cambridge University Press, 1997).

nies such as Paris de Grassis at the papal court in the early sixteenth century. The diary of Grassis offers eloquent testimony both to his desire to do everything by the book and also to the unconventional approach of his master, Pope Julius II, who sometimes refused to genuflect or to wear his stole when the ritual required it.[26]

Moving now to less thickly ritualized occasions, Michel de Certeau examined the dramaturgy of possession by the devil, while Michel Foucault wrote of executions as a 'theatre of terror'. Douglas Hay wrote of 'managing hangings, arranging backstage the precise moment of the emotional climax'. Hay also analysed the dramatic aspects of courts of law, studied more recently by Robert St George in terms of 'courtroom performance'. One might add that some trials – such as the notorious 'show trials' in the Communist world from the 1930s to the 1950s – were more performative than others.[27] Paying more attention to discrepancies between script and practice, Thomas Laqueur criticized both Foucault and Hay for their emphasis on 'judicial dramaturgy' and the view from above. In contrast, he focused on the reactions of the crowd to executions and on the 'unexpected turns' which produced 'a theatre of far greater fluidity'.[28]

Again, it is obvious enough that diplomacy was and is a kind of performance, and that ambassadors needed to learn how to

---

[26] Peter Burke, *Historical Anthropology of Early Modern Italy: Essays on Perception and Communication* (Cambridge: Cambridge University Press, 1987), p. 177.

[27] Michel de Certeau, *La possession de Loudun*, Collections Archives, 37 (Paris: Julliard, 1970), pp. 9, 129–60; Michel Foucault, *Surveiller et Punir* (Paris: Gallimard, 1975), pp. 9–72 (p. 53); Douglas Hay, 'Property, Authority and the Criminal Law', in *Albion's Fatal Tree: Crime and Society in Eighteenth-Century England*, ed. by Douglas Hay and others (London: Allen Lane, 1975), pp. 17–64 (pp. 26–31, 52); Robert St George, 'Massacred Language: Courtroom Performance in Eighteenth-Century Boston', in *Possible Pasts: Becoming Colonial in Early America*, ed. by Robert St George (Ithaca: Cornell University Press, 2000), pp. 327–56. On executions, cf. Pieter Spierenburg, *The Spectacle of Suffering* (Cambridge: Cambridge University Press, 1984), and Richard van Dülmen, *Theater des Schreckens: Gerichtspraxis und Strafrituale in der frühen Neuzeit* (Munich: Beck, 1985).

[28] Thomas W. Laqueur, 'Crowds, Carnival and the State in English Executions, 1604–1868', in *The First Modern Society: Essays in English History in Honour of Lawrence Stone*, ed. by Lee Beier, David Cannadine, and James Rosenheim, Past and Present Publications (Cambridge: Cambridge University Press, 1989), pp. 305–55 (p. 309).

carry themselves on stage.[29] Indeed, treatises were written in the sixteenth and seventeenth centuries in order to teach this art, following the model of the more famous manuals of the behaviour required of courtiers, notably Baldassare Castiglione's *Cortegiano* (1528). In China, foreign diplomats were required to rehearse the *koutou* ('kowtow') and other ritualized gestures at the Board of Ceremonies before being admitted to an imperial audience.[30]

In this domain too things might go wrong, when clashes of interest between two states proved to be more powerful than diplomatic protocol. In London, on 30 September 1661, for instance, there occurred what would now be called a diplomatic 'incident'. A conflict between the Spanish and French ambassadors over precedence led to a traffic accident (as each attempted to take the first place in a procession of carriages in Whitehall), followed by a brawl between the servants of the two protagonists. It is virtually certain that the accident was no accident, but part of a campaign by the French government to make Louis the leading European king.[31]

In other cases it was the cultural distance between the envoys and the ruler to whom they were sent that led to contrasts in expectations and definitions of the situation and so to both accidental and deliberate deviations from protocol. A famous case of such a deviation comes from the British embassy to China in 1793, when the ambassador, Lord Macartney, refused to perform the customary *koutou* and insisted on treating the Emperor as if he were a European monarch, kneeling on one knee instead of touching the ground with his forehead. On other diplomatic occasions, misun-

---

[29] Among the few political historians to discuss these questions are William Roosen, 'Early Modern Diplomatic Ceremonial: A Systems Approach' *Journal of Modern History*, 52 (1980), 452–76; Lucien Bély, *Espions et ambassadeurs au temps de Louis XIV* (Paris: Fayard, 1990), especially pp. 391–416; and James L. Hevia, *Cherishing Men from Afar: Qing Guest Ritual and the Macartney Embassy of 1793* (Durham, NC: Duke University Press, 1995).

[30] John E. Wills, Jr, *Embassies and Illusions: Dutch and Portuguese Envoys to K'ang-hsi, 1666-1687*, Harvard East Asian Monographs, 113 (Cambridge, MA: Harvard University Press, 1984), p. 31.

[31] Peter Burke, 'La reconstruction des rituels politiques au siècle de Louis XIV', in *Le Protocole ou La mise en forme de l'ordre politique*, ed. by Yves Deloye, Claudine Haroche, and Olivier Ihl (Paris: L'Harmattan, 1996), pp. 171–83.

derstanding seems to have played a greater role, as in the cases of the American envoys to Edō in 1857 and the Japanese envoys to Washington in 1860, both groups being unsure what was expected of them in formal audiences.[32]

Even riots have been analysed as performances, from the 'rites of violence' in the French religious wars to a lynching in the American South that has been described as a drama or 'moral scenario'.[33] It is for this reason that sociologists and historians sometimes speak of rioters as following a 'repertoire'.[34] The revolt of Naples in 1647, led by the fisherman Masaniello, has been studied as a form of social drama that went through the four phases distinguished by Victor Turner, ending with a performance of reintegration when the archbishop exorcised the city, thus implying that the rebellion was the work of the devil.[35]

It is possible to take the performative approach still further in the direction of ordinary social behaviour. The insight of Erving Goffman's that everyday life may be viewed in terms of theatre has been pursued by a number of historians. Biographies of famous individuals, from Christopher Columbus to William Butler Yeats, have emphasized their techniques of self-presentation much more than traditional biographies did.[36] Again, social historians have analysed the behaviour of both dominant and subordinate social groups in performative terms. Lawrence Stone, for instance, declared that 'marital litigation has always been a theatrical display', revealing 'domestic dramas'.[37] At one end of the social scale, the deference

---

[32] Hevia, *Cherishing Men from Afar*; Masao Miyoshi, *As We Saw Them: The First Japanese Embassy to the United States (1860)* (Berkeley: University of California Press, 1979), pp. 92–93, 125–41.

[33] Natalie Davis, 'The Rites of Violence' (1971), repr. in *Society and Culture in Early Modern France: Eight Essays* (London: Duckworth, 1975), pp. 152–88; Bertram Wyatt Brown, *Southern Honor* (New York: Oxford University Press, 1982).

[34] Charles Tilly, *Regimes and Repertoires* (Chicago: University of Chicago Press, 2006).

[35] Burke, *Historical Anthropology*, pp. 191–206.

[36] Felipe Fernández-Armesto, *Columbus* (Oxford: Oxford University Press, 1991); Roy Foster, *W. B. Yeats: A Life*, 2 vols (Oxford: Oxford University Press, 1997–2003). Cf Richard Ellmann, *Yeats: The Man and the Masks* (London: Macmillan, 1949).

[37] Lawrence Stone, *Road to Divorce: England, 1530–1987* (Oxford: Oxford University Press, 1990), pp. 30, 211.

exhibited by members of the subordinate classes (slaves, the working classes, servants, peasants and so on) has been studied as a role, sometimes played ironically.[38] At the other end of the scale, it has been argued that the upper classes were concerned with the 'performance of nobility'. The work of Yuri Lotman was mentioned above in the context of cultural theory; however, Lotman also put forward a historical thesis, arguing that Russian nobles became actors in the eighteenth century as a result of the official policy of westernization, which made them self-conscious by obliging them to play new roles (or to play old roles in a new style). In similar fashion, a study of merchants in eighteenth-century Philadelphia emphasizes their use of what the author calls 'the idiom of theatricality' in their letters.[39] In the France of Louis XIV, the Duc de St-Simon was not the only writer to anticipate Goffman and view life as theatre. The Chevalier de Méré, for instance, told his noble readers that they might learn something about self-presentation from professional actors.[40]

A few historians have discussed what theorists call the negotiation of identity, especially individual attempts to be perceived as a member of a different group from their group of origin, in other words 'passing' for white, for middle-class, or for male. For example, two Dutch historians have studied early modern women who dressed as men, often in order to join the army or navy. In order to be successful – and some of these women spent years as soldiers or sailors before being discovered – transvestism had to be accompanied by a full performance of masculinity.[41]

---

[38] Peter Bailey, 'Will the Real Bill Banks Please Stand Up? Towards a Role Analysis of Victorian Respectability', *Journal of Social History*, 12 (1978), 336–53; James C. Scott, *Domination and the Arts of Resistance: Hidden Transcripts* (New Haven: Yale University Press, 1990), pp. 32–36, 39. Cf. Homi K. Bhabha, 'Of Mimicry and Man', in Bhabha, *The Location of Culture* (London: Routledge, 1994), pp. 88–91.
[39] Lotman, 'Theatre', and 'Poetics'; Toby Ditz, 'Secret Selves Credible Personas', in *Possible Pasts*, ed. by St George, pp. 219–42 (p. 221). Cf. David Posner, *The Performance of Nobility in Early Modern European Literature*, Cambridge Studies in Renaissance Literature and Culture, 33 (Cambridge: Cambridge University Press, 1999).
[40] Quoted in Benedetta Craveri, *La civiltà della conversazione*, Collana dei casi, 48 (Milan: Adelphi, 2001), p. 65.
[41] Rudolf M. Dekker and Lotte C. van de Pol, *The Tradition of Female Transvestism in Early Modern Europe* (Basingstoke: Macmillan, 1989).

III

The collective achievement of the last generation of social and cultural historians is an impressive one. However, the purpose of this article is not to celebrate but to question it, attempting to identify opportunities that have been missed or not exploited as fully as they might be. This third section is oriented towards the future, to the possibilities and problems of a performative approach in the strict sense of the term.

Given the point made earlier about the need to distinguish degrees of performance, it may be illuminating to begin with what everyone recognizes as performances, elaborated and institutionalized, moving gradually towards the simple, the everyday and the informal, testing the idea of performance in order to see how far it can usefully go. The frontier zone is an extensive one, but the territory of the spontaneous lies beyond it.

So far as elaborated performances are concerned, we need more dialogue between plain historians on one side and their hyphenated colleagues on the other. From the historian's side of the fence, a question to ask – looking back to *The Singer of Tales* – concerns the importance of semi-improvisation. In the case of music, for instance, how much freedom did performers have to add ornaments to their score? Was what we call 'classical' music closer to jazz than we usually think? In the case of drama, it is well-known that the *commedia dell'arte* was improvised or semi-improvised, the scripts being reduced to plot summaries and the performance aided by stereotyped characters, formulaic speeches and prefabricated actions (known as *lazzi*).[42] Was there also room for extemporization in the case of scripted drama, for responses to the reactions of the audience?

Moving towards the informal, Italian piazzas of the early modern period were common settings for performances of stories by *cantastorie* (singers of tales like the *guslari*). They were also major sites for performances of healing by the *ciarlatani*, as an overture or an advertisement for the sale of their medicines. Again, missions

---

[42] Robert Henke, *Performance and Literature in the Commedia dell'Arte* (Cambridge: Cambridge University Press, 2002).

and the sermons that accompanied them in Counter-Reformation Italy are beginning to be studied as examples of the performance of piety. To what extent were these performances extemporized?[43]

Scholarship too may be studied from this point of view, as the terms 'lecture theatre' and 'anatomy theatre' remind us. The term 'charlatan' has long been used by academics to dismiss the work of their colleagues (notably by the German professor Johann Mencke in an essay published in 1715, *De charlataneria eruditorum*). All the same, Mario Biagioli's study of the performance of knowledge by Galileo at the court of Tuscany remains almost unique in its approach.[44]

Turning from the work of professionals to that of amateurs, the obvious example of performance to cite is that of Carnival in early modern Europe, a festival in which many people from different social groups not only dressed up as kings, beggars and so on but also played the roles in public, an aspect of the festival that has not received as much attention from scholars as it deserves.[45] Charivaris, known throughout Europe (under a variety of different names) were equally performative, whether they are viewed as a form of entertainment or as popular justice.[46]

---

[43] David Gentilcore, 'Performance', in his *Medical Charlatanism in Early Modern Italy* (Oxford: Oxford University Press, 2006), pp. 301-34; Bernadette Majorana, 'Aspetti performativi e spettacolari delle missioni popolari: L'esperienza gesuitica nell'Italia centrale tra Sei e Settecento' (dissertation, Università degli studi di Firenze, ciclo VIII, 1992-1995); Bernadette Majorana, 'Elementi drammatici della predicazione missionaria', in *La predicazione in Italia dopo il Concilio di Trento tra Cinque e Settecento*, ed. by G. Martina and U. Dovere (Naples: n. pub., 1996), pp. 127-52.

[44] Mario Biagioli, *Galileo, Courtier: The Practice of Science in the Culture of Absolutism*, Science and Its Conceptual Foundations (Chicago: University of Chicago Press, 1993). The theatrical aspect of anatomy lessons was already discussed by William S. Heckscher, *Rembrandt's Anatomy of Dr. Nicolaas Tulp: An Iconological Study* (New York: New York University Press, 1958); compare Peter Burke, 'From the Disputation to Power Point: Staging Academic Knowledge in Europe, 1100-2000', in *Inszenierung und Gedächtnis*, ed. by Heidemarie Uhl (Vienna: Oesterreichische Akademie der Wissenschaften, 2014).

[45] Peter Burke, *Popular Culture in Early Modern Europe* (London: New York University Press, 1978), p. 183.

[46] *Le charivari: Actes de la table ronde organisée à Paris (25-27 avril 1977)*, ed. by Jacques Le Goff and Jean-Claude Schmitt (Paris: École des Hautes Études en Sciences Sociales, Mouton 1981).

Turning to the religious sphere, pilgrimages have occasionally been studied, notably by Victor Turner, as performances of piety and even as initiation rituals – though Turner's emphasis on the transformative effect of the pilgrimage experience implies that the pilgrims themselves are the audience as well as the actors.[47] Martyrdoms are another kind of religious performance, even if real blood flows and the actors do not leave the stage.[48]

The idea of martyrdom may be extended to politics, from Thomas More to Jan Palach, whose suicide in Prague in 1969 was a performance of protest against the Russian invasion of his country. Indeed, politics in general deserves to be viewed in terms of performance, not only of display but also of simulation and of dissimulation. The theatre state is not unique to Bali. Until quite recently, however, political historians (unless they worked on the court, discussed above, or occasionally on diplomacy) resisted the performative turn. Much remains to be done.

If the closest analogy to Geertz's Bali in early modern Europe was the Papal States, theatrical elements can be found throughout politics. Courts are not the only stages for political theatre. For example, the proceedings of parliaments and other assemblies, including the speeches, might be studied as performances. Simon Schama's remarks about 'the great theatre of the Estates-General' of 1789 has not been followed up.[49] As for armies and wars, a performative approach might usefully be extended from parades to the choreography of manoeuvres and even battles.[50]

Moving in the direction of everyday life, the history of conversation might be studied from a performative point of view, distinguishing different types of talk, more or less stylized or more

---

[47] Victor Turner and Edith Turner, *Image and Pilgrimage in Christian Culture: Anthropological Perspectives* (New York: Columbia University Press, 1978); Gérard Labrot, *L'image de Rome: une arme pour la Contre-Réforme, 1534–1677* (Lille: Atelier National de Réproduction des Thèses, 1978; second edn, Seyssel: Champ Vallon, 1987).
[48] Some Bulgarian martyrs were studied from this point of view by Kirill Petrov in a paper at the Istanbul conference cited in note 1.
[49] Simon Schama, *Citizens: A Chronicle of the French Revolution* (London: Folio Society, 1989), p. 137; cf. pp. 264, 354, 473, 535, 579.
[50] A beginning has been made by Jan Rueger, *The Great Naval Game: Britain and Germany in the Age of Empire* (Cambridge: Cambridge University Press, 2007).

or less rehearsed. In what has often been described as the golden age of conversation, in France, especially Paris, from the later seventeenth to the later eighteenth century, it may reasonably be suspected that the *bons mots* were generally fabricated beforehand rather than invented on the spot. It was not unknown for the hostess to make notes on the topics of conversation that she would later introduce in her *salon*.[51]

Moving still further toward the everyday, an ethnography of a village in Crete by Michael Herzfeld describes the local coffeehouse as a stage for the daily performance of masculinity through ritualized aggression. Card-playing, for instance, is a form of contest. 'Almost every move', Herzfeld writes, 'is made with aggressive gestures, especially by the striking of the knuckle against the table as each card is flung down ... card games provide a symbolic enactment of concerns that elsewhere might cost men their reputations and even their lives'.[52] Deep play indeed. In similar fashion another anthropologist Robin Fox, has studied what he calls the ritualization of quarrels in the West of Ireland, noting the need for an audience, the stages through which the quarrel proceeds (taking off one's coat marks an important step towards violence), and the holding back of the protagonists by their supporters. Fox's conclusion was that a quarrel appeared to be rehearsed and resembled a ballet.[53]

It might be thought that it is impossible for historians to replicate this kind of anthropological work because the sources are lacking. All the same, it has proved possible to produce a thick description of gambling in early modern Venice.[54] Again, as I discovered when working in the judicial archives in Rome, seventeenth-century Italian quarrels were often performed. They would begin with provocations and responses of a ritualized kind such as the question 'What

---

[51] Craveri, *Civiltà*; Antoine Lilti, *Le monde des salons: sociabilité et mondanité à Paris au XVIIIe siècle* (Paris: Fayard, 2005), especially pp. 273–87.
[52] Michael Herzfeld, *The Poetics of Manhood: Contest and Identity in a Cretan Mountain Village* (Princeton: Princeton University Press, 1985), pp. 155–56.
[53] Robin Fox, 'The Inherent Rules of Violence', in *Social Rules and Social Behaviour*, ed. by Peter Collett (Oxford: Blackwell, 1977), pp. 132–49.
[54] Jonathan Walker, 'Gambling and Venetian Noblemen, c. 1500–1700', *Past and Present*, 162 (1999), 28–69.

are you looking at?' followed by the reply 'I look at whatever I want to'. The dispute would gradually build up to a climax – when a reasonably large audience had assembled, and sometimes when the protagonists were confident that they would be separated by the bystanders before any real damage was done. As in Fox's Ireland, violence was governed by what he calls 'rules' – we might prefer the term 'habitus' today. All the same, as in the case of other ritualized actions, things might go wrong. The archival record of certain quarrels exists because someone was killed or seriously injured.[55]

To conclude, let us return to the central concept of performance and examine its benefits and its costs. The new approach has solved problems, helping historians to move away from determinism, but it has also generated problems of its own. We might say that the reaction against the idea of social constraints has been exaggerated, and also that the central notion of performance has been over-extended.[56]

What, today, is not viewed as performance? If Galileo was performing at court, how should we describe what he did in his study? Pushing towards the frontiers of the concept, how useful is it to treat architecture not only as a setting or stage but as a performance in itself? How useful is it to describe a written text, an image or a building as a performance?[57] Such descriptions have their shock value, which should not be dismissed, but are they useful to work with in the longer term? The meaning of the category depends on the existence of its opposite, 'non-performance', even if it is useful to speak in terms of more or less performativity rather than of its presence or absence.

In order to hold on to the benefits that accrue from our use of the concept without paying too high a price for them, two senses of 'performance' might be distinguished, stronger and weaker, or

---

[55] Burke, *Historical Anthropology*, pp. 11–12.
[56] Cf. Davis and Postlewait, *Theatricality*, p. 4.
[57] Alice Jarrard, *Architecture as Performance in Seventeenth-Century Europe: Court Ritual in Modena, Rome, and Paris* (Cambridge: Cambridge University Press, 2003); Karen-Edis Barzman, 'Early Modern Spectacle and the Performance of Images', in *Perspectives on Early Modern and Modern Intellectual History*, ed. by Joseph Marino and Melinda Schlitt (Woodbridge: University of Rochester Press, 2001), pp. 283–302.

perhaps (more) literal and (more) metaphorical, bearing in mind the difference between improvising and following a script as well as the traditional (if now somewhat blurred) contrast between theatre and 'reality'. In each case, the last half-century of study has produced an important insight. In the first place, everyday behaviour has come to be viewed as a kind of theatre or ritual; but then, in the second place, the informal and unpredictable aspects of theatrical and ritual performances are increasingly emphasized. Two opposite insights, both of them undermining simple distinctions between art and life. Can we live with both?

Another problem that needs to be addressed is that of differences between cultures (including regions and historical periods). Hymes, for instance, distinguished between cultures in which performance is 'salient and common' from cultures in which it is 'subdued and rare', while others have contrasted high and low 'degrees of performance'.[58] The Mediterranean world, for instance, has often been presented as a *società dello spettacolo* and sometimes as a 'theatre culture', contrasted with 'cultures of sincerity' in Northern Europe. The point of the contrast is not that northerners are actually more sincere than Italians (a proposition that could never be tested), but simply that they value sincerity more highly.[59] Alternatively, one might contrast the 'warm' performances of the Mediterranean world with the cooler style of Northern Europe, including the famous British 'stiff upper lip'.

All the same, we must try to avoid simple contrasts between the theatrical and the sincere.[60] In eighteenth-century Britain and in colonial America, orators and actors (notably David Garrick) aban-

---

[58] Hymes, 'Breakthrough', p. 13. Cf. William H. Jansen, 'Classifying Performance in the Study of Verbal Folklore', in *Studies in Folklore: In Honor of Distinguished Service Professor Stith Thompson*, ed. by W. Edson Richmond, Indiana University Publications 9, Folklore Series (Bloomington: Indiana University Press, 1957), pp. 110–18 (p. 112).

[59] Cesare Molinari, *Le nozze degli dèi: un saggio sul grande spettacolo italiano nel Seicento*, Biblioteca teatrale, Studi, 3 (Rome: Bulzoni, 1968), p. 9; Burke, *Historical Anthropology*, pp. 9–13; Silvia Carandini, *Teatro e spettacolo nel Seicento*, Biblioteca universale Laterza, 306 (Rome: Laterza, 1990), p. 7.

[60] *L'anthropologie de la Méditerranée*, ed. by Dionigi Albera, Anton Blok, and Christian Bromberger, Atelier méditerranéen (Paris: Maisonneuve et Larose, 2001), pp. 15–37, 733–52.

doned stereotyped dramatic gestures in the attempt to appear more natural and spontaneous. However, it has been argued that this movement 'led paradoxically to a greater theatricalization of public speaking, to a new social dramaturgy and to a performative understanding of selfhood'. We have returned to the suggestion that what we call 'sincerity' may be viewed and analysed as a 'script'.[61]

It might therefore be more prudent to say that we all perform, although different styles of performing – more or less stylized, expressive or spectacular – are associated with different regions, social groups and, not least, different periods. Even scholarly communication is – and perhaps should be – a kind of performance.[62]

---

[61] Wierzbicka, *Emotions*, pp. 241–46; Jay Fliegelman, *Declaring Independence: Jefferson, Natural Language and the Culture of Performance* (Stanford: Stanford University Press, 1993), pp. 2, 79–94.

[62] Greg Dening, *Performances* (Carlton, Vic.: Melbourne University Press, 1996).

References

Abrahams, Roger D. 'A Performance-Centred Approach to Gossip', *Man*, 5 (1970), pp. 290–301, repr. in his *Man-of-Words in the West Indies: Performance and the Emergence of Creole Culture*, Johns Hopkins Studies in Atlantic History and Culture (Baltimore: Johns Hopkins University Press, 1983).

Abrahams, Roger D. 'Toward an Enactment-Centered Theory of Folklore', in *Frontiers of Folklore*, ed. by William R. Bascom (Boulder: Westview Press for the American Association for the Advancement of Science, 1977), pp. 79–120.

Abu-Lughod, Lila. *Dramas of Nationhood: The Politics of Television in Egypt* (Chicago: University of Chicago Press, 2005).

Austin, John. *How to Do Things With Words* (Oxford: Clarendon, 1962) (but given as lectures in 1955).

Bailey, Peter. 'Will the Real Bill Banks Please Stand Up? Towards a Role Analysis of Victorian Respectability', *Journal of Social History*, 12 (1978), 336–53.

Barzman, Karen-Edis. 'Early Modern Spectacle and the Performance of Images', in *Perspectives on Early Modern and Modern Intellectual History*, ed. by Joseph Marino and Melinda Schlitt (Woodbridge: University of Rochester Press, 2001), pp. 283–302.

Bauman, Richard D. 'Verbal Art as Performance', *American Anthropologist*, 77 (1975), 290–306;

Bauman, Zygmunt. *Liquid Modernity* (Cambridge: Polity Press, 2000).

Bell, Catherine. *Ritual Theory, Ritual Practice* (New York: Oxford University Press, 1992)

Bély, Lucien. *Espions et ambassadeurs au temps de Louis XIV* (Paris: Fayard, 1990).

Bhabha, Homi K. 'Of Mimicry and Man', in Bhabha, *The Location of Culture* (London: Routledge, 1994), pp. 88–91.

Biagioli, Mario. *Galileo, Courtier: The Practice of Science in the Culture of Absolutism*, Science and Its Conceptual Foundations (Chicago: University of Chicago Press, 1993).

Bourdieu, Pierre. *Esquisse d'une théorie de la pratique: précédé de trois études d'ethnologie kabyle*, Travaux de droit, d'économie, de sociologie et de sciences politiques, 92 (Geneva: Droz, 1972).

Brown, Bertram Wyatt. *Southern Honor* (New York: Oxford University Press, 1982).

Burke, Kenneth. *The Grammar of Motives* (New York: Prentice-Hall, 1945)/

Burke, Peter. *Popular Culture in Early Modern Europe* (London: New York University Press, 1978).

Burke, Peter. *Historical Anthropology of Early Modern Italy: Essays on Perception and Communication* (Cambridge: Cambridge University Press, 1987).

Burke, Peter. *The Fabrication of Louis XIV* (New Haven: Yale University Press, 1992).

Burke, Peter. 'La reconstruction des rituels politiques au siècle de Louis XIV', in *Le Protocole ou La mise en forme de l'ordre politique*, ed. by Yves Deloye, Claudine Haroche, and Olivier Ihl (Paris: L'Harmattan, 1996), pp. 171–83.

Burke, Peter. 'Performing History: The Importance of Occasions', *Rethinking History*, 9 (2005), 35–52.

Burke, Peter. 'On the Margins of the Public and the Private: Louis XIV at Versailles', *International Political Anthropology* 2 (2009), pp. 29-36.

Burke, Peter. 'Co-memorations: performing the past', in Karin Tilmans, Frank van Vree and Jay Winter (eds.) *Performing the Past: memory, history and identity in modern Europe* (Amsterdam, Amsterdam University Press, 2010), pp. 105-18.

Burke, Peter. 'Varieties of Performance in 17th-Century Italy', in *Performativity and Performance in Baroque Rome*, ed. by Peter Gillgren and Mårten Snickare (Farnham: Ashgate, 2012), pp.15-23.

Burke, Peter. 'From the Disputation to Power Point: Staging Academic Knowledge in Europe, 1100-2000', in *Inszenierung und Gedächtnis*, ed. by Heidemarie Uhl (Vienna: Oesterreichsche Akademie der Wissenschaften, 2014).

Butler, Judith. *Gender Trouble: Feminism and the Subversion of Identity* (London: Routledge, 1990).

Carandini, Silvia. *Teatro e spettacolo nel Seicento*, Biblioteca universale Laterza, 306 (Rome: Laterza, 1990).

Certeau, Michel de. *La possession de Loudun*, Collections Archives, 37 (Paris: Julliard, 1970).

Craveri, Benedetta. *La civiltà della conversazione*, Collana dei casi, 48 (Milan: Adelphi, 2001).

Davis, Natalie. 'The Rites of Violence' (1971), repr. in *Society and Culture in Early Modern France: Eight Essays* (London: Duckworth, 1975), pp. 152-88.

Dekker, Rudolf M. and Lotte C. van de Pol, *The Tradition of Female Transvestism in Early Modern Europe* (Basingstoke: Macmillan, 1989).

Dening, Greg. *Performances* (Carlton, Vic.: Melbourne University Press, 1996).

Edelman, Murray. *Politics as Symbolic Action: Mass Arousal and Quiescence*, Institute for Research on Poverty Monograph Series (New York: Academic, 1971).

Ellmann, Richard. *Yeats: The Man and the Masks* (London: Macmillan, 1949).

Fernandez, James W. 'The Performance of Ritual Metaphors', in *The Social Use of Metaphor: Essays on the Anthropology of Rhetoric*, ed. by J. D. Sapir and J. C. Crocker (Ann Arbor: University of Michigan Books on Demand, 1977), pp. 100-31.

Fernández-Armesto, Felipe. *Columbus* (Oxford: Oxford University Press, 1991).

Fliegelman, Jay. *Declaring Independence: Jefferson, Natural Language and the Culture of Performance* (Stanford: Stanford University Press, 1993).

Foster, Roy. *W. B. Yeats: A Life*, 2 vols (Oxford: Oxford University Press, 1997-2003).

Foucault, Michel. *Surveiller et Punir* (Paris: Gallimard, 1975).

Fox, Robin. 'The Inherent Rules of Violence', in *Social Rules and Social Behaviour*, ed. by Peter Collett (Oxford: Blackwell, 1977), pp. 132-49.

Fujitani, Takashi. *Splendid Monarchy: Power and Pageantry in Modern Japan*, Twentieth-Century Japan, the Emergence of a World Power, 6 (Berkeley: University of California Press, 1996).

Geertz, Clifford. *The Interpretation of Cultures* (New York: Basic, 1973)

Geertz, Clifford. *Negara: The Theatre State in Nineteenth-Century Bali* (Princeton: Princeton University Press, 1980).

Gentilcore, David. 'Performance', in his *Medical Charlatanism in Early Modern Italy* (Oxford: Oxford University Press, 2006), pp. 301-34.

Goffman, Erving. *The Presentation of Self in Everyday Life* (New York: Doubleday, 1959).

Goldbert, RoseLee. *Performance: Live Art 1909 to the Present* (London: Thames and Hudson, 1979).

Hay, Douglas. 'Property, Authority and the Criminal Law', in *Albion's Fatal Tree: Crime and Society in Eighteenth-Century England*, ed. by Douglas Hay and others (London: Allen Lane, 1975), pp. 17-64.

Heckscher, William S. *Rembrandt's Anatomy of Dr. Nicolaas Tulp: An Iconological Study* (New York: New York University Press, 1958).

Henke, Robert. *Performance and Literature in the Commedia dell'Arte* (Cambridge: Cambridge University Press, 2002).

Herzfeld, Michael. *The Poetics of Manhood: Contest and Identity in a Cretan Mountain Village* (Princeton: Princeton University Press, 1985).

Hevia, James L. *Cherishing Men from Afar: Qing Guest Ritual and the Macartney Embassy of 1793* (Durham, NC: Duke University Press, 1995).

Humphrey, Caroline and James Laidlaw, *The Archetypal Actions of Ritual: A Theory of Ritual Illustrated by the Jain Rite of Worship* (Oxford: Clarendon Press, 1994).

Hymes, Dell. 'Breakthrough into Performance', in *Folklore: Performance and Communication*, ed. by Dan Ben-Amos and Kenneth

S. Goldstein, Approaches to Semiotics, 40 (The Hague: Mouton, 1975), pp. 1-73.

Ihl, Olivier. *La fête républicaine,* Bibliothèque des Histoires (Paris: Gallimard, 1996).

Jansen, William H. 'Classifying Performance in the Study of Verbal Folklore', in *Studies in Folklore: In Honor of Distinguished Service Professor Stith Thompson,* ed. by W. Edson Richmond, Indiana University Publications 9, Folklore Series (Bloomington: Indiana University Press, 1957), pp. 110-18.

Jarrard, Alice. *Architecture as Performance in Seventeenth-Century Europe: Court Ritual in Modena, Rome, and Paris* (Cambridge: Cambridge University Press, 2003);

Labrot, Gérard. *L'image de Rome: une arme pour la Contre-Réforme, 1534-1677* (Lille: Atelier National de Reproduction des Thèses, 1978; second edn, Seyssel: Champ Vallon, 1987).

L'anthropologie de la Méditerranée, ed. by Dionigi Albera, Anton Blok, and Christian Bromberger. Atelier méditerranéen (Paris: Maisonneuve et Larose, 2001).

Laqueur, Thomas W. 'Crowds, Carnival and the State in English Executions, 1604-1868', in *The First Modern Society: Essays in English History in Honour of Lawrence Stone.,* ed. Lee Beier, David Cannadine, and James Rosenheim. Past and Present Publications (Cambridge: Cambridge University Press, 1989), pp. 305-55.

Le charivari: Actes de la table ronde organisée à Paris (25-27 avril 1977), ed. by Jacques Le Goff and Jean-Claude Schmitt (Paris: École des Hautes Études en Sciences Sociales, Mouton 1981).

Leiris, Michel. *La possession et ses aspects théâtraux chez les Éthiopiens de Gondar,* L'Homme; cahiers d'ethnologie, de géographie et de linguistique, n.s., 1 (Paris: Plon, 1958)

Lilti, Antoine. *Le monde des salons: sociabilité et mondanité à Paris au XVIIIe siècle* (Paris: Fayard, 2005).

Lord, Albert B. *The Singer of Tales*, Harvard Studies in Comparative Literature, 24 (Cambridge, MA: Harvard University Press, 1960).

Lotman, Yuri. 'The Theatre and Theatricality as Components of Early Nineteenth-Century Culture' (1973), trans. in Ju. M. Lotman and B. A. Uspenskij, *The Semiotics of Russian Culture*, ed. by Ann Shukman, Michigan Slavic Contributions, 11 (Ann Arbor: Dept of Slavic Languages and Literatures, University of Michigan, 1984), pp. 141–76.

Lotman, Yuri. 'The Poetics of Everyday Behaviour in Eighteenth-Century Russian Culture' (1977), trans. in Iurii M. Lotman, Lidiia Ia. Ginsburg, and Boris A. Uspenskij, *The Semiotics of Russian Cultural History: Essays*, ed. by Alexander D. Nakhimovsky and Alice Stone Nakhimovsky (Ithaca: Cornell University Press, 1985), pp. 67–94.

Majorana, Bernadette. 'Elementi drammatici della predicazione missionaria', in *La predicazione in Italia dopo il Concilio di Trento tra Cinque e Settecento*, ed. by G. Martina and U. Dovere (Naples: n. pub., 1996), pp. 127–52.

Miyoshi, Masao. *As We Saw Them: The First Japanese Embassy to the United States (1860)* (Berkeley: University of California Press, 1979), pp. 92–93, 125–41.

Molinari, Cesare. *Le nozze degli dèi: un saggio sul grande spettacolo italiano nel Seicento*, Biblioteca teatrale, Studi, 3 (Rome: Bulzoni, 1968).

Muir, Edward. *Civic Ritual in Renaissance Venice* (Princeton: Princeton University Press, 1981).

Ozouf, Mona. *La fête révolutionnaire, 1789–1799*, Bibliothèque des Histoires (Paris: Gallimard, 1976).

Posner, David. *The Performance of Nobility in Early Modern European Literature*, Cambridge Studies in Renaissance Literature and Culture, 33 (Cambridge: Cambridge University Press, 1999).

Reddy, William M. *The Navigation of Feeling: Framework for a History of Emotions* (Cambridge: Cambridge University Press, 2001).

Rites of Power: Symbolism, Ritual, and Politics since the Middle Ages, ed. by Sean Wilentz, (Philadelphia: University of Pennsylvania Press, 1985).

Rituals of Royalty: Power and Ceremonial in Traditional Societies. ed. by David Cannadine and Simon Price. Past and Present Publications (Cambridge: Cambridge University Press, 1987).

Roosen, William. 'Early Modern Diplomatic Ceremonial: A Systems Approach' *Journal of Modern History*, 52 (1980), 452-76.

Rosenberg, Bruce A. *The Art of the American Folk Preacher* (New York: Oxford University Press, 1970).

Rueger, Jan. *The Great Naval Game: Britain and Germany in the Age of Empire* (Cambridge: Cambridge University Press, 2007).

Schama, Simon. *Citizens: A Chronicle of the French Revolution* (London: Folio Society, 1989).

Schwartz, Barry. 'The Social Context of Commemoration', *Social Forces*, 61 (1982), 374-402. *Commemorations: The Politics of National Identity*, ed. by John R. Gillis (Princeton: Princeton University Press, 1994).

Scott, James C. *Domination and the Arts of Resistance: Hidden Transcripts* (New Haven: Yale University Press, 1990).

Social Performance: Symbolic Action, Cultural Pragmatics, and Ritual, ed. by Jeffrey C. Alexander, Bernhard Giesen, and Jason L. Mast (Cambridge: Cambridge University Press, 2006).

Spierenburg, Pieter. *The Spectacle of Suffering* (Cambridge: Cambridge University Press, 1984).

Spillman, Lyn. *Nation and Commemoration: Creating National Identities in the United States and Australia* (Cambridge: Cambridge University Press, 1997).

St George, Robert. 'Massacred Language: Courtroom Performance in Eighteenth-Century Boston', in *Possible Pasts: Becoming Colonial in Early America*, ed. by Robert St George (Ithaca: Cornell University Press, 2000), pp. 327–56.

Stone, Lawrence. *Road to Divorce: England, 1530–1987* (Oxford: Oxford University Press, 1990).

Tambiah, Stanley. 'A Performative Approach to Ritual', *Proceedings of the British Academy*, 65 (1979), 113–69.

Theatricality, ed. by Tracy C. Davis and Thomas Postlewait, Theatre and Performance Theory (Cambridge: Cambridge University Press, 2003).

Tilly, Charles. *Regimes and Repertoires* (Chicago: University of Chicago Press, 2006).

Trexler, Richard. *Public Life in Renaissance Florence*, Studies in Social Discontinuity (New York: Academic, 1980).

Turner, Victor. *Schism and Continuity in an African Society: The Study of Ndembu Village Life* (Manchester: Manchester University Press, 1957).

Turner, Victor. *The Anthropology of Performance*, Performance Studies Series, 4 (New York: Performing Arts Journal Publications, 1988).

Turner, Victor and Edith Turner. *Image and Pilgrimage in Christian Culture: Anthropological Perspectives* (New York: Columbia University Press, 1978).

van Dülmen, Richard. *Theater des Schreckens: Gerichtspraxis und Strafrituale in der frühen Neuzeit* (Munich: Beck, 1985).

Voyelle, Michel. *Les metamorphoses de la fête en Provence de 1750 à 1820*, Bibliothèque d'ethnologie historique (Paris: Aubier/Flammarion, 1976).

Wagner-Pacifici, Robin. *The Moro Morality Play: Terrorism as Social Drama* (Chicago: University of Chicago Press, 1986).

Waldstreicher, David. *In the Midst of Perpetual Fetes: The Making of American Nationalism, 1776–1820* (Chapel Hill: Omohundro Institute of Early American History and Culture, University of North Carolina Press, 1997).

Wierzbicka, Anna. *Semantic Primitives*, trans. by Anna Wierzbicka and John Besemeres, Linguistiche Forschungen, 22 (Frankfurt am Main: Athenaum, 1972).

Wierzbicka, Anna. *Emotions across Languages and Cultures: Diversity and Universals* (Cambridge: Cambridge University Press, 1999).

Wills, John E., Jr. *Embassies and Illusions: Dutch and Portuguese Envoys to K'ang-hsi, 1666–1687*, Harvard East Asian Monographs, 113 (Cambridge, MA: Harvard University Press, 1984).

Wortman, Richard. *Scenarios of Power: Myth and Ceremony in Russian Monarchy*, Studies of the Harriman Institute, 2 vols (Princeton: Princeton University Press, 1995–2000).

3: TRANSLATING KNOWLEDGE, TRANSLATING CULTURES

One of the many shifts or turns in historical thought and historical writing in the last generation has been the turn from intellectual history to cultural history, from the history of ideas to the history of meanings. Like most such shifts or turns, this one is not complete. Some intellectual historians continue as they did before, while others produce what we might call 'hybrid' studies. That is, they approach topics that used to be viewed as part of intellectual history – the history of ideas, the history of knowledge – from a broader, cultural or socio-cultural point of view. This broader approach is the central theme of this paper.

I

It is a commonplace to note that the topics that historians choose to study are related to the problems, anxieties, hopes and debates occurring at the time that they are writing. In today's 'information society', historians are turning to the study of information – how and why it is collected, how it is organized, classified, criticized and employed for a variety of purposes, in short, turned from information that is more or less 'raw' into knowledge that has been processed or 'cooked'.[1]

---
[1] P. Burke, A Social History of Knowledge (Cambridge, 2000).

What is History Really About? A Historian Reflects on Theory and Practice

In an age of globalization, in which the internationalization of knowledge is visible on the screens of our computers and televisions, historians are coming to view past knowledge as the result of an international or even an intercontinental process of cultural exchange or cultural transfer. To offer a recent example from the area and the period on which I usually work, between 1997 and 2002, the European Science Foundation sponsored a programme devised by the French historian Robert Muchembled and entitled 'Cultural Exchange in Early Modern Europe'. One of the four international teams, the one of which I was a member, was concerned with information and communication.[2]

As is usually the case with a new turn or a new trend, problems arise in the course of research, leading us to question the very concepts with which we started. It might for example be better to use the term 'knowledge' in the plural than in the singular, to speak of different knowledges or systems of knowledge in different parts of the world or among different social groups – professors and artisans, men and women, young and old, etc.

Again, the idea of a 'transfer' of knowledge is less helpful than the idea of the transfer of technology on which the concept was modelled. For one thing, when there is an encounter between two cultures, information usually flows in both directions, even if in unequal amounts. We might therefore speak of intellectual or cultural 'exchanges'.

But even the term 'exchange' is unsatisfactory in some ways. Like the old term 'tradition', it implies handing over something that remains more or less unchanged. However, it has become increasingly apparent in the last generation, in studies ranging from sociology to literature, that 'reception' is not passive but active. Ideas, information, artefacts and practices are not simply adopted but on the contrary, they are adapted to their new cultural environment. They are first decontextualized and then re-contextualized, domesticated or 'localized'. In a word, they are 'translated'.

---

[2] R. Muchembled (ed.) Cultural Exchange in Early Modern Europe (4 vols, Cambridge 2007).

II

The phrase 'cultural translation' can be heard on many lips today, including those of anthropologists, linguists, literary critics and students of religion as well as cultural historians. The metaphor now seems an obvious one, and it goes back at least eighty years. In the 1920s, the anthropologist Bronisław Malinowski, for example, claimed that 'the learning of a foreign culture is like the learning of a foreign tongue' and that he was attempting 'to translate Melanesian conditions into our own'. A few years later, in the Thirties, the Hungarian sociologist Karl Mannheim, complaining about the difficulty of explaining the sociology of knowledge to the British, remarked on 'the urgent need and the great difficulty of translating one culture in terms of another'.[3] He should know. Mannheim was himself translated to England (in the sense of transferred, as a refugee). Indeed he was part of what we might call the great *Translatio Studii* in which Central European scholars, mainly German-speaking and Jewish, took refuge from the Hitler regime, mainly in Britain and the USA.

In a broader, looser sense, the idea of cultural translation is still older, taking us back to the Renaissance. John Florio, the Anglicized Italian who translated Montaigne's *Essais* into English (1603), justified his translation in his preface to the reader with a kind of *captatio benevolentiae*, by saying that we all translate, even the writers of 'original' works. If there is nothing new under the sun, 'What do the best, then, but glean after others' harvest? Borrow their colours, inherit their possessions? What do they but translate?'

However, the more precise idea that understanding an alien culture was analogous to the work of translation first became current among anthropologists in the 1950s and 1960s in the circle of Edward Evans-Pritchard. As one of them has claimed, 'Anthropology is an art of translation'.[4] We might say the same thing about history, since 'the past is a foreign country' where they do things

---

[3] Bronisław Malinowski, Argonauts of the Western Pacific (London, 1922), 90; Karl Mannheim, Conservatism, ed. David Kettler, Volker Meja and Nico Stehr (London, 1997), 118–19.

[4] Malcolm Crick, Explorations in Language and Meaning (London, 1976), 164.

differently and perhaps think differently as well.[5]

As translators know, the passage of a text from one language to another is not a smooth or easy one. It requires negotiation.[6] Many words in one language lack exact equivalents in another. Keywords or *Grundbegriffe* are part of a given culture and resist translation. Translators learn to live with a dilemma: should they be faithful to the original text from which they are translating, or intelligible to the readers of the text they are writing?

There are two opposite solutions to the problem, two strategies to follow, the maximalist and the minimalist. The maximalist strategy is better known as domestication, while the minimalist has become known as 'foreignizing'. In the famous words of Friedrich Schleiermacher, the choice lies between taking the text to the reader, in other words adapting it to the culture in which it is a 'guest', or taking the reader to the text, that is, producing a version that allows or encourages the new readers to become aware of the text's alien or foreign qualities.[7] One strategy follows the model of cultural translation, the other rejects or resists it.

To take a couple of examples from the field of Catholic missions, especially the practice of the Jesuits. Christian missionaries, like translators, faced a dilemma when adapting (or as was said at the time, 'accommodating') the Christian message to the culture in which they were working. In China, Matteo Ricci chose the maximalist solution. He translated the word 'God' by the neologism *Tianzhu*, literally 'Lord of Heaven', and allowed Chinese Christians to refer simply to *Tian*, 'Heaven', as Confucius had done. Ricci also discovered that if he dressed as a priest no one would take him seriously, so he dressed like a Confucian scholar instead, thus 'translating' his social position into Chinese. He allowed the Chinese whom he converted to pay reverence to their ancestors in the traditional manner, arguing that this was a social custom rather than a religious one.

---

[5] The quotation, repeated by many historians, is from the first sentence of Leslie P. Hartley's novel The Go-Between (London, 1953).

[6] Umberto Eco, Mouse or Rat? Translation as Negotiation (London, 2003).

[7] On the term 'foreignizing', Lawrence Venuti (ed.) Rethinking Translation (London, 1992). On the 'guest' culture, Lydia H. Liu, Translingual Practice (Stanford, 1995).

Translating Knowledge, Translating Cultures

In Rome, the Jesuits were accused of having been converted to the religion of the Chinese rather than converting them to Christianity. What appeared in Beijing to be a good cultural translation looked more like a mistranslation in Rome. Other Jesuit missionaries chose the other horn of the dilemma from Ricci, the minimalist one, keeping their traditional black robes and also the Latin word *Deus*, glossing rather than translating it into different languages, from Huron to Tagalog.

III

It is time for a case-study, turning to the translation of knowledge in early modern Europe and using the term 'translation' in both the literal and the metaphorical sense. To link the two kinds of translation is indeed my main purpose here, stressing the point that interlingual translation is one of the most visible or audible parts of cultural translation. In other words, we need a historical anthropology of interlingual translation.[8]

Translation between languages is obviously of central importance in any history of cultural exchange, including exchanges of information about history, geography, politics, natural philosophy, architecture and so on. A historical anthropology of translation might focus on two questions: What was translated? How was it translated?

What was translated, and where, reveals what one culture finds of interest in another, separated from it either in space or time. Take the case of historical writing. Ancient historians were translated more than any modern authors. In different European vernaculars, nearly 300 translations of 25 ancient historians were published between the invention of printing and the end of the eighteenth century. To this figure we have to add the translations of Greek historians into Latin.[9] The leading historians translated were Sallust, Valerius

---

[8] Hans J. Vermeer, 'Übersetzen als kultureller Transfer', in Mary Snell-Hornby (ed.) Übersetzungswissenschaft (Tübingen, 1986), 30–53; Catherine Tihanyi, 'An Anthropology of Translation', American Anthropologist 106 (2004), 739–42.

[9] Peter Burke, 'The Popularity of Ancient Historians 1450–1700', *History and Theory* 5 (1966), 135–52; id., 'Translating Histories', P. Burke and R. Hsia (eds.) Cultural Translation in Early Modern Europe (Cambridge, 2007), 125–41.

Maximus and Caesar, in that order, a choice that says something about the difference between the early modern and later periods.

Among 'modern' historians, from Leonardo Bruni onwards, I have so far discovered more than 550 published translations of texts by 289 historians, and there may well be many more. Italian, French and Latin were the languages from which most historians were translated. English, Latin, French, Dutch and German led the languages into which texts were translated. The importance of translations from the vernacular into Latin is worth noting, as a major means for the dissemination of information across Europe.[10] The historians most translated were Commynes (eleven translations in the period), and the Jesuit missionary Martino Martini's account of the fall of the Ming dynasty in China (nine translations). Four texts tie for third place because they were translated eight times each: Francesco Guicciardini's *History of Italy*, the Italian bishop Paolo Giovio's *History of His Own Time*, Sleidan's *Commentaries* – which might be described as a political history of the Reformation – and Sarpi's *History of the Council of Trent*.

How were these texts translated? In other words, what was the dominant 'regime' or 'culture' of translation in the early modern period? Despite frequent references to the 'laws' of translation, the early modern culture of translation was one of relative freedom. Translators generally followed what Venuti calls the 'fluent strategy', the one that 'domesticates the foreign text', offering the reader 'the narcissistic experience of recognizing his or her culture in a cultural other'.[11] If they still used that once fashionable term, anthropologists might describe what these translators were doing as a form of 'acculturation'.

Translations were often made indirectly, at second hand, as titlepages ('shamelessly', as we might say) admit. French was a common medium: Italian or Spanish texts were translated into English via French, while English texts followed the same route into German. Modern texts were not infrequently considered capable of improvement by their translators (Rawlinson's version of Lenglet

---

[10] Peter Burke, 'Translations into Latin in Early Modern Europe', in P. Burke and R. Hsia (eds.) Cultural Translation in Early Modern Europe (Cambridge, 2007), 65–80.
[11] Venuti (1992), 5.

du Fresnoy's method for studying history, published in 1728, was described on the title-page as 'translated and improved'). What were described at the time as 'translations' often differed from the originals in major respects, whether they abridged the texts or amplified them. Major changes of this kind were often made without warning the reader.

The borderline between translation and imitation was drawn less sharply than it would be in the nineteenth century. In some cases the context was shifted from one locale to another, a process that may be described in musical terms as 'transposition' or – following the practice of current translators of software – as 'localization'. The translation of Machiavelli's *Arte della Guerra* into Spanish displaced the dialogue from Italy to Spain and turned the speakers into two Spaniards, the Great Captain Gonzalo Fernández de Cordoba and the Duke of Najara, perhaps because Spanish readers of the period would not have expected to learn anything about war from Italians.

Even more shocking for modern readers, translators of works of history or natural philosophy sometimes allowed themselves to express opinions that the original author would have repudiated. With characteristic boldness, when Cardinal de Retz, who had been a rebel himself, translated Agostino Mascardi's history of the conspiracy by Count Fieschi, he contradicted his source text by turning the protagonist from a villain into a hero.

However, no dominant regime lacks opposition, whether in translation or in politics. Attempts at foreignization can be found long before the nineteenth century, most obviously in the case of the Bible: some translations of the Old Testament into English and Dutch took pains to imitate Hebrew formulae and syntax. Nicolas D'Ablancourt is notorious for the freedom of his French translations from the classics, but even he retained some technical terms such as 'cohort' or 'centurion' when translating ancient writers, since their armies, he explained, were very different from 'ours'. The reason for this temporary shift into foreignization, which led D'Ablancourt to provide his translation of Appian with a glossary, was probably that he was writing for noblemen who took considerable interest in the details of military organization.

IV

What follows is concerned with the cultural translation of the Turks by western travellers writing in their own language and also with the translations of those translations into other languages, especially Latin, Italian, French, English, German and Dutch. In Spanish, relatively little on the Turks appeared in print at this time, whether original works or translations.[12] However, a number of translations remained in manuscript, together with one fascinating sixteenth-century text, the *Viaje de Turquía*. Scholars are still discussing who wrote the *Viaje* and whether it represents first-hand observation or should be treated as a work of fiction based on secondary sources.[13]

The problem for all the writers discussed here was that of deciding which technical terms to translate (and how) and which were better left in the original Turkish. When their books were translated into other languages, translators had to make the same decision, crucial for the transmission of both information and ideas.

In early modern Europe, let us say from 1453 to 1789, the Ottoman Empire and Turkish culture were translated in two very different ways. On one side we see the persistence of traditional stereotypes. On the other, we find examples of a fresher vision, generally the result of direct observation at close quarters. Some individuals combine or at any rate juxtapose schematic and fresh perceptions.

The stereotyped ways in which western Europeans viewed the Ottoman Empire in the early modern period are well known. The medieval stereotype of Muslims as 'the scourge of God', 'the enemy of the Cross', 'perfidious infidel', 'the new barbarian' 'was carried over to the Ottomans'.[14] These ideas form part of the discourse

---

[12] Giovio's book on the Turks appeared in Spanish in 1543 but it is a rare book with only one edition; Sagredo's history was published in Spanish translation in 1684.
[13] Marie-Sol Ortola (ed.) Viaje de Turqía (Madrid, 2000); pp.117–24 discuss the Turkish terms in the text. Cf. Jeremy Lawrance, 'Europe and the Turks in Spanish Literature of the Renaissance', in Nigel Griffin et al. (eds.) *Culture and Society in Habsburg Spain* (Woodbridge 2001) 17–34.
[14] Robert Schwoebel, *The Shadow of the Crescent: the Renaissance Image of the Turk* (Nieuwkoop, 1967), 147; cf. Almut Höfert, *Den Feind beschreiben* (Frankfurt, 2003).

of 'orientalism' described by Edward Said 30 years ago, though with more emphasis on cruelty and less on passivity – unsurprisingly enough, since the Turks conquered and colonized Eastern Europe, not the other way round.[15] What was new at this time was the emphasis on the Ottoman political regime. Five keywords in different languages recur to describe this regime: tyranny, despotism, absolutism, slavery and lordship (the sultan as *il grande signore*, owning all the land in the Ottoman Empire).

Another kind of stereotyping was associated with Renaissance humanism. Take the case of Pietro Bembo, author of a Latin history of Venice which naturally had much to say about the neighbours of the Venetians. Bembo was a purist who believed that Latin prose should imitate Cicero. Hence Bembo calls the Turkish galleys *biremes*, the spahis *equites*, the admiral of the Turkish fleet *prefectus classis Thraciae* and the sultan *Rex Thracium*.[16] The janissaries were often described as the 'praetorian guards', *praetoriani milites*.

V

A different style of translating the Turks was based on relatively close encounters and on more or less first-hand information from former prisoners, ambassadors or consuls who had lived in the Ottoman Empire. These writers generally 'foreignized' the Turks by keeping technical terms, especially the names for different kinds of official, in their original language – as anthropologists do in their ethnographies – explaining rather than translating them, even when writing Latin and referring to *dragomani, bassae, janizari* and so on.

In the case of the vernaculars, domestication was even less common than in the case of Latin, although a few translators were supporters of linguistic purism. Take the case of the Italian bishop Paolo Giovio, for instance, whose Italian account of the Turks had at least eight Italian editions in the sixteenth century as well translations into Latin, German, English and Spanish. Giovio left terms such as *aga, beylerbey* or *timariot* in Turkish. The prevalence of for-

---

[15] Carlo Dionisotti, 'La Guerra d'Oriente nella letteratura veneziana de Cinquecento', rpr his *Geografia e Storia della letteratura italiana* (Turin, 1967), 201–26.
[16] Pietro Bembo, *Historia Veneta* (1551, new edn Venice 1611), 176, 340.

eignizing might be linked to the increasing interest in foreign manners and customs shown by Europeans from the sixteenth century onwards.

In the seventeenth century, foreignizing becomes still more obvious. Take the case of Paul Rycaut, an Englishman of Flemish descent who lived in Istanbul and Smyrna (Izmir) from 1661 to 1678, as consul or secretary to the ambassador (incidentally, Rycaut was a translator himself, from the Spanish). Rycaut saw the Ottoman Empire from the point of view of a merchant and diplomat interested in peace and trade.[17]

In his *The History of the Present State of the Ottoman Empire* (1667), several times reprinted as well as being translated into French, Dutch, German, Polish, Italian and Russian, Rycaut called the Turks 'men of the same composition with us', so that they 'cannot be so savage and rude as they are generally described'. He noted the danger of 'contempt of the Turk', of treating them as 'barbarous'. Indeed, echoing Montaigne, he wrote of the 'prejudice' of treating as barbarous whatever is 'differenced from us by diversity of Manners and Custom, and are not dressed in the mode and fashion of our times and Countries'.

When he comes to speak of the political regime, he shows his concern for cultural specificity. 'The Constitution of the Turkish Government being different from most others in the World', he wrote, 'hath need of peculiar Maxims and Rules, whereon to establish and confirm itself'. For this reason Rycaut used many Turkish terms, explaining them in the text or margin as he goes. Some of these terms are religious (*mufti, mullah, dervish, hoja, imam*), some are military (*Spahees*) and a high proportion are political and administrative (among them *Bey, Defterdar, Divan, Kadi, Pasha, Pashalik*).

The translation of books from Turkish into western languages (and vice versa) was rare in the sixteenth and seventeenth centuries. One of the rare exceptions was the *Annals* [*Tac al-Tevarikh*, literally 'The Crown of Histories'] of Khojah Efendi [also known as Sa'duddin Bin Hasan Can, 1535-99].

---

[17] Paul Rycaut, The History of the Present State of the Ottoman Empire (London, 1667).

Translating Knowledge, Translating Cultures

The English translation of Khoja Efendi was made by the clergyman William Seaman, who had served as an embassy chaplain in Istanbul and translated the New Testament into Turkish. Despite the interest in missionary activity revealed by his Bible translation, Seaman did not domesticate the text. He retained the system of dating by the year of the Hegira (adding the year of Our Lord), left technical terms such as *sanjak bey* or *bassalik* in the original language, filled up his margins with Turkish words in the Arabic script, and went so far as to retain the term 'unbelievers' to refer to Christians.

What is more, in the preface, Seaman justified his approach in words which may remind modern readers of Schleiermacher's famous formulation of the translator's task, taking the reader to the text rather than vice versa, or as Seaman puts it, 'desiring rather a little to change our propriety to fit theirs, than much to alter their phrase to put it in ours'.

We should not imagine that we, or even our early twentieth-century predecessors, were the first people to be interested in what is specific to particular cultures and to try to preserve that specificity in translation. Some early modern writers were already of the opinion that among the most efficacious strategies for understanding other cultures is precisely the refusal to translate their keywords.

4: THE HISTORY AND THEORY OF RECEPTION

Quidquid recipitur, ad modum recipientis recipitur. – Thomas Aquinas

In what follows I shall argue (1) that the concept of reception (German *Rezeption*, French *réception*, Italian *recezione*, etc.) is older than is generally thought; (2) that, even so, the recent 'turn' in this direction is a significant one; (3) that the concept of 'cultural translation' is useful in reception studies; (4) that a number of problems plague scholars who try to tracethe history of the reception of particular texts or other cultural artefacts; and (5) that despite the problems, this approach continues to illuminate intellectual history. Examples from the cultural relations between Europe and East Asia will be privileged, on the grounds that the more distant two cultures are from each other, the more visible the reception process becomes.

1

In common with so many apparently new ideas, the idea of reception-has a longer history than we may think. As a term of art, it was current in scholarly circles, especially in Germany, about a hundred years ago, in the contexts of Roman law and of Renaissance humanism.[1]

---
[1] Carl Adolf Schmidt, *Die Reception des Römischen Rechts in Deutschland* (1868: repr Leipzig: Zentralantiquariat der DDR, 1969); Paul Laband, *Rede über die Bedeutung der Rezeption des römischen Rechts für das deutsche Staatsrecht* (Strasbourg: University of Strasbourg, 1880); Max Herrmann, *Die Reception des Humanismus in Nürnberg* (Berlin:Wiedmann, 1898); Stefan Schuler, *Vitruv im Mittelalter: Die Rezeption von "De Architectura"von der Antike bis in die frühe Neuzeit* (Cologne: Böhlau, 1999).

The term was also used by English-speaking literary scholars and, a little later, by some historians of religion.[2] The idea of reception has also attracted interest from students of literature, art and ideas who did not make use of the word. Classicists in particular speak of 'tradition'.[3] In Germany, an alternative term is 'afterlife'(*Nachleben* or *Fortleben*).[4] In Italy, the favoured term was and is *fortuna*.[5] Some writers in English preferred and indeed still prefer 'influence', especially in studies of literature, but in intellectual history and art history as well.[6] Others chose and still choose 'legacy'.[7]

Most if not all of the studies mentioned so far have looked at reception essentially from the point of view of the donor, treating recipients as relatively passive, as followers: Machiavellians, Erasmians, Lutherans and so on. Terms such as 'transmission' or 'transfer' (as in the case of the 'transfer of technology') also emphasize donors.[8] Studies of reception, transfer, tradition, and legacy generally depend on the assumption of fidelity or continuity, taking it for granted that

[2] William Frederic Hauhart, *The Reception of Goethe's Faust in England in the First Halfof the 19th Century* (New York: Columbia University Press, 1909); Lawrence M. Price, *The Reception of English Literature in Germany* (Berkeley: University of California Press, 1932); Thomas A. Brady, *The Reception of Egyptian Cults by the Greeks* (Columbia: Universityof Missouri, 1935); Charles D. Cremeans, *The Reception of Calvinistic Thought in England* (Urbana: University of Illinois Press, 1949).
[3] Anthony Grafton, Glenn W. Most and Salvatore Settis, eds., *The Classical Tradition* (Cambridge MA: Harvard University Press, 2010).
[4] Otto Immisch, *Das Nachleben der Antike* (Leipzig: Dieterich, 1919); Jacob Walter, *William Blakes Nachleben in der englischen Literatur des neunzehnten und zwanzigsten Jahrhunderts* (Schaffhausen: Bachmann, 1927).
[5] For example, Vincenzo Luciani, *Francesco Guicciardini e la fortuna dell'opera sua* (Florence: Olschki, 1949); Giuliano Procacci, *Studi sulla fortuna del Machiavelli* (Rome:Istituto Storico Italiano per l'età moderna e contemporanea, 1965).
[6] Alfred E. Taylor, *Platonism and its Influence* (London: Harrap, 1925); Thomas F. Scanlon, *The Influence of Thucydides on Sallust* (Heidelberg: Winter, 1980); Henry H. Reed, *Palladio's Architecture and its Influence* (New York: Dover, 1980); Mordechai Feingold, Joseph S.Freeman and Wolfgang Rother, ed., *The Influence of Petrus Ramus* (Basel: Schwabe, 2001).
[7] Richard W. Livingstone, ed., *The Legacy of Greece* (Oxford: Clarendon Press, 1921); Cyril Bailey, ed., *The Legacy of Rome* (Oxford: Clarendon Press, 1923); Joseph V. Femia, ed., *The Machiavellian Legacy* (Basingstoke: Macmillan, 1998).
[8] Michel Espagne, *Les Transferts culturels franco-allemands* (Paris: Presses Universitaires de France, 1999).

what was received or inherited was the same as what was given or handed over. In this respect scholars follow the people they were studying, from classical antiquity to early modern times, when favoured terms were *traditio* and *translatio* (in the sense of 'transfer').

Traditions might of course be criticized as corrupt, as reformers criticized the traditions of the Catholic Church, but the criticism implied that purification or a return *ad fontes* was possible. A similar point might be made about the critique of some translations as unfaithful, as in the famous debate in seventeenth-century France about *les belles infidèles*.[9] Although the famous epigram attributed to Karl Marx, "I am not a Marxist", has been circulating for a long time, the implications for intellectual history of the distance between founders and followers have rarely been made explicit.[10]

A few scholars have found fault with these approaches, more especially with the concept of 'influence'. As early as 1945, R. G. Collingwood criticized what he called "the frivolous and superficial type of history which speaks of 'influences' and 'borrowings' and so forth and...never asks itself what there was in A that laid it open to B's influence, or what there was in A which made it capable of borrowing from B". Quentin Skinner made a similar point in 1969 and Michael Baxandall in 1985: "'Influence' is a curse of art criticism primarily because of its wrong-headed grammatical prejudice about who is the agent and who the patient...If one says that X influenced Y it does seem that one is saying that X did something to Y rather than that Y did something to X...If we think of Y rather than X as the agent, the vocabulary is richer and more attractively diversified: draw on, resort to, avail oneself of, appropriate from, have recourse to, adapt, misunderstand, refer to".[11]

---

[9] Jean-Pierre Massaut, *Critique et tradition à la veille de la Réforme en France* (Paris:Vrin, 1974); Roger Zuber, *Les "belles infidèles" et la formation du goût classique* (Paris: Colin,1968).
[10] For an important exception, see Benjamin Schwartz, "Some Polarities in Confucian Thought," in *Confucianism in Action*, ed. David Nivison and Arthur Wright (Chicago: University of Chicago Press, 1959).
[11] Robin G. Collingwood, *The Idea of Nature* (Oxford: Oxford University Press, 1945), 128. Cf Quentin Skinner, "Meaning and Understanding in the History of Ideas," *History and Theory* 8 (1969): 3–53; Michael Baxandall, *Patterns of Intention* (New Haven CT: YaleUniversity Press, 1985), 58–9. Skinner and Baxandall (like Jauss, discussed below) quote Collingwood with approval.

2

As if in response to these criticisms, a new wave—not to say flood—of reception studies arrived in the late twentieth century. What was important was not so much the increase in number, creating a trend or, as critics would say, an academic 'fashion', but the change in the way in which followers or receivers were viewed. Instead of being regarded as passive recipients of 'influence' or at best as lacking ideas of their own, followers were now accorded agency and the emphasis fell on 'uses' or 'responses', viewed from the side of the recipient. Hence one might speak of a 'turn' towards reception, on the analogy of the more famous linguistic, visual and other turns. Changes in language make a sensitive indicator of the trend. Scholars working on the Renaissance in particular have found themselves using more and more words beginning with 're': not only 'reception', but also 're-reading', 'rewriting', 're-employment', 'reframing','re-interpretation' and 'recontextualization'.[12]

In the case of literature, this turn is associated with the rise of 'Reception Theory' and with two German theorists in particular, Hans-Robert Jauss and Wolfgang Iser.[13] Jauss stressed what he called the "aesthetics of reception", while Iser emphasized "reader-response", viewing meaning as the product of the interaction between reader and text, but the two men are often linked as leaders of the 'School of Konstanz', the new German university where they both taught. Iser's work in particular has become well known in the English-speaking literary world, thanks in part to his appointment as a professor at the University of California at Irvine in the later 1970s.

---

[12] Maryanne C. Horowitz, Anne J. Cruz and Wendy A. Furman, eds., *Renaissance Rereadings* (Urbana: University of Illinois Press, 1988); Centre Interuniversitaire de recherche sur la Renaissance italienne, *Réécritures: commentaires, parodies, variations dans la literatureitalienne de la Renaissance* (3 vols., Paris: Université de la Sorbonne Nouvelle, 1983-7);Claire Farago, ed., *Reframing the Renaissance* (New Haven CT: Yale University Press, 1995).

[13] Hans-Robert Jauss, *Literaturgeschichte als Provokation* (Frankfurt: Suhrkampf, 1970);Wolfgang Iser, *Der Akt des Lesens: Theorie ästhetischer Wirkung* (Munich: Fink, 1976). Robert C. Holub, *Reception Theory: a Critical Introduction* (London: Methuen, 1984) remains a useful guide.

Perhaps the most distinctive feature of this approach is the concern with the 'horizon of expectations' (*Erwartungshorizont*), the argument being that the different expectations brought to a text by different readers shape the different ways in which a given text is understood. To give an example from intellectual history, a study of the German Enlightenment argues that in the 1770s and 1780s James Steuart was taken more seriously as an economic writer than Adam Smith, noting the attraction of Steuart's *Inquiry* for readers accustomed to the ideas of German writers such as J. H. G. Justi on the same subject. In other words, Smith was beyond their horizon.[14] The metaphor of 'horizon' is a traditional one in German philosophy, passed down from Edmund Husserl to his student Martin Heidegger, Heidegger's student Hans-Georg Gadamer and Gadamer's student Iser — although it was not always employed in the same manner by these four individuals. Another concept common to Gadamer, Jauss and Iser is that of *Wirkung*, the effect of a message on readers (or listeners). The distinction between *Rezeption* and *Wirkung* remains unclear.[15]

In the strict sense of the term, 'Reception Theory' refers to this German approach. However, there was a parallel movement in France, a broader movement in the sense that it was never confined to literary studies. Major figures in this movement were the philosopher Paul Ricoeur and the polymath Michel de Certeau. Both scholars stressed the agency of recipients. Ricoeur launched the concept of 'appropriation' for this purpose, a term which should perhaps be preferred to 'reception' precisely because of its associations with activity rather than passivity. As for Certeau, his favourite concept was 're-employment' (*ré-emploi*). Reacting against a common sociological view of ordinary people as passive consumers of mass-produced goods, Certeau argued that individuals exercise freedom of choice in selecting what to buy and inventiveness in using it afterwards, combining it with other items and so domesticating or customizing their acquisitions. Making

---

[14] Keith Tribe, *Governing Economy: the Reformation of German Economic Discourse, 1750–1840* (Cambridge: Cambridge University Press, 1988), 140.
[15] Holub, *Reception Theory*, xi.

reference to Claude Lévi-Strauss's idea of intellectual *bricolage* but developing it further, Certeau asserted that consumptionmight be regarded as a form of production.[16]

In literary studies, Julie Kristeva launched the idea of 'intertextuality', emphasizing the ways in which one text refers to others (by imitation, refutation, parody, and so on), in other words literary *bricolage*, while Gérard Genette developed the idea, distinguishing transtextuality, metatextuality, paratextuality and so on.[17]

Reception still attracts more interest in literary departments than in other parts of the campus, with the possible exception of departments of communication, especially following a well-known study of the reception of the soap opera *Dallas* in different parts of the world that argued that the same images viewed by different groups could scarcely have been understood more differently.[18]

In other fields too there is increasing interest. Historians of art, for instance, study the reception of particular painters or kinds of art (Japanese art in the West, for instance), and some historians of architecture are concerned with re-employment in a more literal sense than Certeau, with the use of fragments of old buildings in new ones.[19] Intellectual historians have also been moving in this direction. Heidegger and Jauss were among the inspirations of the 'conceptual history' (*Begriffsgeschichte*) practised by Reinhart Koselleck and underlying the massive volumes of the *Geschichtliche*

---

[16] Paul Ricoeur, "Appropriation," in Ricoeur, *Hermeneutics and the Human Sciences: Essays on Language, Action and Interpretation*, 182-93 (Cambridge: Cambridge UniversityPress, 1981); Michel de Certeau, *L'invention du quotidien* (Paris: Union Générale d'Éditions,1980).

[17] Julia Kristeva, "Bakhtine, le mot, le dialogue et le roman," *Critique* 239 (1967): 438-65. Cf. Michael Worton and Judith Still, eds., *Intertextuality: theories and practices* (Manchester: Manchester University Press, 1990), especially 1-44; Graham Allen, *Intertextuality* (London: Routledge, 2000), especially 30-60, 97-115.

[18] Tamar Liebes and Elihu Katz, *The Export of Meaning: Cross-Cultural Readings of Dallas* (New York: Oxford University Press, 1990).

[19] Elisa Evett, ed., *The Critical Reception of Japanese Art in Late Nineteenth-Century Europe* (Epping: Bowker, 1982); Lucilla de Lachenal, *Spolia: uso e reimpiego dell'antico dal III al XIV secolo* (Milan: Longanesi, 1995).

Grundbegriffe. Koselleck in particular made frequent use of the idea of a horizon of expectations.[20] More generally, a shift towards reception is visible in the history of science, the history of political thought and the history of religion. In the case of science, Darwinism and Copernicanism have attracted particular attention.[21] In the domain of political thought, some studies of John Locke exemplify the new trend.[22]

In the case of religion, one might compare and contrast two studies of Erasmus and his followers that were published half a century apart. In his classic study of Erasmus and his writings in sixteenth-century Spain, Marcel Bataillon wrote of *érasmisme, mouvement érasmien, evangélisme érasmien* and so on and asked a fundamental question in reception studies, Why here? "How was it that this erasmian form of Christianity flourished more spectacularly in Spain than elsewhere?" Fifty years later, Silvana Seidel Menchi produced an important monograph on Erasmus's readers in Italy which both followed and differed from Bataillon's work. Unlike Bataillon, Seidel Menchi used the term *ricezione,* and in tune with recent reception studies, she criticized the term *erasmismo* as "a category worn out by too much use", stressing instead the use made of Erasmus by Italians who had their own agenda, to disguise Protestant beliefs or to legitimate a political attack on the Papacy.[23]

There are parallel or connected movements in other disciplines. Classicists, for instance, are examining Greek and Roman tradi-

---

[20] Otto Brunner, Werner Conze and Reinhart Koselleck, eds., *Geschichtliche Grundbegriffe,* 8 vols. (Stuttgart: Klett, 1972-97). Reception and horizon are discussed in ReinhartKoselleck, *Futures Past: on the Semantics of Historical Time,* trans. Keith Tribe (CambridgeMA: MIT Press, 1985), 7, 46, 56, 64, 106, 186, 196-7, 200, 267-88.

[21] Thomas F. Glick, ed., *The Comparative Reception of Darwinism* (Austin: Universityof Texas Press, 1974); Rienk Vermij, *The Calvinist Copernicans: the Reception of the NewAstronomy in the Dutch Republic, 1575-1750* (Amsterdam: Koninklijke Nederlandse Akademie van Wetenschappen, 2002).

[22] Mark Goldie, ed., *The Reception of Locke's Politics* (London: Pickering and Chatto, 1999).

[23] "Comment ce christianisme érasmien a-t-il fleuri en Espagne plus brillament qu'ailleurs?": Marcel Bataillon, *Erasme en Espagne* (1937; revised edn, Geneva: Droz, 1991), 846. Cf Silvana Seidel Menchi, *Erasmo in Italia: 1520-1580* (Turin: Bollati Boringhieri, 1987).

tions through the lens of reception.[24] Historians and critics of literature now pay more attention to readers and their responses than they used to do.[25] A recent study of the fortunes of Cervantes in seventeenth-century England begins with the question, "what did the first English-speaking readers of *Don Quixote* perceive?" and goes on to note that English writers "put *Don Quixote* to work toward their own ends".[26]

Certeau is one of the inspirations of Roger Chartier's research on the history of reading, while a number of historians have studied annotations in order to analyse the reception of texts by Castiglione, Montaigne, Copernicus and other writers.[27] In similar fashion, art historians have come to focus on viewers, and musicologists to listen to listeners.[28] Economic historians pay more attention to consumption than they used to, while many social and even political historians have turned to history 'from below', emphasizing the agency of ordinary people.

As so often happens in the history of historical thought, changes in the present, from populism to the concern with the environ-

---

[24] Charles Martindale, *Redeeming the Text: Latin poetry and the Hermeneutics of Reception* (Cambridge: Cambridge University Press, 2003); Martindale and Richard F. Thomas,eds., *Classics and the Uses of Reception* (Oxford: Blackwell, 2006); Philip Ford, *De Troie à Ithaque; réception des épopées homériques à la Renaissance* (Geneva: Droz, 2007).
[25] Iser, *Akt des Lesens*; Susan Suleiman and Inge Crosman, eds., *The Reader in the Text* (Princeton: Princeton University Press, 1980); Robert Darnton, "History of Reading," in *New Perspectives on Historical Writing*, ed. Peter Burke, 157–86 (2nd edn., Cambridge: PolityPress, 2001); Guglielmo Cavallo and Roger Chartier, eds., *A History of Reading in the West*, trans. Lydia G. Cochrane (Amherst: University of Massachusetts Press, 1999).
[26] Dale B. J. Randall and Jackson C. Boswell, *Cervantes in Seventeenth-Century England:the Tapestry Turned* (Oxford: Oxford University Press, 2009), xv, xxxvii.
[27] Roger Chartier, *Cultural History between Practices and Representations*, trans. Lydia G.Cochrane (Cambridge: Polity Press, 1988), 40–1; Peter Burke, *The Fortunes of the Courtier* (Cambridge: Polity Press, 1995); Warren Boutcher, "Marginal Commentaries: the Cultural Transmission of Montaigne's *Essais* in Shakespeare's England", in *Shakespeare et Montaigne*, ed. Pierre Kapitaniak and Jean-Marie Maguin, 13–27 (Paris: Société FrançaiseShakespeare, 2003); Owen Gingerich, *The Book Nobody Read: Chasing the Revolutions of Nicolaus Copernicus* (New York: Walker, 2004).
[28] Wolfgang Kemp, ed., *Der Betrachter ist im Bild* (Cologne: DuMont, 1985); David Freed-berg, *The Power of Images* (Chicago: University of Chicago Press, 1989); James H. Johnson, *Listening in Paris: a cultural history* (Berkeley: University of California Press, 1995).

ment, have encouraged scholars to ask different questions about the past. In the case of the classics, for instance, where reception studies have gained a good deal of ground, especially in the last decade, the need to respond to the decline in the study of Greek and Latin is obvious enough. The growing interest in the metaphorical re-employment of the *Odyssey* or the *Aeneid* might be construed uncharitably as a reaction to the need for the literal re-employment of ex-classicists.

Unlike the reception studies of the years around 1900, the new movement is—or at least was, back in the 1970s—subversive, shocking, even scandalous because it shifted the emphasis from passive or faithful reception to active or creative reception. Reception scholars were helping to unmask the illusion of perfect communication, undermining the importance of the intentions of writers, artists and philosophers, and calling into question the notion of fixed meaning. Some of the scholars involved in the movement had no such ambitions, but, appropriately enough in this context, their studies too were received in this way.

However shocking the reception approach seemed to some critics, the stress on readers and viewers as appropriators was not completely new. The concept of cultural 'borrowing' is an old one that emphasizes recipients, even if it was often assumed that what was borrowed was identical to what was lent. For this reason, writing about the Renaissance in the 1920s, the iconoclastic Lucien Febvre had rejected the concept of borrowing on the grounds that the artists and writers of the time "have combined, adapted, transposed" producing "something that was composite and original at the same time".[29] Some Brazilian writers made a similar point at about the same time, even more vividly. In his *Manifesto antropófago* (1928) Oswald de Andrade, playing with the European stereotype of Brazilians as cannibals, addressed the question whether writers like himself should or should not follow European models. Oswald attacked what he called "importers of canned consciousness" and suggested that Brazilians were capa-

---

[29] "ont combiné, adapté, transposé": "quelquechose de composite et d'original à la fois": Lucien Febvre, "La Première Renaissance française," reprinted in Febvre, *Pour une histoire à part entière* (Paris: SEVPEN, 1962), 529–603, at 584.

ble of digesting foreign ideas, thus making them their own.[30]

In fact the assumption of fidelity had been challenged long before, by Thomas Aquinas. In his famous *Summa Theologiae*, Aquinas formulated the principle that *Quidquid recipitur, ad modum recipientis recipitur:* "whatever is received is received according to the manner of the receiver".[31] As Thomas well knew, some of the Fathers of the Church (Basil, Origen, Jerome and Augustine) had responded in a similar way to a difficult problem: What was to be done with pagan traditions in a Christian world? Their solution was to stress what we now call selective appropriation, or in their much more vivid vocabulary, "loot" (*spolia*). Augustine, quoting *Exodus* iii.22, "*spoliabitis Egyptum*", compared the Christian use of the classics to the people of Israel plundering Egypt's treasure when they left. For their part, Origen and Jerome, quoting *Deuteronomy* xxi.11-13, used the striking sexist metaphor of the beautiful captive: Christian readers could make the pagan classics serve their own purposes, just as the Israelites had used the Egyptian women they captured and enslaved, shearing their hair and paring their nails.[32] Basil of Caesarea used the metaphor of bees who "neither approach all flowers equally, nor try to carry away those they choose entire, but take only what is suitable for their work and leave the rest untouched".[33]

The Church Fathers make a bridge to reception theory because two of the major French theorists, Paul Ricoeur and Michel de Certeau, were well-read in patristics. Ricoeur's discussion of appropriation, like Certeau's presentation of re-employment, was itself a translation or creative adaptation of the ideas of Augustine and Jerome. In his most famous study of reception, Certeau referred like Augustine to readers "looting the goods of Egypt to enjoy them themselves".[34]

---

[30] Carlos A. Jauregui, *Canibalia. Canibalismo, calibanismo, antropofagia cultural y consumo en América Latina* (2nd edn, Madrid: Iberoamericana, 2008).
[31] Thomas Aquinas, *Summa theologiae* (Cologne: Hieratus, 1604), 1a, q. 75, a. 5; 3a, q. 5.
[32] Henri de Lubac, *Exegèse médiévale: les quatre sens de l'écriture*, 4 vols. (Paris: Aubier,1959-64), 1: 290-304.
[33] Werner Jaeger, *Early Christianity and Greek Paideia* (Cambridge, MA: Harvard University Press, 1962).
[34] "ravissant les biens d'Egypte pour en jouir": Certeau, *L'Invention du quotidien*, 292.

3

There are other traditions of reception studies besides the German and the French. In literary studies in the USA, a landmark was Harold Bloom's *The Anxiety of Influence* (1973), which focused not on the influential older writer but on the anxious younger one, torn between admiration for a classic and the drive towards originality.

Another approach originated not in literature but in social anthropology. In the 1950s, Edward Evans-Pritchard described the task of interpreting one culture to another as "cultural translation". His approach has been criticized for neglecting the power relations embedded in the translation process, but the same point has been made about interlingual translations, so the analogy still holds.[35] Evans-Pritchard's concept was gradually extended from the anthropologist as translator to refer to acts of translation taking place within the culture being studied.[36] A vivid example of the latter process comes from the American anthropologist Laura Bohannan, describing a story-telling session in a West African village in which she was doing fieldwork. When her turn to tell a story came round, she decided to summarize the plot of *Hamlet*. However, the village elders kept interrupting her and "correcting" the story. In the process they localized *Hamlet*, adapting it to their environment and so transforming the play into a West African folktale.[37]

Bohannan was writing in the 1960s, when the idea of cultural translation was more or less confined to anthropology. Since then, of course, it has spread to scholars in other disciplines. The point that we are all translators whenever we adapt ideas or artefacts to new purposes is made more and more frequently in the age of what has been called the 'translational turn' of the 1990s. Just as translation is viewed as a kind of negotiation, so negotiation may

---

[35] Talal Asad, "The Concept of Cultural Translation", in *Writing Culture*, ed. James Clifford and George Marcus, 141-164 (Berkeley, University of California Press, 1986).
[36] Edward E. Evans-Pritchard, *Social Anthropology* (London: Routledge, 1951), 81-82; Thomas O. Beidelman, ed., *The Translation of Cultures* (London: Tavistock, 1970).
[37] Laura Bohannan, "Shakespeare in the Bush," (1966), reprinted in *Critical Essays on Shakespeare's Hamlet*, ed. David S. Kaston (New York: Prentice-Hall, 1995).

be regarded as a form of translation.[38]

In religious studies, for instance, it has become almost commonplace to present missionaries as translators between cultural systems. They face a dilemma resembling the dilemma of translators, walking a tightrope between fidelity to the original text and intelligibility to the new audience. For example, in his study of Maurice Leenhardt, a French Protestant missionary in New Caledonia who later became an anthropologist, James Clifford wrote about "the idea of a cross-culturally translatable Christianity".[39]

For a vivid example, or series of examples, of this process of tightrope-walking one might take the case of Matteo Ricci, the Italian Jesuit who became the leading figure in the China mission in the sixteenth century. In the first place, Ricci had to translate himself. He began by wearing the robes of a Buddhist monk, which made him acceptable in his new environment at the price of being treated as someone of low status. Worse still for the mission, the Chinese perceived Catholic doctrine "through the lens of Buddhism", viewing images of the Virgin Mary, for instance, as representations of the local deity Guanyin.[40]

Reacting against what he perceived to have been a cultural mistranslation, Ricci took off his monk's clothes and put on the robes of a Chinese scholar. He also began to present Christianity as consistent with the ideas of Confucius, "accommodating" it, as he put it, to the local culture. Hencehe described the Christian God to the Chinese as "Lord of Heaven" (*Tianzhu*) or "High Sovereign" (*Shangdi*), since references to Heaven and to the High Sovereign occur in the

---

[38] Anthony Pym, 'Negotiation Theory as an Approach to Translation History: an Inductive Lesson from 15thc Castille', in Yves Gambier and Jorna Tommola, eds., *Translation and Knowledge*, 27–39 (Turku: Grafia Oy, 1993); Umberto Eco, *Mouse or Rat? Translation as Negotiation* (London: Weidenfeld and Nicolson, 1993).
[39] James Clifford, *Person and Myth: Maurice Leenhardt in the Melanesian World* (Berkeley: University of California Press, 1982), 79. Cf. Cristina Pompa, *Religião como tradução.Missionários, Tupi e Tapuia no Brasil colonial* (São Paulo: ANPOCS, 2003).
[40] Ronnie Po-chia Hsia, *A Jesuit in the Forbidden City. Matteo Ricci, 1552–1610* (New York:Oxford University Press, 2010), 92, 168. Cf. Qiong Zhang, "The Politics of Cultural Translation and Interpretation in the Early Jesuit Mission," in *Tokens of Exchange: the Problem of Translation in Global Circulation*, ed. Lydia Liu, 74–106 (Durham, NC, 1999).

Confucian classics. Ricci also faced the difficult decision whether to treat the cult of ancestors as a form of religion, in which case his converts would have to abandon it, or as a social custom, in which case it would be retained. Ricci and his successors in the mission chose the latter option. In this way they made more converts — at the price of being denounced by rival missionaries as unchristian.[41]

Another field in which the idea of cultural translation has become prominent is film studies. After all, in the world of the cinema adaptations of texts are commonplace, while some adaptations involve not only a change of medium, but also a transfer from one country or one period to another.[42] A spectacular example of such a transfer in space, time and culture is Akira Kurosawa's *Throne of Blood* (1957), a film that translates Shakespeare's *Macbeth* (itself a cultural translation from eleventh-century Scotland to Jacobean England) into the feudal world of sixteenth-century Japan.

The metaphor of translation has the great advantage of emphasizing agency, drawing attention to the work of adaptation performed by individual mediators between cultures, academic disciplines and so on. It also reminds students of reception to look for what is 'lost in translation', or what is distorted: as Cervantes memorably wrote, reading a text in translation is "like viewing Flemish tapestries from the wrong side".[43]

4

The idea of reception, as it has been elaborated and developed over the last generation, offers insights and opportunities to intellectual historians, although problems come in its train. Reception theory still bears the marks of the contexts in which it originated. In the case of Jauss and Iser, this context includes German literary studies in the late 1960s, when the theorists belonged to a new generation in revolt against an older one. Again, the ideas of Harold

---

[41] Po-chia Hsia, *A Jesuit*, 81, 138, 158, 293–8.
[42] Brian McFarlane, *Novel to Film: an Introduction to the Theory of Adaptation* (Oxford:Clarendon Press, 1996), especially 8–10.
[43] Miguel de Cervantes, *Don Quixote*, ed. Francisco Rico (Barcelona: Instituto Cervantes, 1999), Part 2, ch. 62.

Bloom about the anxiety of influence, presented as universal, are formulated with reference to poets of the nineteenth and twentieth centuries. However, these ideas still have their uses for historians if they are suitably adapted. A study of poets of the Renaissance, for instance, would have to begin by recognizing that attitudes to imitation were not the same as later romantic and post-romantic ones.

Reception studies enrich intellectual history by encouraging scholars in the field not to limit themselves to the reconstruction of the intentions of major thinkers, but to ask a much wider range of questions about recontextualizations, responses, uses, and so on. A comparative approach is particularly illuminating, focusing on the warm or cool reception of the same text or author in different countries, for instance, or that of different authors in the same country. However, even in the case of one text in one country it may be prudent to speak of 'receptions' in the plural: witness, for instance, the divided British responses to Salman Rushdie's *Satanic Verses* when it first appeared in 1988.

As usual, new opportunities are accompanied by new problems, two in particular. In the first place, what shapes reception? To what extent does it depend on affinities, resonances or merging horizons of expectation? Apparent affinities, or the recognition of the self in the other, have played an important part in the cultural relations between Japan and the West. For example, the interest in Japanese art in France at the end of the nineteenth century was related to the rise of Impressionism. Camille Pissarro, an enthusiast for the work of Utagawa Hiroshige, described him as "a marvellous Impressionist". Conversely, a Japanese art historian, Yukio Yashiro, published a book on Botticelli in 1925 in which he compared his work to that of Japanese artists such as Kitagawa Utamaro.

Insofar as reception can be shaped, the bibliographer Don McKenziehas noted the importance of the physical layout of books (the size of pages, the fount of the type, etc) as part of the message of the text. As he put it, "forms effect meanings". In similar fashion, as we have seen, the French critic Gérard Genette emphasized 'paratexts' — dedications, epigraphs, introductions, prefatory verses, illustrations, notes, indexes and so on — as so many means, available to authors, editors and publishers, of managing the responses of readers. Again, book reviews have helped to shape the expectations of other readers (and of some non-readers), from the invention of the genre in the learned journals of the late seventeenth century until today.[44]

When a text is translated, the translator has the power to shape reception, especially when the domesticating mode of translation is adopted. This was generally the case for early modern translators, who allowed themselves to omit and add passages and even to transpose the text from one locale to another.[45] When Machiavelli's *Arte della Guerra* was translated into Spanish, the dialogue was displaced from Italy to Spain while the speakers, originally the Roman Fabrizio Colonna and the Florentine Cosimo Rucellai, were turned into two Spaniards, the Great Captain Gonzalo Fernández de Cordoba and the Duke of Najara. Why? Presumably Spanish readers in the age of the famous *tercios* would not have expected to learn anything about war from Italians. Such an idea was beyond their horizon, and so cultural translation was necessary.

Thomas More's *Utopia* makes a particularly interesting case of the reception process because it might be described, like Castiglione's *Cortegiano*, as founding a genre to which it did not itself belong. *Utopia* was not written as a blueprint for an ideal society any more than the *Cortegiano* was written as a guide to good manners. They were transformed into such guides or blueprints by their printers, editors, translators and imitators. A recent collective study of More's *Utopia* in early modern Europe shows very clearly how editions and translations may be analysed to reveal the history of reception, based as it is on a careful analysis of the German, Italian, French, English, Dutch and Spanish translations of the text together with the paratexts that appear, disappear and on occasion reappear in different editions.[46] It would be good to see Bodin's major works treated in the same way.

---

[44] Donald F. McKenzie, *Bibliography and the Sociology of Texts* (London: British Library, 1986); Gérard Genette, *Seuils* (Paris: Seuil, 1987).
[45] Peter Burke, "Cultures of Translation in Early Modern Europe," *Cultural Translation in Early Modern Europe*, ed. Peter Burke and R. Po-chia Hsia, 7–38 (Cambridge: Cambridge University Press, 2007).
[46] Terence Cave, ed., *Thomas More's Utopia in Early Modern Europe* (Manchester: Manchester University Press, 2008).

Another illuminating case-study is concerned with the reception of the writings of Adam Ferguson in eighteenth-century Germany, focusing on problems of translation from one 'discourse' (in the sense of a network of interconnected concepts) into another. When Ferguson's key concept of "civil society" was rendered as *bürgerliche Gesellschaft*, for instance, it changed its meaning because the German phrase, unlike the English one, "did not contain a definite space for the citizen". Again, the use of terms such as *Seele* (soul) to translate "Mind" moved the text in the direction of German Pietism.[47]

Speaking more generally, it might be argued that the law of unintended consequences in history is as valid in the history of reception as it is elsewhere, and that even if translators intend to be faithful to the original, the language and indeed the culture into which they translate serve to condition their work, resulting in a hybrid product.

Such a hybrid product is often seen as a mistranslation, raising a second problem that might be called 'the problem of "mis"': not only mistranslation but also misunderstanding, misinterpretation, misreading, misrecognition or misuse — whether or not qualified by the term 'creative'. In the last generation, a number of studies have been devoted to this topic. Harold Bloom, for instance, devoted a book to what he called "misreading". The Brazilian critic Roberto Schwarz wrote a famous essay on "misplaced ideas" (*ideias fora do lugar*). The study of German responses to the writings of Adam Ferguson, cited above, was described by its author as a study of "misreception".[48]

The essay on misplaced ideas focuses on what the author calls "the disparity between the slave society of Brazil and the principles of European liberalism". It offers a brilliant critique of Brazilian culture, but fails to recognize that the problem is not one for

---

[47] Fania Oz-Salzberger, *Translating the Enlightenment: Scottish Civic Discourse in Eighteenth-Century Germany* (Oxford: Clarendon Press, 1995), 142-4, 158-9.
[48] Harold Bloom, *A Map of Misreading* (New York: Oxford University Press, 1975); Roberto Schwarz, "Misplaced Ideas", in *Misplaced Ideas: Essays on Brazilian Culture* (1977), ed. John Gledson, 19-32 (London: Verso, 1992); Oz-Salzberger, *Translating the Enlightenment*, 2-3, 77-85.

Brazilians alone, especially in an age of increasing "cultural mobility".[49] Whenever ideas are taken to new places, they are necessarily 'out of place'. Again, to speak of "misreception", as the study of Ferguson does, implies that a correct reception is possible, even though all reception involves some element of adaptation and recontextualization.

Rather than setting up a binary opposition between correct and incorrect, it might be more useful to speak of degrees of distance from the original. In any case, historians need to take account of the opposite points of view of donors and recipients. For donors, any adaptation or translation looks like an error. On the other hand, recipients often perceive their adjustments as corrections, like the West African elders cited above who corrected Shakespeare's *Hamlet*. It is sometimes reasonable to speak of 'mistranslation', or of 'misunderstandings' between individuals or groups, but the term 'misreception' remains problematic.

The study of Ferguson also raises the old problem of translatability, discussed by Iser among others.[50] In many languages, perhaps in all, there are certain words that the natives deem to be untranslatable. They have a special aura, a richness of associations that is lost in translation. Unfortunately for foreigners, these terms usually play a central role in a given culture, so much so that Rushdie could remark in another of his novels, *Shame*, that "to understand another culture, look at its untranslatable words".

The problem is so acute that it has led the author of one penetrating study of translation to describe that activity as a "wager"; to speak of equivalent terms in different languages as "constructed" rather than found; and even to abandon the central concept altogether, replacing "translation" by "translingual practice", defined as "the process by which new words, meanings, discourses and modes of representation arise, circulate and acquire legitimacy within the host language due to, or in spite of, the latter's contact/

---

[49] Elias J. Palti, "The Problem of 'Misplaced Ideas' Revisited," *Journal of the History of Ideas* 67 (2006): 149-79; Stephen Greenblatt et al., *Cultural Mobility: a Manifesto* (Cambridge: Cambridge University Press, 2010).
[50] Budick and Iser, *Translatability*.

collision with the guest language".[51] In similar fashion, historians and philosophers of science, notably Thomas Kuhn, have argued that successive theories or paradigms were incommensurable, changes of world view that made rational comparison impossible.[52]

Once again, though, a binary opposition, in this case between translatable and untranslatable, commensurable and incommensurable, oversimplifies a complex situation. We are better served by notions of a better or worse fit or of greater or lesser translatability or commensurability between words, languages and cultures. This conclusion has been reinforced by an exemplary study of nineteenth-century Japan, inspired in part by the work of Koselleck.[53]

After 1868, the new rulers of Japan set out to modernize the country by following western models, partly in order to protect themselves from the West. Scholars lent a hand in the process, translating certain books from English into Japanese, among them works by Charles Darwin, T. H. Huxley, Herbert Spencer and John Stuart Mill, whose essay *On Liberty* was translated in 1871. In Mill's case, the central problem was the translation of the word "liberty" itself. The translator searched for an equivalent term in the Japanese tradition and chose *jiyu*, a word that had already been used in early modern times to translate the Latin *libertas* and the Dutch *vrijheid*. However, *jiyu* carried a heavy negative connotation, associated as it was with selfishness and wilfulness in a culture that, unlike that of the West, favours the community over the individual. This example reveals with exemplary clarity some of the cultural as distinct from the linguistic obstacles to successful translation.

It is likely that the first Japanese readers failed to understand Mill's praise of liberty. On the other hand, their successors probably

---

[51] Lydia H. Liu, *Translingual Practice* (Stanford: Stanford University Press, 1995), 26; Liu,ed., *Tokens of Exchange* (Durham, NC: Duke University Press, 1999), 5, 34.
[52] Thomas S. Kuhn, *The Structure of Scientific Revolutions* (Chicago: University of Chicago Press, 1962), 110-11.
[53] Douglas Howland, "Translating Liberty in Nineteenth-Century Japan," *Journal of the History of Ideas* 62 (2001): 161-81. Cf. Howland, *Translating the West: Language and PoliticalReason in Nineteenth-Century Japan* (Honolulu: University of Hawaii Press, 2002). Cf. JörnLeonhard, "Language, Experience and Translation: towards a comparative dimension", in Javier Fernández Sebastián, ed., *Political Concepts and Time*, 245-72 (Santander: CantabriaUniversity Press, 2011).

understood him better a generation later after the new meaning of *jiyu* had established itself. Generalizing, perhaps rashly, from this example, one might suggest that when foreign words enter a given semantic field they are likely to be domesticated, transformed by the force of the other terms in the field.[54] In the course of time, however, the field itself may be transformed by these newcomers.

In making this suggestion I am myself re-employing the ideas of a distinguished anthropologist, Marshall Sahlins, whose reflections on the impact of Captain Cook, and more generally of British culture, on Hawaii from the late eighteenth century onwards distinguish two phases. In the first phase, the events which took place in Hawaii were "ordered by culture". The Hawaiians saw Cook's visit in terms of their own cultural traditions, thus "reproducing" the contact with another culture in the image of their own (or to use the language of this chapter, making a cultural translation). However, in the course of this re-ordering or reproducing, Hawaiian culture was transformed or re-ordered.[55] What seems to have happened in the Japanese case is that in a first phase the new idea of liberty was absorbed into a traditional linguistic field. At a certain point, though, once a critical threshold was passed, the field was re-ordered.

As these examples suggest, translation, whether between languages or cultures, is not a marginal topic for historians, even if it has entered their agenda only recently. If "the past is a foreign country", historians are all translators from the language of the past into that of the present. One might even say that this activity is their *raison d'être*. Like other translators, they face a central dilemma, between fidelity to the language they are translating from and intelligibility to the public for whom they are translating. In other words, the dilemma is not confined to the history of reception: it is built into the enterprise of history itself.

---

[54] On semantic fields, Howland, *Translating the West*, 28–9.
[55] Marshall Sahlins, *Islands of History* (Chicago: University of Chicago Press, 1985), 136–56.

5: IMAGES AS EVIDENCE IN SEVENTEENTH-CENTURY EUROPE

In memory of Francis Haskell

This essay is concerned with one aspect of the European antiquarian movement between the early Renaissance and the so-called "scientific" archaeology of the early nineteenth century. As a cultural practice, antiquarianism may be defined by its concern for the material remains of the past, together with a wide conception of that past, including everyday life, since the evidence of artefacts, combined with that of texts, allowed a more detailed and accurate reconstruction of "customs" (modes of eating and drinking, marriage and burial, etc), than had been possible from texts alone. It may sound anachronistic to attribute a concern with "total history" to early modern scholars, but their aim was indeed a reconstruction of the past out of surviving fragments, a restoration, in the words of the numismatist-diplomat Ezechiel Spanheim, of "the wholeness of history" (*historiae integritatem*).[1]

Like the humanist movement out of which it developed, antiquarianism was originally text-centred, focussed on the reading

---

[1] Ezekiel Spanheim, *Dissertatio de praestantia et usu numismatum antiquorum* (Rome, 1664), 97.

of inscriptions on monuments and coins, marble and metal. However, in the course of time the antiquaries – some of them at least – made what we might call a "visual turn", becoming more and more interested in the material culture of the past, including images.[2]

This territory was surveyed in a masterly fashion by Arnaldo Momigliano more than half a century ago, in a famous article which stressed the antiquaries' "revolution in historical method" and their interest in "non-literary evidence". More recently, Francis Haskell devoted several chapters of his *History and its Images* to a discussion of early modern antiquaries.[3]

In order to complement the work of Momigliano and Haskell, rather than simply repeat what they have argued so well, this article will adopt a comparative approach to the study of what might be called the "three antiquities", classical, Christian, and barbarian. In the second place, it will concentrate on the seventeenth century and on some scholars whom neither Momigliano nor Haskell discussed, such as Ole Worm and Jean-Jacques Chifflet. In the third place, like other articles in this collection, it will focus as sharply as possible on the question of evidence, especially on what the scholars of the time considered to be reliable evidence. Considering material culture in this way means placing Stuart Piggott alongside Momigliano and Haskell, and replacing the antiquaries in the history of archaeology.

Antiquarians or archaeologists?

It is impossible, and indeed undesirable to disentangle the history of the early modern antiquarian movement from the history of ar-

---

[2] Annie Laming-Emperaire, *Origines de l'archéologie préhistorique en France* (Paris, 1964), 77; cf. Alain Schnapp, *La conquête du passé: aux origines de l'archéologie* (Paris, 1993).

[3] Arnaldo D. Momigliano, "Ancient History and the Antiquarian" (1950, rpr *Studies in Historiography*, London 1966, 1–39); Francis Haskell, *History and Its Images* (New Haven, 1993). Cf. Roberto Weiss, *The Renaissance Discovery of Classical Antiquity* (Oxford, 1969).

chaeology, – or as some would say, its prehistory, describing the age before 1800 as "the pioneer, preparatory and speculative period".[4] The opposite dangers which any study in this domain must try to avoid are those of dismissing the work of the antiquaries as "pre-scientific" and of identifying their concerns with those of contemporary archaeologists. A third way might take its cue from Michel Foucault and sketch what he would have called an archaeology of archaeology.

Looking for changes in the linguistic field, it is easy to notice the increasing use of such terms as "antiquities" (*antiquitates*), "remains" (*vestigia*), "monuments" (*monumenta*), and "archaeology" itself, a seventeenth-century term for the study of antiquities, linguistic as well as material. Sir Henry Spelman, for instance, used the term *Archaeologus* for his glossary of medieval words, published in 1626, just as Edward Llwyd called his comparative study of the Celtic languages *Archaeologia Britannica* (1707). The French antiquary Jacques Spon proposed the alternative terms *archaeologia* and *archaeographia* to describe the science of antiquities, including numismatics, epigraphy, glyptography and iconography, as well as *angeiographia*, Spon's name for what we call the history of technology.[5]

The basic point which emerges from this brief linguistic survey is that the antiquarians were not specialists in one approach, like archaeologists today. For the most part amateurs working in their spare time, they were not confined to a single discipline but could move back and forth as they wished between literary and non-literary evidence, Romans and barbarians.

Turning from concepts to methods, it should be noted that many of the "fragments" which the antiquaries tried to fit together originally came to light by accident, often in the course of digging the

---

[4] For the first view, Glyn Daniel, "Edward Lhwyd: Antiquary and Archaeologist", *Welsh History Review* 3 (1966-7), 345-59, and Bruce G. Trigger, *A History of Archaeological Thought* (Cambridge, 1989); for the second, Stuart Piggott, "Antiquarian Thought in the 16th and 17th Centuries", in *English Historical Scholarship*, ed. Levi Fox (London, 1956), 93-114; Ole Klindt-Jensen, *A History of Scandinavian Archaeology* (London, 1975); Schnapp, *La conquête*, especially 11-12, 275-6, and Ingo Herklotz, *Cassiano del Pozzo und die Archäologie des 17. Jhts* (Munich, 1999), especially 9-10, 284-306.

[5] Jacques Spon, *Miscellanea erudita antiquitatis* (Lyon, 1685), preface.

foundations of buildings. In Rome in particular, ancient artefacts were constantly being turned up in this way. Building work at the Vatican, in 1544, for example, led to the discovery of the tomb of Maria, wife of the emperor Honorius, while some of the catacombs were discovered during the construction of the new St Peter's in the late sixteenth and early seventeenth centuries. Road works on the Via Flaminia near Rome led to the discovery of a painted room underground in 1674. The city of Pompei came to light in 1594 (although it was not identified till 1763) in the course of the construction of an aqueduct while Herculaneum was discovered in 1709 by workers digging a well.

In France, the construction of fortresses designed by Vauban led to the discovery of Roman amphitheatres at Metz and Besançon. In the Spanish Netherlands, the digging of the foundations of a hospital at Tournai in 1653 revealed the tomb of the Frankish ruler Childeric. In Britain, finds included the Alfred Jewel, discovered at North Petherton in Somerset in 1693, and the Stonesfield Pavement, unearthed in Oxfordshire in 1712.[6]

However, in the course of the period, an increasing number of antiquaries were turning to "digging up the past" in deliberate and more or less systematic fashion. Early examples include the excavation of a dolmen near Roskilde in 1588, the dig in Uppland organized by the Swedish antiquary Olof Verelius in 1663, the one at Björkö by his colleague Johan Hadorph in the 1680s, and the excavations conducted by Lhwyd in Britain.[7]

The History of Evidence

The concern for system and method was associated with a concern for evidence, a concept which scholars have recently been

---

[6] Simon Keynes, "The Discovery and First Publication of the Alfred Jewel", *Somerset Archaeology and Natural History* 136 (1992), 1–8, a reference for which I should like to thank my Emmanuel colleague David Pratt; Joseph M. Levine, "The Stonesfield Pavement: Archaeology in Augustan England", *Eighteenth-Century Studies* 11 (1977–8), 340–60.
[7] Daniel, "Lhwyd".

replacing in its historical context. In English, "evidence" is part of a cluster of terms including "testimony", "document", "fact", "inference" and "proof", which were coming to be defined with increasing care by lawyers, natural philosophers and others.[8] A similar point could probably be made about *preuve* and *témoignage* in French, *Beweis* and *Zeugnis* in German, and so on, but these usages still await systematic investigation.

The same goes for Latin, the language in which the majority of the texts discussed in this article were written. For a preliminary survey one might turn to the lawyers, who needed to make careful distinctions in this domain, for example to the Italian civil lawyer Giacomo Menochio, whose treatise on the topic, which went through at least fourteen editions in the century following its publication in the 1580s, may therefore be described as a standard work. Following Aristotle and the pseudo-Ciceronian *Ad Herennium*, Menocchio distinguishes different degrees of proof from the slightest, *suspicio*, through the more probable *praesumptio* and *probatio artificialis* to the most certain, *probatio directa*, and discusses not only direct *testimonia* but also indirect *indicia*, *signa* or *vestigia*. Similar points were made by Menochio's contemporary Giuseppe Mascardi, whose treatise on evidence (*probationes*) was published in 1593 and distinguishes *indicia* according to their evidential weight as *levia*, *gravia* and *gravissima*, and also as *credibilia*, *remota*, and so on.[9]

The last cluster of terms refers to the mute but eloquent story told either by facial expressions or by material remains. In a passage which has often been quoted in the last thirty years, the fifteenth-century Byzantine humanist Manuel Chrysoloras used the term *autopsia* – in other words eyewitnessing, seeing with one's own eyes – to refer to the evidence of material remains such as sculptures for "what kinds of arms the ancients had, what kind of clothes they

---

[8] Ian Hacking (1975); Barbara Shapiro, *A Culture of Fact: England, 1550-1720*, (Ithaca, 2000); Richard W. Serjeantson,'Testimony and Proof in Early Modern England', *Studies in the History and Philosophy of Science* 30 (1999), 195-236.

[9] Giacomo Menochio, *De praesumptionibus, coniecturis, signis et indiciis* (Lyon, 1588); Giuseppe Mascardi, *De probationibus* (3 vols, Frankfort 1593), especially voil.1, 23-5.

wore ... how they formed lines of battle, fought, laid siege".[10] His point was increasingly re-iterated in the following centuries.

For example, a series of writers on coins justified their studies on similar grounds.[11] In 1559, the Venetian Sebastiano Erizzo noted that the medals of the Roman Empire "reveal the whole history of these emperors", including facts which are not mentioned in the literary sources.[12] In 1587, the Spaniard Antonio Agustín declared that he had "more trust in medals, tablets and stones than in anything written".[13] In 1664, it was the turn of Ezekiel Spanheim to emphasise the importance of coins as historical evidence because they survive better than manuscripts, because they are less biased than texts, and because they fill gaps in the historical record with their images of houses, ships and so on.[14] Spon made a similar point in 1673, describing monuments as books with pages of marble or bronze which resolved contradictions between the textual sources of Roman history and were written with the chisel instead of the pen (the same metaphor had been used a few decades earlier by the Italian Jesuit Agostino Mascardi.[15] In 1697, John Evelyn described medals as 'the most Authentic and certain Reporters, preferable to any other'.[16]

Other antiquaries, as we shall see, treated different kinds of material object, from buildings to images, as "remains", "traces" or "vestiges" of the past, to be examined alongside texts. Developed in the course of studying Roman antiquity, this "materialist" method was applied in turn to early Christianity and to the other antiquities here classified (following the usage of the scholars of the time) as "barbarian".

---

[10] Quoted in Michael Baxandall, *Giotto and the Orators* (Oxford, 1971), 80–1. Cf. Haskell, *History*, 90–2, and Patricia F. Brown, *Venice and Antiquity* (New Haven, 1996) 76–7.
[11] Momigliano, "Ancient History".
[12] Sebastiano Erizzo, *Discorso sopra le medaglie de gli antichi* (1559: Venice, 1568), 2.
[13] Agustín quoted in Momigliano, "Ancient History", 16. Cf. Michael H. Crawford (ed.) *Antonio Agustín between Renaissance and Counter-Reform* (London, 1993).
[14] Spanheim, *Dissertatio*, 96–7.
[15] Jacques Spon, *Recherche des antiquités et curiosités de la ville de Lyon* (Lyon, 1673), preface; Mascardi quoted in Haskell, *History*, 94.
[16] John Evelyn, *A Discourse on Medals* (London, 1697), 243.

Images as Evidence in Seventeenth-Century Europe

The Discovery of Classical Antiquity

The antiquarian movement was of course a part of the wider movement we call the Renaissance. It included the imaginative reconstruction of ancient cities, and their buildings, especially Rome, stimulated by the discovery of ancient objects in the ground, from statues such as the Farnese Hercules to corpses such as the embalmed body of a girl found on the Via Appia in 1485 and described with enthusiasm by the humanist Bartolomeo della Fonte. It also included a series of learned monographs on the history of material culture in ancient Greece and Rome, beginning in the sixteenth century with treatises such as those of Guillaume Budé on coins, Lazare du Baïf on clothing and ships, Lilio Giraldi on tombs and many more.

In the seventeenth century, the study of ancient costume may be exemplified by the controversies about the Roman toga in which Ottavio Ferrari and Albert Rubens (the son of the painter) took part.[17] Baïf's work on ancient ships was continued in the books published by Johannes Gerhard Scheffer, a scholar from Nuremberg who was invited to court by Queen Christina of Sweden.[18] Ancient tombs and funeral customs were discussed in works such as Johann Kirchmann's *De funeribus romanorum*.[19] The different types of ring or bracelet used in antiquity were the objects of special attention.[20]

Today, these attempts to write the history of ancient togas, tri-

---

[17] Ottavio Ferrari, *De re vestiaria libri vii* (1642; second edn., Padua, 1685); Albert Rubens, *De re vestiaria veterum* (Antwerp, 1665).

[18] Lazare de Baïf, *De re navali* (1536); Johann Scheffer, *De militia navali veterum libri iv* (Uppsala, 1654); Herklotz, *Cassiano*, 166–72, 179–80.

[19] Lilio Giraldi, *De sepulchris* (1539); Johan Kirchmann, *De funeribus romanorum libri iv* (Lübeck, 1636); Thomas Browne, *Hydriotaphia: Urn Burial; or, a Discourse of the Sepulchral Urns lately found in Norfolk* (1658: Everyman edition, London 1906); cf. Stuart Piggott, "Sir Thomas Browne and Antiquity", *Oxford Journal of Archaeology*, 7 (1988), 257–70.

[20] Johann Kirchmann, *De anulis* (1623; second ed., Leiden 1672); Fortuni Liceto, *De anulis antiquis* (1645); Thomas Bartholin, *De armillis veterum* (Copenhagen, 1647); Johan G. Scheffer, *De antiquorum torquibus* (Stockholm, 1656); Giorgio Longo, *De annulis signatoris antiquorum* (Leiden, 1672).

remes, chariots, bracelets or lamps are likely to seem insufferably trivial and pedantic. Some writers already mocked these attempts at the time, Robert Burton for example, whose satirical essay "Democritus to the Reader" in his *Anatomy of Melancholy*, refers to "curious antiquaries" who concern themselves with topics such as "what clothes the senators did wear in Rome, what shoes, how they sat, where they went to the close-stool", and so on. The reference to shoes is probably to a book by Nigronius, *De caligula veterorum*, published in 1617, three years before the first edition of Burton, and the reference to "how they sat", to a book on the *triclinium* by the Spanish scholar Pedro Chacón.[21] In similar fashion, one character in Addison's *Dialogues on Medals* pokes fun at scholars who "are amazed at a man's ignorance, who believes that the toga had any sleeves to it till the declension of the Roman Empire".[22]

The critics surely had a point, since despite their references to the 'integrity' of the past, the work of many antiquaries was as fragmentary as the material remains they collected and studied with such enthusiasm. Yet some of them at least were concerned with major themes such as Roman religion, warfare and slavery. Pignoria's study of slavery, for instance, is exemplary in its use of visual evidence, including the collars worn by slaves who had attempted to escape.[23]

Some of the subjects the antiquaries studied were of topical interest. The Italian priest Onofrio Panvinio, for instance, discussed ancient Roman spectacles at the time of the Counter-Reformation critique of the theatre.[24] The reconstruction of the ancient art of painting was obviously of contemporary relevance during the Re-

---

[21] Robert Burton, *Anatomy of Melancholy* (1620: Everyman edition, London 19xx) 1, 113. Pedro Chacón, *De triclinio romano* (Rome, 1588); cf. Anthony Blunt, "The Triclinium in Religious Art", *Journal of the Warburg Institute* 2 (1938–9), 271–6; Herklotz, *Cassiano*, 295ff.
[22] Joseph Addison, *Dialogues upon the Usefulness of Ancient Medals* (London, 1726), 16–17.
[23] Lorenzo Pignoria, *De servis* (Augsburg, 1613), 22.
[24] Onofrio Panvinio, *De ludis circensibus libri ii* (Venice, 1600); cf. Federico Taviani (ed) *La commedia dell'arte e la società barocca* (Rome, 1970), li, and Jean-Louis Ferrary, *Onofrio Panvinio et les antiquités romaines* (Rome, 1996).

naissance, when artists were attempting to imitate the example of antiquity.²⁵ The humanist Justus Lipsius wrote on ancient Roman warfare at a time when his former pupil Maurice of Nassau was reforming the Dutch army by introducing forms of discipline on Roman lines.²⁶ Given his connections with the court of Sweden, Scheffer's concern with naval warfare may well have had a similar aim.

Trained in the humanist tradition of philology, these scholars generally began by collecting all the classical texts they could find relating to their subject. Even when they looked at monuments, from coins to triumphal arches, they concentrated on their inscriptions. They often began their treatises with the etymology of the Latin and Greek words describing the objects they were studying. They were sometimes led to their specific topics by the desire to clarify the meaning of a passage in an ancient writer. In the case of the history of clothes, for example, doubts about the meaning of technical terms such as *chlamys* or *latus clavus* were a major stimulus to research. Some major studies of antiquities, lacked illustrations altogether including Johan Kirchmann on ancient funerals, Johannes Meursius on ancient games, John Selden on the gods of the Syrians and Elias Schedius on those of the Germans.²⁷

However, the woodcuts and engravings which appear in many treatises offer us evidence of a gradual emancipation from logocentrism and an increasing concern with the testimony of images. In the later sixteenth century, at a time when new books were increasingly illustrated with frontispiece portraits of the authors, the Roman scholar Fulvio Orsini tried to identify reliable portraits of ancients such as Aristotle or Seneca.²⁸ The works of Ferrari, Scheffer and others were illustrated with engravings of the statues and coins on which they depended for much of their evidence. The

---

²⁵ Franciscus Junius, *De pictura veterum* (1636); cf. Rolf H. Bremmer Jr (ed.), *Franciscus Junius and his Circle* (Amsterdam and Atlanta, 1998).
²⁶ Justus Lipsius, *De militia romana* (1595, new ed. Antwerp 1598); cf. Gerhard Oestreich, *Neostoicism and the Early Modern State* (Cambridge, 1982, 76-89).
²⁷ Kirchmann, *De funeribus*; Johannes Meursius, *De ludis graecorum* (Leiden, 1622); Elias Schedius, *De dis Germanis* (Amsterdam, 1648).
²⁸ J. H. Jongkees, *Fulvio Orsini's Imagines and the Portrait of Aristotle* (Groningen, 1960).

increasing use of illustrations of this kind should be linked to the rise of private collections of classical sculpture and of cabinets of curiosities, especially cabinets of coins and medals. More intellectually ambitious than most collectors, the Roman cleric Cassiano del Pozzo attempted to collect images of all the remains of classical antiquity into his famous "paper museum", well-known to scholars in his day although unpublished.[29]

To symbolise the shift from text to object as evidence about the classical past, one might contrast the famous treatise by the French humanist Franciscus Junius, *De pictura veterum* (1637), which attempted to reconstruct ancient painting from literary sources, with the Italian critic Gianpietro Bellori's *Le pitture antiche* (1706), studying recently-found paintings in Roman grottoes.

The Uses of Trajan's Column

As a case-study of the uses of ancient remains as evidence it may be illuminating to focus on Trajan's Column. The accuracy of detail in the reliefs on the column, down to the eye-protectors for the horses of the Dacian cataphracts, are well known to ancient historians.[30] This accuracy did not escape the notice of Renaissance artists and antiquaries. Mantegna, Raphael and Giulio Romano all made use of the reliefs in order to represent Roman armour and weapons as accurately as possible. In his richly-illustrated study of Roman warfare, the French antiquary Guillaume Du Choul drew on the evidence provided by the Column, to show the Roman shield roof or *testudo*, for example. So did Justus Lipsius in his book on Roman machines or war, which also illustrated the *testudo*.[31] A few years later, Girolamo Aleandro drew on the evidence of the column in order to interpret the iconography of an ancient marble tablet.

---

[29] Elizabeth Cropper and Charles Dempsey, *Nicolas Poussin: Friendship and the Love of Painting* (Princeton, 1996); Herklotz, *Cassiano*.
[30] Ian Richmond, *Trajan's Army on Trajan's Column* (1935, rpr London 1982), 4n.
[31] Guillaume Du Choul, *Discours sur la castrametation et discipline militaire des Romains* (Lyon, 1557); Justus Lipsius, *Poliorceticon* (1596: second ed., Antwerp 1599), 32.

Studies devoted specifically to the Column appeared in print from the later sixteenth century onwards. The Spanish Dominican Alfonso Chacón published a description of the column in 1576 under the title of *The History of the Dacian Wars*, drawing the reader's attention in a prefatory note to the value of the Column's evidence for the history of armour and weapons, military discipline, and so on. His description was written in order to accompany a set of engravings of the reliefs, made by Girolamo Muziano.[32]

In the later seventeenth century, the artist Pietro Sante Bartoli made a new series of engravings of Trajan's Column with an accompanying text by Bellori and a note by the printer remarking on the value of the reliefs as evidence.[33] The ecclesiastical lawyer Raffaello Fabretti produced a new account of the column in 1683, richly illustrated with woodcuts of details, together with discussions of the history of Roman warfare and religion. Fabretti also checked older images of the column against the original reliefs and criticised the illustrations of 1576 as "perhaps more elegant than accurate", as well as pointing out mistakes on the part of Du Choul and Chacón and misreadings of the inscriptions by other scholars.[34]

The Discovery of the Early Church

In the age of the Counter-Reformation, there was a turn to a second antiquity, to the material remains of early Christianity. Fulvio Orsini, for example, dedicating to pope Sixtus V the treatise on the Roman *triclinium* by Pedro Chacón, remarked on the value of Roman antiquities for purposes such as the understanding of passages in Scripture, in this case a passage in St Luke (7, 36) about the woman anointing Christ's head when he reclined to eat. The combination of devotion to Christ's passion with antiquarian interests

---

[32] Alfonso Chacón, *Historia utriusque belli dacici* (Rome, 1576); cf Haskell, *History*, 93, and Herklotz (1999), 222-7, 257-60.
[33] GianPietro Bellori and Pietro Sante Bartoli, *Colonna Traiana* (Rome, 1673).
[34] Raffaello Fabretti, *De columna traiani syntagma* (Rome, 1683), 2, 51, 53, 92, 204; *Dizionario Biografico degli Italiano*, sub voce.

produced more than a century of scholarly debate on modes of crucifixion, in which Lipsius and the Dane Thomas Bartholin were the best-known participants. Gallonio's still more gruesome *Instrumenti di martorio* (1591), should be linked to the contemporary scenes of torture shown in the church of San Stefano alla Rotonda in Rome, to prepare missionaries for their possible future fate. [35]

However, the great stimulus to what has come to be known as "christian archaeology" was the discovery of the catacombs. The first of these underground cemeteries was found in 1578, on via Salaria Nuova in Rome, and it was soon followed by a series of similar discoveries. The excitement of the finds was evoked by Cesare Baronio, whose famous history of the Church described his visit to the cemetery of Priscilla. Particularly exciting to scholars were the paintings found in the catacombs, which dated from the third and fourth centuries.[36]

Alfonso Chacón, for example, copied some of the images himself and employed six artists to assist him. A friend of Chacón's, Antonio Bosio, began to explore the cemeteries from 1593 onwards. His treatise *Roma sotterranea*, published posthumously in 1632, gained him the later title of 'the Columbus of the Catacombs'. Drawing on the pictures made by Chacón and the Flemish artist Philips van Winghe as well as on his own observations, Bosio discussed such antiquarian topics as the sandals of the apostles, early gestures of prayer, and the meaning of images of lambs, doves, cocks, palms, cypresses, images of Orpheus (whom he identified with Christ) and so on.[37]

The special importance of the finds was their contribution to the controversy over the use of images in the primitive church. The Cambridge divine William Perkins, for instance, attacking Catholic images as "idols", had argued that "Images were not established in churches in these West parts, till after 700 years".[38] To this argu-

---

[35] Justus Lipsius, *De cruce* (Antwerp, 1593); Thomas Bartholin, *De cruce Christi* (Amsterdam, 1670).
[36] Cesare Baronio, *Annales ecclesiastici* (Rome, 16xx), A. D. 130. Cf. Haskell, *History*, 102–11.
[37] Antonio Bosio, *Roma Sotterranea* (Rome, 1632),
[38] William Perkins. *A Reformed Catholic* (London, 1617), 141.

ment Bosio's treatise was a reply, emphasizing the value of sacred images and giving a history of the cult of images which was continued by Catholic scholars such as Louis Maimbourg and Noël Alexandre.[39] Despite the many illustrations in Bosio's book, it has been argued that he too was a logocentric humanist who put 'text before trowel'.[40] A famous critique of Maimbourg and Alexandre by Friedrich Spanheim – who was the brother of the famous numismatist Ezekiel – ignored images and based itself on texts. Other Protestants denied the visual evidence, claiming, for instance, that the catacombs were not christian or that the paintings came from a later period, the "Gothick".[41]

The Discovery of the Barbarians

Alongside the concern with the classical and christian past, there was a gradual rise of interest in what might be called "alternative antiquities". The best-known example is that of ancient Egypt, its hieroglyphs and its mummies, which attracted the interest of scholars such as the Italian canon Lorenzo Pignoria, the French magistrate Nicolas-Claude Fabri de Peiresc and the German Jesuit Athanasius Kircher.[42] The Spanish scholar Benito Arias Montano wrote on Jewish antiquities (temples, altars, candelabra, the tabernacle and so on), the Englishman John Selden published a treatise on the gods of the Syrians, and the French Protestant pastor Samuel Bochart studied the Carthaginians.[43] The spread of information about the "Indies" led to an interest in their antiquities on the part of a few scholars. Pignoria, for instance, studied the gods

---

[39] Bosio, *Roma*, especially Book 4, ch. 5. Cf Louis Maimbourg, *Histoire de l'hérésie de l'iconoclasme* (Paris, 1674).
[40] Simon Ditchfield, 'Text before Trowel: Antonio Bosio's *Roma Sotterranea* Revisited', *Studies in Church History* 33 (1997), 343–60.
[41] Haskell, *History*, 106.
[42] Eric Iversen, *The Myth of Egypt and its Hieroglyphs in European Tradition* (1961: second ed., Princeton 1993); Sydney H. Aufrère, *La momie et la tempête: Nicolas-Claude Fabri de Peiresc et la curiosité egyptienne en Provence au début du 17e siècle* (Avignon, 1990).
[43] Montano; Selden; Bochart.

of the Mexicans and the Japanese as well as those of the Greeks and Romans.[44]

Of these alternative antiquities, the one which attracted most interest in seventeenth-century Europe was "barbarian antiquity", from what we call "prehistory" to the early Middle Ages or even later. Despite the contempt for the Middle Ages on the part of early humanists, their successors found the "barbarians" increasingly fascinating, largely because they viewed the ancient Britons, Gauls, Franks, Lombards and so on as their ancestors. The Danes identified themselves with the Cimbri, the Dutch with the Batavians, the Hungarians with the Huns and so on. The Swedish cult of the Goths and the Polish cult of the Sarmatians have attracted particular attention from scholars, but these examples are only the most spectacular instances of a general trend.[45]

The scholars who turned to the study of these national antiquities generally began from texts. They learned dead languages such as Gothic and Anglo-Saxon and edited collections of laws or chronicles such as Gregory of Tours on the Franks, Jornandes on the Goths, or Paul the Deacon on the Lombards. They studied non-classical epigraphy, notably the runes.

However, the relative paucity of texts, compared to those surviving from the other two antiquities, encouraged the students of barbarian antiquity to pay more attention to material objects. In Britain, the artefact or collection of artefacts which inspired most interest was of course Stonehenge, whether it was viewed as classical or barbarian. Inigo Jones thought it Roman, Walter Charleton ascribed it to the Danes while John Aubrey thought it the work of the Druids.[46] Thomas Browne's essay on urn burial

---

[44] Lorenzo Pignoria, "Discorso", in Vincenzo Cartari, *Imagini degli Dei delli antichi* (Padua, 1626); cf. Caterina Volpi, 'Lorenzo Pignoria', *Nouvelles de la République des Lettres* 2 (1992), 71–118.

[45] Johannes Nordström, *De yverbornes ö* (Stockholm, 1949); Kurt Johannesson; *The Renaissance of the Goths in Sixteenth-Century Sweden* (1982, English translation Berkeley 1991); Stanislaw Cynarski, "The Shape of Sarmatian Ideology in Poland", *Acta Poloniae Historica* 19 (1968), 5–17.

[46] Stuart Piggott, *Ancient Britons and the Antiquarian Imagination* (London, 1989); Graham Parry, *The Trophies of Time: English Antiquarians of the Seventeenth Century* (Oxford, 1995), 281–7.

also deserves to be noted here as a serious contribution to the study of antiquities as well as a meditation on mortality. When it first appeared in print, this essay included a frontispiece illustrating four urns, which later editions have generally failed to reproduce or even to mention. It discusses whether the urns were "British, Saxon or Danish" (though Browne thought they were probably Roman), and should be placed in the context of a European interest in urns and funeral customs which seems to have been particularly strong in Germany, where it attracted Leibniz among others.[47]

It is striking how often British antiquaries such as Aubrey, Browne and Lhwyd refer to their Danish and Swedish contemporaries. The point is that in the study of the third antiquity, Danish and Swedish scholars were playing a particularly important role in the seventeenth century. Even the state was involved in these studies, which were already associated with national identity. In 1622, for instance, Christian IV of Denmark issued an edict protecting antiquities, while in Sweden a *Riksantikvariat* or "State Office of Antiquities" was founded in 1630, a chair in antiquities at Uppsala University in 1662 and a College of Antiquities in 1666. A circle of scholars specialized in the study of what were known as "Swedish-Gothic" antiquities.

Johan Bure, for instance, collected runic inscriptions. Olof Verelius was another leading specialist in "runology" (to use his own term), and so was Johan Hadorph. The excavations directed by Verelius and Hadorph have already been mentioned. Verelius and the polymath Olof Rudbeck were both aware of the significance of what was later known as "stratigraphy", and so were Martin Lister and Edward Lhwyd in Britain, thus blurring the line between "scientific" and "pre-scientific" archaeology.[48]

In Denmark, the early artefacts found in Sleswig and Roskilde had already caused excitement in the sixteenth century. The leading Danish antiquary of the seventeenth century was Ole Worm, who interested himself in runes, megalithic tombs, urns and ship-

---

[47] Piggott, "Browne"; Parry, *Trophies*, 249–58. Cf. Hans Gummel, *Forschungsgeschichte in Deutschland* (Berlin, 1938), 26–33, 101.

[48] Hunter, "Royal Society"; Klindt-Jensen, *Archaeology*; Daniel, "Lhwyd", 353.

burials, and employed assistants to draw objects for him.[49] Worm was equally well known for his collection of antiquities and other objects, the Museum Wormianum in Copenhagen.[50] The Danish circle of antiquaries also included Thomas and Caspar Bartholin and Johan Rhode.

Among the signs of increasing sensitivity to visual evidence are Worm's engravings of graves, stones, swords, spurs and especially the famous golden horn. Worm was summoned by King Christian IV, whose physician he was, to view a golden drinking-horn soon after its discovery in Gallehus in Jutland in 1639. He published a study of it soon afterwards, discussing the scenes represented on the horn and comparing it to other objects of the same kind. Today, the engraving from Worm's book is the best evidence for the appearance of the horn, since it was stolen from the royal collection in 1802 and destroyed.

The Discovery of Childeric

An even more spectacular discovery of the time was that of Childeric. Childeric, who died in 481, was a Merovingian ruler, the father of Clovis. His grave was discovered at Tournai in 1653, by accident, when the foundations of a new hospital were being dug.[51]

The magnificence of the many objects which came to light on this occasion made Tournai, in Piggott's phrase, "The Sutton Hoo of the day". With Childeric there were found, in the words of Sir Thomas Browne (following Chifflet), "his sword, two hundred rubies, many hundred Imperial Coyns, three hundred golden Bees, the bones and horse shoe of his horse interred with him, accord-

---

[49] Sten Lindroth, *Svensk Lärdomshistoria: Stormaktstiden* (Stockholm, 1975), 235–348, the fullest survey; cf. Klindt-Jensen, *Archaeology*, and Schnapp, *La conquête*,156–67, 199–201.

[50] On Worm, *Dansk Biografisk Leksikon* (Copenhagen, 1979), sub voce; Klindt-Jensen, *Archaeology*; Schnapp, *La conquête*, 160–7.

[51] On the political implications, Fritz Wagner, *Die politische Bedeutung des Childerich-Grabfundes von 1653* (Munich, 1973).

ing to the barbarous magnificence of those dayes in their sepulcral Obsequies".[52]

Jean-Jacques Chifflet was a scholar from Besançon who became physician to the archdukes in Brussels. His work as antiquarian dealt with all three antiquities. He wrote on a Roman port in the Low Countries. He made an early contribution to the unending debate over the Turin Shroud. In a study published in 1624, the year in which the shroud was exhibited in public in Turin, Chifflet claimed that both the Besançon and the Turin shrouds as authentic, illustrating them in parallel and arguing that they were used respectively before and after the burial. Chifflet pointed out that the shroud was not painted (as a French bishop had claimed in the fourteenth century), because there were no traces of brush-strokes to be found. His book was illustrated with engravings of coins and mosaics as well as a folding plate comparing the Turin shroud with that of Besançon.[53]

A later book, *De ampulla remensi* (1651), on the ampulla preserved in Rheims holding the holy oil used to consecrate the kings of France, dismissed the story of the dove bringing the oil to Clovis as a "pious fable", making not only a scholarly point about evidence but a political point against France (Chifflet was of course a subject of Philip IV of Spain). In the context of the history of evidence, however, it is Chifflet's use of the testimony of coins and of two images of the baptism of Clovis which most deserves to be noted.[54]

Chifflet's most famous book is his *Anastasis Childerici I Francorum Regis* (1655). This study of the discovery or "resurrection" (*anastasis*) of the Merovingian ruler is also a good example of the antiquarian's attempt to resurrect the past. After describing the finds, which are fully illustrated, Chifflet identifies the dead man as Childeric on the evidence of his seal-ring. He notes that the king had been buried outside the city "with barbarian ritual" (*ritu barbarico*), and argues that Childeric's tunic and *chlamys* show that the ancient custom of dressing up the dead for burial had been taken over by the Franks.

[52] Browne, *Hydriotaphia*, 107. Cf. Edward James, *The Franks* (Oxford, 1988), 58–67.
[53] Jean-Jacques Chifflet, *De linteis sepulchralibus Christi* (Antwerp, 1624).
[54] Jean-Jacques Chifflet, *De ampulla remensi* (Antwerp, 1651), 56, 74.

Chifflet's analysis of the contents of the grave draws on a range of secondary literature by the antiquarians of his day, including Liceti, Kircher, and Albert Rubens. He makes considerable use of literary sources, including Salvian, Sidonius, Gregory of Tours and the laws of the Visigoths. However, his attention is focussed on the objects themselves and the social customs associated with them. He quotes a saying of Peiresc's that coins and seals are "uncorrupted witnesses of Antiquity" (*testes esse Antiquitatis incorruptos*).[55] Discussing rings and their uses, he concludes that the ring with Childeric's name and portrait was a signet ring. A golden object is identified as a writing instrument, to be used with wax tablets, and leads to a digression on the history of writing. The golden bees are interpreted both as an "emblem, or hieroglyphic enigma" and as "symbols of kings". Chifflet is also extremely interested in the weapons and the horse buried with the king, discussing details of the harness ornaments.

Chifflet has recently been criticized for his lack of a sense of archaeological context.[56] He did not show the interest in stratigraphy of a Verelius or a Rudbeck, but few scholars did at that time. In any case, he did not carry out an excavation, but tried to interpret the objects which had been discovered by accident. In the course of his work, Chifflet appeals to the testimony of other artefacts. For example, he compares Childeric's sword and axe with the weapons of the Dacians as represented in the reliefs on Trajan's Column.[57] His book shows very clearly how some antiquaries combined the evidence of texts and images. As in the case of Worm and the golden horn, Chifflet's treatise is the best evidence which remains of the appearance of some of the objects from Childeric's tomb, which were stolen from the Bibliothèque royale in 1831 (having been offered to Louis XIV by the emperor Leopold I in 1665).

---

[55] Jean-Jacques Chifflet, *Anastasis Childerici I Francorum Regis* (Antwerp, 1655), 113, with a reference to Gassendi's biography of Peiresc.
[56] Schnapp, *La conquête*, 204.
[57] Chifflet, *Anastasis*, 204, 209.

The Eighteenth-Century Synthesis

In the outpouring of scholarly monographs in the seventeenth century, the ideal of the "integrity" of history expressed by Spanheim was sometimes in danger of being forgotten. A synthesis of literary and non-literary evidence was much needed, and various attempts were made. Francesco Bianchini, for instance, described his universal history as 'based on the evidence of monuments' (*provata con monumenti*), and reproduced some at the beginning of each chapter, although he made little use of them in his text.[58] To provide a synthesis and "concilier les monumens avec l'histoire" was the life work of the French Benedictine Bernard de Montfaucon. It was around 1693 that Montfaucon began collecting prints and drawings of antiquity, and by the early 1720s he had between 30, 000 and 40, 000 of them. Part of his "paper museum", unlike Cassiano del Pozzo's, was printed in the fifteen volumes of his *Antiquité expliquée* (1719-24), which opened with the complaint that the work of the antiquarians was fragmented and that virtually no one had the knowledge of "all the parts of antiquity".

The use which Montfaucon made of the evidence of Trajan's Column may serve as an example of his method. Following Fabretti for the most part, but showing himself to be aware of earlier commentators, Montfaucon calls the column as a witness for the history of costume, for instance, as well as reproducing a long series of engravings of the column, juxtaposed to other evidence, in his section on the history of war, not forgetting the famous *testudo*.[59]

The indefatigable Montfaucon then carried out a similar enterprise by publishing the "monuments" of France. The most famous section of his work is that reproducing and discussing what is now known as the Bayeux Tapestry, though Montfaucon, working from a copy, calls it a "painting", while his informant Antoine Lancelot described it as the "toilette du Duc Guillaume". The Tapestry might be described as the Trajan's Column of barbarian history, a fine example of the contribution of the study of antiquities to

---

[58] Francesco Bianchini, *La Istoria universale provata con monumenti* (Rome, 1697).
[59] Bernard de Montfaucon, *Antiquité expliquée* (10 vols. in 15, Paris 1719-24), vol. 2, 82; vol. 3, 294; vol. 4, 22, 32-3, 98-112, 143-5. Cf. Haskell, *History*, 131-5.

the history of events, and Montfaucon compared its evidence with that of the chronicles.[60]

Montfaucon was also well aware of the importance of the grave of Childeric, which he calls one of the great discoveries of the seventeenth century. He combines a narrative of the king's reign derived from Gregory of Tours with a description of the grave goods and four plates all derived from Chifflet, although he disagrees with his predecessor on several interpretations, arguing that the golden bull's head is an ornament rather than an idol, and identifying what Chifflet thought to be a writing instrument as a buckle. He takes coins seriously as evidence, noting that the quantity of Roman coins in the grave "proves that this money circulated among the French".[61]

Evidence and Interpretation

Like texts, material objects posed problems of authenticity. Treatises on medals and coins in particular discussed how to detect fakes, but inscriptions and other monuments sometimes fell under suspicion as well, from the ancient shield owned by the English antiquary John Woodward to the Spanish "lead books" offering testimony about the early medieval past.[62]

Another problem was that the iconography of ancient images was often mysterious to post-classical eyes. The early history of iconography remains to be written. Here I will only mention a few early attempts to solve iconographical problems, including Stephanus Pighius's analysis of a bas-relief of the seasons belonging to cardinal Granvelle; Lorenzo Pignoria's study of a bronze tablet of Isis and his interpretation of a Roman fresco discovered in

---

[60] Bernard de Montfaucon, *Les Monumens de la Monarchie Françoise* (5 vols, Paris 1729-33, vol. 1, 371ff; Haskell, *History*, 138-44.

[61] Monfaucon, *Monumens*, vol. 1, 8-16. On the buckle, cf James, *Franks*, 61.

[62] On medals, Enea Vico, *Discorsi sopra le medaglie de gli antichi* (Venice, 1555), chapter 22: Antonio Agustín, *Dialogos de medallas, inscrpciones y otras antiguedades* (Tarragona, 1587), chapter 11. On other monuments, Joe Levine, *Dr Woodward's Shield* (1977: second edn., Ithaca 1993), and Julio Caro Baroja, *Las falsificaciones de la historia* (Madrid, 1992).

1606, the Aldobrandini Wedding; Girolamo Aleandro's "explanation" of an ancient marble tablet; Bosio's study of the paintings in the catacombs; Claude Menestrier's study of the symbolism of the many-breasted goddess Diana of Ephesus; and Lukas Holsten's study of a picture of a nymphaeum.[63]

Attempts at decoding such as these should be related not only to the aristocratic fashion for collecting antiquities but also to the interest in encoding exemplified in another fashion of the period, emblem-books. Pignoria annotated a new edition (published in 1621) of the most famous of emblem-books, that of Andrea Alciato, and added an appendix to the 1626 edition of Cartari's *Imagini degli dei antichi*, a guide to encoding like Cesare Ripa's even more famous *Iconologia* (1593).

The method employed in these iconographical studies was essentially a humanist one, juxtaposing quotations from classical texts to the problem-image, although Aleandro, for instance, drew on the testimony of Trajan's Column as well as that of ancient writers. Today, more attention is probably given to comparisons between different images, but in its essentials the humanist method is one which students of iconography still follow, even if our knowledge of both the classics and the Bible is probably less than theirs.

The difficulties of iconographical interpretation in this period – difficulties which have not yet vanished – may be illustrated from the attempts to read the paintings discovered in the catacombs. A figure now regarded as Noah in the Ark, for instance, was first interpreted as St Marcellus in the pulpit.[64] The successes of the approach included Peiresc's recognition of the emperor Tiberius on the cameo preserved in the Sainte Chapelle at Paris and traditionally known as 'Joseph', together with the identification of the classical equestrian figure in Rome traditionally believed to be Constantine

---

[63] Stephanus Pighius, *Mythologia* (Antwerp, 1568); Lorenzo Pignoria, *Mensa Isiaca* (1605: rpr Amsterdam 1669); *id, Antiquissima pictura* (Padua, 1630); Girolamo Aleandro, *Antiquae tabulae marmoreae explicatio* (1616: rpr Paris, 1617); Bosio, *Roma*; Claude Menestrier, *Symbolica Dianae Ephesiae Statua* (posthumous, 1657; rpr Rome, 1688); Lukas Holsten, *Vetus pictura nymphaeum referens explicata* (posthumous, Rome 1676).
[64] Bosio, *Roma*; cf Haskell, *History*, 107.

(or sometimes Commodus, Hadrian or the Ostrogothic ruler Theoderic) as the emperor Marcus Aurelius. Proposed in the fifteenth century by the Italian humanist Bartolomeo Platina, it was in the seventeenth century that this identification came to be accepted.[65]

Working out the uses of ancient artefacts was not always easy. Even the identification of an object as an artefact, a flint arrowhead or dagger for example, was sometimes problematic. Solving these problems was facilitated by the increasingly widespread knowledge of ethnographic parallels, a by-product of European exploration and colonisation. The Danish scholar Johan Laverentzen, for example, compared axes found in Denmark to those of the Indians of Louisiana. Lhwyd noted similarities that the ancient Britons used "just the same chip'd flints the natives of New England head their arrows with to this day".[66]

Despite the problems, artefacts, including images, were taken increasingly seriously as evidence of what were increasingly called historical "facts".[67] William Camden read crop marks as signs of vanished structures, long before aerial photography made the task a relatively simple one.[68] The remarks by numismatists on the testimony of medals have already been quoted. Aubrey declared that barrows "would be evidence to a Jury", while the stones of Stonehenge and elsewhere "give evidence for themselves".[69] In these ways the study of antiquities, as Momigliano noted fifty years ago, supplied ammunition for the refutation of historical sceptics or 'pyrrhonists' and aided what has been described as the eighteenth-century "rehabilitation of history".[70]

---

[65] Francis Haskell and Nicholas Penny, *Taste and the Antique* (New Haven, 1981) 252-5; Haskell, *History*, 115.
[66] Ole Klindt-Jensen, "Archaeology and Ethnography in Denmark: Early Studies", in *Towards a History of Archaeology*, ed. Glyn Daniel (London, 1981), 14-19; Lhwyd quoted in Piggott, "Antiquarian Thought", 111.
[67] Shapiro, *Fact*, 51-3.
[68] Stuart Piggott, *William Camden and the Britannia* (London, 1953).
[69] Quoted Michael Hunter, *John Aubrey and the Realm of Learning* (London, 1975), 180, 183.
[70] Momigliano, "Ancient History"; cf. Judith Shklar, "Jean D'Alembert and the Rehabilitation of History", *Journal of the History of Ideas* 42 (1981), 643-64; Peter Burke, 'Two Crises of Historical Consciousness', *Storia della Storiografia* 33 (1998), 3-16.

Artists and Physicians

A social history of the antiquarian movement, were one to be written, might profitably investigate the influence of the occupations of antiquaries to their attitude to visual evidence. Despite the place of material *indicia* in court, and the interest of many lawyers in scholarship, there were relatively few of them in this field (among them Agustín, Peiresc, Selden and Fabretti). Two occupational groups which stand out are the artists and the physicians.

As trained observers, artists obviously had an important role to play both in recording and in interpreting the material remains of the past.[71] A number of artists were employed, as we have seen, by antiquaries such as Alfonso Chacón, Cassiano del Pozzo and Ole Worm. Philips van Winge, Santi Avanzino and Francesco Fulcaro were among the painters and engravers involved in recording the images painted in the catacombs. Matthieu Ogier of Lyon illustrated the works of Spon with magnificent engravings. Wenceslas Hollar, a friend of Aubrey, drew the plates for Dugdale's *Monasticon*.[72] Pietro Sante Bartoli, a pupil of Poussin, illustrated Bellori's work on Trajan's Column.

However, to break away from the text-dominated approach to the past, it was surely necessary either for antiquaries to become artists or for artists to become antiquaries. Scholar-artists included Aubrey, Lhwyd, Worm, and Bure (who drew rune-stones and made his own woodcuts). On the other side, the most famous examples of seventeenth-century artist-scholars are those of Poussin and Rubens. Poussin consulted Bosio on early christian history and knew Cassiano well. Rubens also knew Cassiano, and Lipsius and Peiresc too, sharing their interest in stoicism and antiquities, collecting medals and making sketches of Roman gems and Egyptian mummies. Franciscus Junius sent his book on painting to both Rubens and van Dyck for comment.[73] Inigo Jones both drew and wrote about Stonehenge.

---

[71] Stuart Piggott, *Antiquity Depicted: Aspects of Archaeological Illustration* (London, 1978), 27, 35.
[72] Parry, *Trophies*, 232–8.
[73] Philipp Fehl, "Access to the Ancients", in Bremmer, *Junius*, 35–70, at 35, 42, 44–5.

As for physicians, a study of their place in early modern culture, along the lines of William Bouwsma's essay on the lawyers, is much to be desired.[74] Like artists, they were trained observers, and it is striking how many of them – especially those trained at Padua – doubled as antiquaries in this period. Among these antiquary-medics were Liceto, Chifflet, the Frenchmen Patin and Spon, the Danes Worm, Bartholin, and Rhode, the Englishmen Browne, Charleton and Lister and the Scotsman Sir Robert Sibbald.

Given this predominance of medical men, it may be suggested that the habit of interpreting symptoms aided emancipation from logo-centrism and served as an alternative model to the legal model of evidence for the interpretation of antiquities. Carlo Ginzburg's famous discussion of the pursuit of 'clues', pointing to the seventeenth-century physician-connoisseur Giulio Mancini's careful observation of small details, has important implications for the study of the antiquarian movement. In 1950, Momigliano had already noted that the physicians Spon and Patin 'brought something of the method of direct observation into historical research'. A nineteenth-century scholar had gone further still by remarking of Spon, 'Ce qu'il cherche dans un monument, c'est l'interprétation du signe'.[75]

An early meaning of the term 'evidence' is, of course, 'sign'. The epistemological problem of signs was a subject of some interest in the seventeenth century, and even the word 'semiotics' was in use at this time, in Latin, Italian, French and English, especially in a medical context. Nicholas Culpeper's *Semeiotica uranica* (1651), for instance, discussed the 'astronomical judgement of diseases'. The growing literature on physiognomy – Mascardi's *De affectibus* (1639) for example – discussed not only the form of faces but expression, posture, gesture and even the hairstyle and clothing as so many signs of character and emotions. John Evelyn's book on

---

[74] William J. Bouwsma, "Lawyers and Early Modern Culture" (1973, rpr *A Usable Past: Essays in European Cultural History* (Berkeley and Los Angeles, 1990), 129–53.
[75] Samuel Rocheblave, *Essai sur le comte de Caylus* (Paris, 1889), 253; Momigliano, "Ancient History". Cf Carlo Ginzburg, "Clues: Roots of an Evidential Paradigm" (1978, rpr in his *Myths, Emblems, Clues*, London 1990), 96–125, and Arnaldo Momigliano, 'La storia tra medicina e retorica', in his *Tra storia e storicismo* (Pisa, 1985), 11–24.

medals included what he called a 'digression' on physiognomy, discussing what he called 'semiotics and configurations' and suggesting that the face of Tiberius, for example, recorded on his medals, was a clue to his character.[76]

Some writers showed a still wider interest in material signs. The physician-philosopher Camillo Baldi studied the handwriting and the language of letters from this point of view, while the Jesuit rhetorician Agostino Mascardi explained how to infer emotional states from the study of the hands, the voice, clothing, gait and so on. In England, John Wilkins described communication by gestures under the heading 'Semaeology', while John Locke discussed signs or 'marks' and what he called *'semiotike* or the Doctrine of Signs' in the *Essay Concerning Human Understanding*.[77]

The rise of a concern with non-visual evidence in the seventeenth century, palpable as it is, should not be exaggerated. No general semiotics developed out of Locke's suggestions. Neither Montfaucon nor anyone else formulated the general rules for interpreting visual evidence in the way in which his colleague Jean Mabillon formulated the rules of documentary evidence (Scipione Maffei's *Ars critica lapidaria* was concerned only with epigraphy).[78]

The failure of the antiquaries to go further in this direction should not surprise us. No systematic training in the use of visual evidence was yet available, as was the case for philology. No wonder then that some humanist antiquaries focussed on words even when ostensibly dealing with things. Even Montfaucon has been described as relatively lacking in 'visual curiosity', and as considerably less critical in his use of images than in his use of texts, although he deserves the credit for 'footnoting' images in the sense of making the provenance of each image clear to the reader.[79]

---

[76] Evelyn, *Discourse*, 292–342.
[77] Camillo Baldi, *Trattato come da una lettera missiva si conoscano la natura e qualità dello scrittore* (Carpi, 1622); Agostino Mascardi, *Romanae dissertationes, de affectibus sive perturbationibus animi, earumque characteribus* (Paris, 1639); John Locke, *Essay Concerning Human Understanding* (London, 1690), Book 4, ch. 20. Cf. Hacking, *Probability*, 39–62.
[78] Momigliano, "Ancient History ", 17.
[79] Haskell and Penny (1981), 43–4; cf. Schnapp, *La conquête*, 277, and Haskell, *History*, 131–44.

All the same, the examples of Worm and Aubrey as well as a succession of numismatists support the idea of a revaluation of objects (as opposed to texts) in the assessment of evidence about the past. The change in the methods of English antiquarians in the 1680s has been noted, the rise of more careful descriptions of excavations for instance.[80] Important observations about method were also made. For example, the polymath Peiresc made the point that the study of ancient artefacts was necessary precisely because ancient writers 'never wrote consciously or deliberately' about the topics which to them were 'well known and trivial'.[81] The remarks by Claude Chifflet or John Evelyn on the value of 'a perfect and uninterrupted series' of coins or medals also deserve to be emphasized.[82] Aubrey, Laverentzen and Lhwyd all adopted a comparative approach to artefacts.[83] In ways such as these the visual turn of the early modern period not only extended the subject-matter of history but also refined historical methods. Let us hope that the same will be said about the visual turn of the 1980s and 1990s.

---

[80] Michael Hunter,"The Royal Society and the Origins of British Archaeology", *Antiquity* 65 (1971), 113–21, 178–91.
[81] Quoted in Herklotz, *Cassiano*, 233–4.
[82] Claude Chifflet, *De numismate antiquo* (Louvain, 1628), 15; Evelyn (1671).
[83] Schnapp, *La conquête*, 192.

6: REFLECTIONS ON THE CULTURAL HISTORY OF TIME[1]

It was in 1988 that Stephen Hawking published his now famous *Brief History of Time*, from the point of view of a theoretical physicist, or a cosmologist. However, this is not the only possible history of time. An alternative is to write the history of time from the point of view of a cultural or social historian, drawing on the "endlessly multiplying" studies by anthropologists in particular and looking at systems of time reckoning and time perception (*Zeitbewusstsein*) as social or cultural constructions.[2] In what follows I should like to reflect on the development of this cultural approach.

Historians know all too well how dangerous it is to claim that anything started at a particular moment, but it may be useful to take that risk and suggest that the idea of 'social time' began to be taken seriously by scholars around the year 1900, with Durkheim

---

[1] This article originated as a contribution to a conference on 'Calendar Reform and Religious Reformation', held in 2003 at the Center for Medieval and Renaissance Studies, UCLA. It was subsequently given as a paper to a seminar on time at the Institute of Historical Research, London, organized by Michael Hunter, Miri Rubin and Laura Gowing. My thanks to the organizers and to the members of the audience who asked pertinent and difficult questions.

[2] Nancy D. Munn, "The Cultural Anthropology of Time", *Annual Review of Anthropology* 21 (1992) 93–123.

and his followers in France and Weber and some of his colleagues in Germany.[3] The idea is surely implicit in Marx, and it has certainly been developed by some Marxists. All the same, Marx did not give time the systematic attention that either Durkheim or Weber did, confining himself, in the tenth chapter of *Capital*, to a discussion of the extension of the working day in the age of capitalism.[4]

Why did an interest in social time develop at that moment? One historian has noted an analogy between the temporal relativism of Durkheim and that of Albert Einstein, put forward only a few years later.[5] Another possibility is that awareness of difference was a paradoxical side-effect of standardization. World Standard Time was introduced in 1884 and thereafter one country after another adopted Greenwich Time. These changes may have made western observers more conscious of the variety of non-Greenwich times preceding this process of globalization.

In the course of the last century or so there have been three main approaches to this sociology, anthropology or socio-cultural history of time. The scholars who have pursued these approaches share a concern with what might be called "time communities", viewing them first as communities in a weak sense of the term, that is, whole societies or cultures; later as communities in a stronger or more precise sense, social groups in conflict within the same society; and finally, relatively recently, as small groups employing different notions of time in different domains of activity. In this article the three approaches will be discussed in order of appearance.

---

[3] Emile Durkheim and Marcel Mauss, "Primitive Classification" (1901-2, English translation, ed. Rodney Needham, Chicago and London 1963); Max Weber, *The Protestant Ethic and the Spirit of Capitalism* (1904: ed. Johannes Winckelmann, Munich and Hamburg 1965; English translation, London 1930); Werner Sombart, *Der Bourgeois* (1913, English translation *The Quintessence of Capitalism*, London 1915).

[4] Karl Marx, *Capital* (London, 1867), chapter 10; Christopher Hill, "The Uses of Sabbatarianism", in his *Society and Puritanism in Pre-Revolutionary England* (London 1964), 145-218.

[5] Stephen Kern, *The Culture of Time and Space, 1880-1918* (1983: second edition, Cambridge, MA, 2003), 19-20.

Times and Cultures

The first approach is associated with Emile Durkheim and his disciples Marcel Mauss and Henri Hubert. Hubert noted that periods of time are often defined by particular activities. True to his view of categories as "social facts" (*choses sociales*), Durkheim described time as a collective representation, "thought by everyone in a given culture" (*pensé par tous les hommes d'une meme civilization*) and reflecting the organization of a given society, "borrowed from social life", as he puts it. "It is the rhythm of social life that is the basis of the category of time" (*Ce qui est à la base de la catégorie de temps, c'est le rythme de la vie sociale*).[6]

This group of French scholars was followed at a certain distance by their compatriots Marc Bloch, Lucien Febvre, Maurice Halbwachs, famous for his discussion of the "social framework of memory" and the young Pierre Bourdieu in his North African phase, while Georges Gurvitch and Jacques Le Goff diverged from it, as we shall see. Using the metaphor of floating, both Bloch and Febvre emphasized the vagueness of the sense of time in traditional societies, while Bourdieu described the Kabyle as submitting to time "scanned in the rhythm of nature"[7] Outside France, a similar approach was followed by Max Weber, the American generalist Lewis Mumford, his sociological colleagues Pitirim Sorokin and Robert Merton, the German literary historian Richard Glasser, the British anthropologists Bronisław Malinowski and Edward Evans-Pritchard, and – much later – by the

---

[6] Durkheim and Mauss, *Classification*; Henri Hubert, "Etude sommaire de la représentation du temps" (1905, rpr *Mélanges d'histoire des religions*, Paris 1909, 189-229); Durkheim, *Les formes élementaires de la vie religieuse* (Paris 1912: English translation, New York 1961), introduction; cf. François A. Isambert, "Henri Hubert et la sociologie du temps", *Revue française de sociologie* 20 (1979) 183-201.

[7] "Cette sorte de perpetuel flottement du temps": Marc Bloch, *La société féodale* (2 vols., Paris 1939-40), vol. 1, 117; Lucien Febvre, "Temps flottant, temps dormant", in *Le problème de l'incroyance: la religion de Rabelais* (Paris 1942), 426-34; Maurice Halbwachs, "La mémoire collective et le temps", *Cahiers Internationaux de Sociologie* (1947) 3-31; Pierre Bourdieu, "The Attitude of the Algerian Peasant towards Time", in Julian Pitt-Rivers (ed.) *Mediterranean Countrymen* (Paris and the Hague 1963), 55-72.

German sociologist Norbert Elias.[8]

It should also be noted that the Swedish classicist Martin Nilsson published a comparative study of time reckoning as early as 1920. His book was concerned with nature rather than society, with the rise of "calendrical science" in different parts of the globe. He therefore dismissed the reckoning of time by everyday events as unscientific. All the same, he offered an example that illustrates very well the concerns of the Durkheim circle. "In Madagascar 'rice-cooking' often means half an hour, 'the frying of a locust', a moment".[9]

The many vivid examples cited by the scholars listed above are both fascinating and illuminating, but they raise a serious problem. In principle, it should surely be possible to discover various conceptions of time or systems of time reckoning in different cultures. In practice, however, what these scholars chose to discuss was almost always a binary opposition between two kinds of society and two kinds of time, irrespective of whether the context was ancient Greece, medieval Europe, sixteenth-century France, the Nuer or the Kabyle.

The basic binary opposition underlying these studies was the one between self and other, presented as a contrast between traditional and modern, between what Febvre called *le temps vécu* and *le temps-mesure*.[10] Time in traditional societies, according to the model used by these scholars, is qualitative, concrete, local, imprecise, or in a word, organic. Time in modern societies, on the other hand, is quantitative, abstract, uniform and exact, as mechanical as the clocks and watches used to measure it. The semi-exception to this

---

[8] Lewis Mumford, *Technics and Civilization* (New York 1934), 12–18; Pitirim A. Sorokin and Robert K. Merton, "Social Time: a Methodological and Functional Analysis", *American Journal of Sociology* 42 (1937), 615–29; Richard Glasser, *Studien zur Geschichte des französischen Zeitbegriffs* (1936, translated as *Time in French Thought*, Manchester 1972); Bronisław Malinowski "Lunar and Seasonal Calendars in the Trobriands", *Journal of the Royal Anthropological Institution* 57 (1927) 203–15; Edward Evans-Pritchard, "Nuer Time-Reckoning" (1939); id., "Space and Time", in *The Nuer* (Oxford 1940), 94–138; Norbert Elias, *On Time* (1987, English trans. Oxford 1992)..

[9] Martin P. Nilsson, *Primitive Time Reckoning* (Lund 1920), 41–3.

[10] Febvre, *Incroyance*, 431. Cf. Eugène Minkowski, *Le temps vécu* (1933, English translation as *Lived Time*, Evanston 1970).

rule, the article by Sorokin and Merton, noted that even in modern societies people continue to measure time – at least some of the time – in terms of social activities and events.

Traditional time is the time of experience, organized and measured by tasks, especially agricultural tasks. Malinowski, for instance, described gardening as "the real measure of time" for Trobrianders, who dated the events of a given year by the different gardening activities, and the years themselves by the fields under cultivation at that time.[11] Again, in his ethnography of the Nuer, a pastoral society of the Sudan, Evans-Pritchard wrote vividly of the "cattle clock".[12] In the longer term, decades, that of generations or centuries, time is often remembered by local events, whether natural, like floods or droughts, or political, like reigns or invasions. A number of anthropological studies of more or less traditional villages in the Mediterranean and elsewhere make this point.[13]

In his famous study of the religion of Rabelais, Febvre discussed conceptions of time in the sixteenth century in a similar fashion. For example, he analysed the references to time in the journal kept by the Norman country squire the Sieur de Gouberville, who would use such phrases as "around sunrise" (*environ soleil levant*), for instance, or "it was the time of the woodcock's flight" (*il était vol de vitecoq*). Alternatively, Gouberville would refer to the time of an *Ave Maria* or *Pater Noster*. Moving from days to years, Febvre drew attention to the same lack of precision, pointing out for instance that Erasmus, Lefèvre d'Etaples and Rabelais did not know the year of their birth. He noted that the long "duel", as he calls it, between traditional and modern conceptions of time was already in progress in the sixteenth century, but his emphasis fell on the traditional side.[14]

Modern time, by contrast, according to these scholars, was exact

---

[11] Bronisław Malinowski, *Coral Gardens and Their Magic* (2 vols., London 1935), vol. 1, 52-5.
[12] Evans-Pritchard, The *Nuer*.
[13] Anna Collard, "Investigating Social Memory in a Greek Context", in *History and Ethnicity*, ed. Elizabeth Tonkin et al. (London 1989) 89-103.
[14] Febvre, *Incroyance,* 426-34 (English translation, 393-400).

time, measured by the clock, a sense of time appropriate to commercial and industrial societies, with a different work rhythm from pastoral or agricultural communities.

For Max Weber and Christopher Hill alike, a major consequence of the Protestant Reformation was to ease the transition from traditional to modern time. Weber noted that Protestants – he quoted Benjamin Franklin, but argued more generally – compared time to money, whether it was '"spent" or "saved", and he discussed the secularization of time discipline as part of the "this-worldly asceticism" (*innerweltliche Askese*), that he considered to have been essential to the rise of capitalist society.[15] In similar fashion, sixty years later, Christopher Hill noted that the frequency and irregularity of holidays in honour of saints was an obstacle to productivity, while describing "the regular day of rest and meditation", on the contrary, as "suited to the regular and continuous rhythms of modern industrial society".[16]

One major topic in the social history of time – the idea of the future – has been omitted so far, because it was not placed on the historian's agenda until the later twentieth century. It was the German historian Reinhart Koselleck who argued that attitudes to the past and the future were linked and that they changed together in Europe in the late eighteenth century, the great *Sattelzeit* or turning-point as he calls it. Around the time of the French Revolution, Koselleck suggested, the idea of a future more or less like the past was replaced by the expectation of a future which was open, subject to human manipulation or as he described it, "constructible" (*verfügbar*). As one of his former students has claimed, the future was 'invented' some two hundred years ago, in the period 1770–1830, justifying the claim with references to the *Zukunftsroman* (the novel set in the future) and the *Zukunftstaat* (the state that is organized around calculations of the future, managing change).[17]

---

[15] Weber, *Ethik*, 40–1 (English translation, 48–50).
[16] Hill, *Society and Puritanism*, 146.
[17] Reinhart Koselleck, *Vergangene Zukunft* (1979: English translation, *Futures Past: on the Semantics of Historical Time*, Cambridge, MA, 1985), especially part 1; Lucian Hölscher, *Die Entdeckung der Zukunft* (1999).

Temporal Relativism

There is a sense in which the historians and sociologists who discovered social time a century or so ago had been anticipated by those medieval and early modern people for whom awareness of alternative systems of time reckoning was part of everyday life. Early Christians were aware of pagan time and some medieval Christians were aware of Muslim and Jewish time.[18]

In medieval cities differences of this kind would have been particularly clear, especially in a Mediterranean city in which Christians, Jews and Muslims followed different religious calendars, with their own annual holidays, feasts and fasts, and even their own divisions of the day. Inside and outside the gates of the ghetto or the *morería* different time systems prevailed. To walk through such a city would have been a journey through several time zones.

All the same, the awareness of different orders of time was probably more intense and more widespread in the early modern period than it had been in the Middle Ages. It also included greater varieties of time reckoning, such as the Chinese and the Japanese. Missionaries, merchants and administrators carried western time to other parts of the globe, but the carriers became aware in their turn of indigenous systems of time. There were clashes between Christian time and indigenous time in sixteenth-century Mexico, for instance.[19] Correspondence between continents surely affected perceptions of time, since a year might elapse between writing a letter and reading it.

Again, the shift from the Julian to the Gregorian calendar, like the shift to World Standard Time, must have been a shock for many people, even if we do not know how long the shock lasted. Printed calendars spread the knowledge of differences in time systems. Scholars took an increasing interest in comparative chronology, working out equivalents between years in the Greek, Roman, Arabic, Chinese and other systems.[20] At the level of the day, the

---
[18] At the Los Angeles conference, these topics were discussed by Anne Prescott and Michele Salzman.
[19] Serge Gruzinski, *La pensée métisse* (Paris, 1999), 67-8.
[20] Anthony Grafton, *Joseph Scaliger*, vol. 2, *Historical Chronology* (Oxford, 1993).

German Jesuit Athanasius Kircher's image of the "Ignatian Tree" (modelled on the Tree of Jesse) and showing the world distribution of Jesuit establishments, included illustrations of different time zones: "at the fork of most branches is placed the face of a sundial oriented to show local time in relation to 'Roman mean time'" (a modern reader may be reminded of the hotel foyers with clocks showing the time in London, New York, Los Angeles and Tokyo).[21]

Qualifying the Model

In the process of working out the cultural history of time, especially western time, the original simple paradigm has proved to be less than adequate. It has become necessary to introduce a few epicycles into the original model.

For example, the rise of the mechanical clock, so often invoked in histories of social time, no longer looks as simple a phenomenon as it once did. Even the place of technology in the story is problematic. Did the invention of the mechanical clock lead to a new sense of time, or was the clock invented, like the printing press, when there was a demand for it? The use of clocks and watches spread only slowly from one part of Europe or one social group to another. The consequences of the regular use of the clock for the perception of time are still under discussion.[22]

As for the future, the idea of its manipulability was implied by the practices of merchants, in particular lending money at interest and taking out insurance (first, in the later Middle Ages, on ships, and later, in the seventeenth century, on houses and lives).[23]

Generally speaking, earlier assumptions of relatively swift change, a "Great Divide" between traditional and modern concep-

---
[21] Steven Harris, 'Mapping Jesuit Science: The Role of Travel in the Geography of Knowledge', in John W. O'Malley and Gauvin Bailey (eds.) *The Jesuits* (Toronto 1999), 212–40, at 219.
[22] Carlo Cipolla, *Clocks and Culture 1300–1700* (New York 1967); David Landes, *Revolution in Time* (Cambridge. Mass. 1983); Stuart Sherman, *Telling Time: Clocks, Diaries and English Diurnal Form, 1660–1785* (Chicago 1996).
[23] Geoffrey Clark, *Betting on Lives: The culture of life insurance in England, 1695–1775* (Manchester, 1999).

tions and experiences of time, have been replaced by the conviction that the shift was gradual.

In the first place, it has become clear that traditional attitudes persisted well into the 'modern' period, especially in remote regions of the countryside. At the level of the year, the point is made in a recent social history of the calendar that focuses on France from 1450 to 1800. At the level of hours, Thomas Hardy offered a vivid illustration of this persistence in his *The Return of the Native*, set in the rural West of England in the early nineteenth century, in which he described the variety of local times, despite some access to clocks and watches. "On Egdon there was no absolute hour of the day. The time at any moment was a number of varying doctrines professed by the different hamlets, some of them having originally grown from a common root, and then become divided by secession, some having been alien from the beginning. West Egdon believed in Blooms-End time, East Egdon in the time of the Quiet Woman Inn. Grandfer Cantle's watch had numbered many followers in years gone by, but since he had grown older faiths were shaken."[24]

Again, the rise of time discipline, once associated with early Protestants, has been moved forward into the nineteenth century, placing more emphasis on the rise of factories and their time-sheets and also railway time-tables, viewed as examples of what has been called the "industrialization" of time. The rise of capitalism is still viewed as a motor of change but the stress has shifted from commercial to industrial capitalism.[25]

On the other side, it is increasingly recognized that major changes in the experience and perception of time began earlier than used to be thought and were spread over centuries. Where Weber stressed the Protestant Reformation, his academic colleague Wer-

---

[24] Thomas Hardy, *The Return of the Native* (1878: new ed., London 1972), 137; Francesco Maiello, *Storia del calendario: la misurazione del tempo, 1450–1800* (Turin 1994).
[25] Edward P. Thompson, "Time, Work-Discipline and Industrial Capitalism" (1967, rpr *Customs in Common*, 1991, second ed. Harmondsworth 1993, 352–403). Cf. Paul Glennie and Nigel Thrift, "Reworking E. P. Thompson's 'Time, Work-Discipline and Industrial Capitalism'", *Theory and Society* 5 (1996) 275–300. On time-tables, Wolfgang Schivelbusch, *Geschichte der Eisenbahnreise* (1977, English translation *The Railway Journey*, Oxford 1980).

ner Sombart noted the importance of Renaissance Italy. The idea of time as money is clearly expressed in some fifteenth-century texts, from the humanist Leon Battista Alberti's dialogue on the family to the *Zibaldone* (notebook) of the Florentine merchant Giovanni Rucellai. More recently, scholars have moved still further back into the past, noting comparisons between time and money in the fourteenth, thirteenth and even the twelfth century.[26] Again, it has been pointed out that the timetables of the nineteenth-century railways were preceded by the timetables of Dutch barges in the eighteenth century and of coaches in the seventeenth century.[27]

These arguments about the modern elements in traditional culture and the traditional elements in modern culture may not be as inconsistent as they appear, but they have encouraged historians to abandon the assumption of homogeneity within a given culture and consider instead what Georges Gurvitch called the "multiplicity of social times", distinguishing between the attitudes of different social groups.

Times and Groups

For historians, a landmark in the development of this second approach to the cultural history of time was Jacques Le Goff's famous article on church time and merchant time, first published in *Annales* in 1960.[28]

Le Goff's article arose out of his work in the fifties on universities and merchants. It focussed on an academic debate of the later Middle Ages, whether or not time can be sold. But it drew out wid-

---

[26] Jacques Le Goff, "Merchants' Time and Church's Time in the Middle Ages" (1960, reprinted in his *Time, Work and Culture in the Middle Ages* (Chicago 1980), 29–42; Arnold Borst, *The Ordering of Time* (1990, English translation Cambridge 1993); Alexander Murray, "Time and Money", in *The Work of Jacques Le Goff*, ed. Miri Rubin (Woodbridge 1997), 1–26.
[27] Jan de Vries, *Barges and Capitalism* (Utrecht 1981); Wolfgang Behringer, *Im Zeichen des Merkur. Reichspost und Kommunikationsrevolution in der Frühen Neuzeit* (Göttingen 2003), 645.
[28] Georges Gurvitch, *La multiplicité des temps sociaux*, (1958: English translation, *Spectrum of Social Time*, Dordrecht 1964); Le Goff, "Merchants' Time".

er social implications of the conflict between conceptions of time, describing the clock on the town hall as an "instrument of domination" by merchants. Where Durkheim had contrasted whole societies, Le Goff contrasted different groups within the same society. Of course Weber and Sombart might be said to have linked time to social classes, notably modern time with the bourgeoisie, but they did this implicitly, without discussing other social groups.

Where Le Goff emphasized difference, Edward Thompson stressed conflict, notably contests over time in nineteenth-century England, interpreting the cult of "St Monday" as an informal holiday as an expression of resistance to the new work discipline.[29] More recent studies have also noted the clashes resulting from employers trying to impose modern time discipline on workers, often workers recently arrived in the city from the countryside, whether in Italy, Japan or the United States.[30] Their point has been developed and given a new twist by historians of imperialism, especially historians of Africa, who have discussed the conflict between concepts of time in cases where employers and employed come from two different cultures. After all, it was the Africans who joked that the clock is the god of the Europeans.[31]

Le Goff's view of time has in turn been criticized as too simple.[32] It was an advance on the simple binary opposition, but it created another simple binary opposition, between churchmen and merchants. This may not have been intentional but was a side-effect of the success of the article, its virtual "canonization".

---

[29] Thompson, "Work-Discipline", especially 373-7.
[30] Franco Ramella, *Terra e tela* (Turin 1984); Thomas C. Smith, "Peasant Time and Factory Time in Japan", *Past & Present* 111 (1986) 165-97. David Brody, "Time and Work during Early American Industrialism", *Labor History* 30 (1989) 5-46.
[31] Keletso E. Atkins, "Kaffir Time: Pre-industrial Temporal Concepts and Labor Discipline in Nineteenth-Century Colonial Natal', *Journal of African History* 29 (1988), 229-44; Frederick Cooper, "Colonizing Time", in Nicholas Dirks (ed.) *Colonizing Cultures* (Ann Arbor 1995).
[32] Gerhard Dohrn van Rossum, *History of the Hour* (1992: English translation Chicago 1996); Natalie Davis, "The Sacred and the Body Social in Sixteenth-Century Lyon", *Past &Present* 90 (1981), 40-70 at 60-2; Chris Humphrey, "Time and Urban Culture in Late Medieval England", in Humphrey, and W. M. Ormrod (eds.) *Time in the Medieval World* (York 2001), 105-18, at 106.

The question, Whose time? is clearly a crucial one. But when it is answered, it is surely useful to distinguish more than two rival times. The idea of "Church time" fails to distinguish between monks and the secular clergy. The idea of "merchant time" does not distinguish between bankers, say, and shopkeepers.

Again, peasant time is not identical with that of either clergy or merchants. The quotation from Hardy's *Return of the Native* illustrates the gap between the author's own middle-class time and the time of the villagers about whom he is writing.[33] Lawyer's time is distinctive in some cultures at least.[34] In the case of England, one thinks of the common-law concept of "time out of mind" or "time immemorial", whether this meant no more than "unknown" or was interpreted to mean (as it sometimes was by lawyers) the accession of Richard I in 1189.[35]

A case may also be made for distinguishing male from female time in a given society. Stereotypes of punctuality apart, "Women's ways of dating events and things", it was recently argued, "are different from men's". For example, women tend to remember the past by private or domestic events rather than public ones.[36]

Different religious groups often hold different conceptions of time, as in the case of the Christian, Jewish and Muslim time zones, mentioned above, or Catholics and Protestants following the Reformation. The Protestants secularized time, abandoning the traditional references to saints. A striking local example of change comes from the village of Morebath in Devonshire, where the vic-

---

[33] István G. Tóth, "Chimes and Ticks: the concept of time in the minds of peasants and the lower gentry class in Hungary in the 17th and 18th centuries", *CEU History Dept Yearbook* (1994-5), 15-37.
[34] Chris Wickham, "Lawyer's Time: History and Memory in Tenth- and Eleventh-Century Italy", in Henry Mayr-Harting and Robert I. Moore (eds.) *Studies in Medieval History Presented to R. H. C. Davis* (London 1985), 53-71; Paul Brand, "Lawyers' Time in England in the Later Middle Ages", in Humphrey and Ormrod, *Time,* 73-104.
[35] Alan Wharam, "The 1189 Rule", *Anglo-American Law Review* 1 (1972), 262-79.
[36] Jorma Kalela, 'The Challenge of Oral History', in Ann Ollila (ed.) *Historical Perspectives on Memory* (Helsinki 1999), 139-54, at 145. Cf. Julia Kristeva, "Women's Time" (1979: English translation in Toril Moi (ed.) *The Kristeva Reader*, Oxford 1986, 187-213).

ar dated his parish accounts by saints' days until 1568, and then switched to secular dates such as the 17th of November.[37]

Within Protestantism, however, there were different conceptions of time, indeed debates about it. Some opposed the "difference between the times, sacred and common" and wanted spontaneity, to "pray when the spirit moves us".[38] It was only after a period of conflict that there was a general acceptance of what we might call Weber's model of the rejection of festival time and greater emphasis on the Sabbath. There are Protestant communities such as the Amish in the United States today, who, like Orthodox Jews, cling to their traditional forms of time, "slow time" as it has been called, and reject the faster rhythms of the secular world surrounding them.[39]

The example of the Amish, a traditional island in the ocean of modern society, reminds us that what have been called "total institutions" may have their own organization of time, not only the monasteries discussed above but also prisons, factories, ships, regiments and schools, with Reveille, roll calls, "Lights Out" and so on. One of the leading analysts of these institutions, Michel Foucault, was apparently less interested in time than he was in space, but his history of discipline did include a discussion of "the employment of time", arguing that monasteries provided a model for other institutions in their rejection of "free" or idle time and their imposition of time-tables.[40] The school time-table is older than the timetables of coaches, barges and trains.

Despite these important differences between social groups, times are not hermetically sealed but contaminate one another. As Natalie Davis once remarked, "sometimes the 'temps de l'eglise' reinforces the 'temps de marchand' rather than being in tension

---

[37] Eamon Duffy, "Seasons and Signs: the Liturgical Year", in his *The Stripping of the Altars* (New Haven 1992), 11–52; id., *The Voices of Morebath: reformation and rebellion in an English village* (New Haven 2001), 181–2.
[38] Henry Burton, quoted in David Cressy, *Birth, Marriage and Death* (Oxford 1997), 303. Cf. Davis, "The Sacred", 62.
[39] Fabienne Randaxhe, "Temporalités en regard", *Annales: Histoire, Sciences Sociales* 57 (2002), 251–74.
[40] Michel Foucault, *Surveiller et punir: naissance de la prison* (Paris, 1975), 151–

with it".[41] There were centuries of negotiation between agricultural time and ecclesiastical time. The influence of the Church on the laity is visible in the spread of 'books of hours' or the Sieur de Gouberville's calculation of time in terms of prayers.[42] Siesta comes from Sext, paradoxically enough, since monks were vowed to wakefulness.[43]

Again, lawyers' time might affect other social groups like the nuns of Port-Royal in the seventeenth century, often the daughters of judges and magistrates. It has been pointed out that when the nuns were persecuted for their adherence to Jansenism, "their petitions for redress from heaven were made with full forms of law", down to the timing. "In 1679 a nun was buried with an *appel* to the Risen Saviour between her hands; and forty days later, since that was the proper legal interval, a *relief d'appel* was lowered into her tomb".[44]

The Reformation and Counter-Reformation have their place in this story of negotiation. Calendar reform, with its exactitude of calculation, suggests that the churches were adapting themselves to merchant time. On the other hand, dating by saint's days survived in Lutheran Germany. The Protestant churches also supported the traditional Julian calendar until the eighteenth century, precisely because it was a pope who had proposed reform.[45]

This list of examples confirms the suggestion that "Time is a medium for expressing social differences". This quotation comes from a book by the anthropologist Kevin Birth, *Any Time is Trinidad Time*, an engaging report on his fieldwork on that island. At one level, he is concerned, like the first group of scholars discussed in this paper, with the whole culture in contrast to others. The proverb "any time is Trinidad time" and the notices displayed in rum shops, "opening and closing hours: any day and any time" are interpreted as examples of the Trinidad or more generally the Caribbean way of life.

---

[41] Davis, "The Sacred", 61n.
[42] Maiello, *Calendario:* Febvre, *Incroyance, loc. cit.*
[43] I owe this point to Andy Kelly.
[44] Ronald Knox, *Enthusiasm* (Oxford 1950), 201.
[45] George V. Coyne (ed.) *Gregorian Reform of the Calendar* (Vatican City 1983).

Times and Occasions

At another level, like my second group of scholars, Birth emphasizes differences in conceptions of time and conflicts over time between Creoles and Indians, between men and women and also between age-groups, etc.[46] However, the book goes on to suggest a third possibility, approach or model, that of multiple and competing times at the level of the individual or small group as well as a social class or a whole society. The author notes the 'multiple routines' for different activities, work, school, the home etc.[47] He redefines punctuality to mean arriving at an appropriate time for a given activity. "Each time has its own form of punctuality".[48]

New ideas are often older than one thinks. Le Goff, discussing the Christian merchant, noted in passing that 'The time in which he worked professionally was not the time in which he lived religiously', but he did not take this insight any further. It will be interesting to see how historians will work with this idea in the near future. In the case of the calendar, for instance, there is something of interest to say about the rise in the eighteenth century, in Paris at least, of specialized printed calendars for different occupations, such as fruit-sellers or shoemakers, and for different activities such as the theatre.[49] The histories of the hunting season, the fighting season, the legal season, the university season, theatre season and the social season – to mention no more – all deserve investigation.

This third approach to the history of time is part of a more general turn in historical practice that might be described – borrowing and redefining a term from seventeenth-century theology – as 'occasionalism'. It involves taking account of the fact that the same people behave differently according to the occasion or situation. For example, sociolinguists have long been interested in the phenomena of diglossia and code-switching.[50] More recently, art histo-

---

[46] Kevin K. Birth, *Any Time is Trinidad Time* (Gainesville 1999), 143–62, the quotation at 166.
[47] Birth, *Any Time*.
[48] Birth, *Any Time*, 141.
[49] Maiello, *Calendario*, 176–80
[50] Charles Ferguson, "Diglossia", *Word* 15 (1959), 325–40.

rians have discussed painters or sculptors who switched between Gothic and Renaissance styles when they worked for different patrons, rather than 'evolving' from one style to the other.[51] The shift has wide implications that have been pursued in more detail and depth elsewhere. Here it may be sufficient to suggest that future discussions of the cultural or social history of time are likely to place increasing emphasis on occasions.[52]

---

[51] Thomas Kaufmann, *Court, Cloister and City: The Art and Culture of Central Europe, 1450-1800* (London 1995).
[52] Peter Burke, "Performing History: the Importance of Occasions", forthcoming, *Rethinking History*.

7: THE CULTURAL HISTORY OF INTELLECTUAL PRACTICES[1]

Today, anyone who wishes to study the history of ideas is quickly confronted with two rival models. In the German-speaking world, there is the *Begriffsgeschichte* associated with Reinhart Koselleck and his former students and institutionalized in the multi-volume *Geschichtliche Grundbegriffe*. In the English-speaking world, there is 'intellectual history', as practiced along what we might call the 'Cambridge-Baltimore axis' by John Pocock, Quentin Skinner, and their numerous followers.[2] For a long time, a cultural as well as a linguistic frontier separated these two approaches to ideas, although, thanks to the diplomatic efforts of Melvin Richter in particular, this frontier has recently become more open to traffic.[3]

It is certainly not my intention to suggest that these two illuminating approaches are obsolete, although it may well be that after a generation of success, intellectual returns from both of them are diminishing, as the returns from the 'History of Ideas' practiced by Arthur Lovejoy and his circle were diminishing at the time that

---

[1] A summary of this chapter appeared as 'La historia intelectual en la era del giro cultural', *Prismas* 2 (2007), 159–64.
[2] For a recent celebration and re-assessment of Skinner's work, see Annabel Brett and James Tully (eds.) *Rethinking the Foundations of Modern Political Thought* (Cambridge, Cambridge University Press, 2006).
[3] Melvin Richter, *The History of Political and Social Concepts: a critical introduction* (New York, Oxford University Press, 1995).

Koselleck and Pocock put forward their alternatives. The claim to be made in what follows is simply that there is a valuable 'third way', another approach – if not a paradigm – closer than the other two to cultural history as it is currently practiced.

Although intellectual history and cultural history have developed in rather different directions, especially since the rise of the so-called 'New Cultural History' in the 1980s, the frontier between them is transgressed more and more frequently. The resulting hybrid might be described by the phrase 'the cultural history of ideas', along the lines of the 'social history of ideas' proposed in the 1960s and 1970s by Peter Gay and Robert Darnton (even if these two scholars did not give the phrase quite the same meaning). The 'cultural history' part of the phrase should be understood in the wide or anthropological sense of 'culture' associated with the idea of 'historical anthropology'.[4]

Alternatively, and more precisely, we might speak of 'the cultural history of intellectual practices', especially everyday practices as famously studied by Michel de Certeau.[5] Remembering the well-known definition of cultural history by Roger Chartier (who learned from Certeau) in terms of practices and representations, the body of work to be discussed below may be located on the frontier between intellectual and cultural history, understanding the term 'frontier' in this context as a 'contact zone' rather than a line of separation.[6]

In a book dedicated to the memory of Reinhart Koselleck, who wrote on historical perspective and discussed the concepts of the *Standort* and *Sehe-puncklen* associated with Johann Martin Chladenius, readers will be all the more aware than usual that this survey is written from a particular point of view, that of an Englishman who has spent his career working on the cultural history of early modern Europe.[7]

---

[4] Lynn A. Hunt (ed.), *The New Cultural History* (Berkeley: University of California Press, 1989); Peter Burke, *What is Cultural History?* (Cambridge: Polity Press, 2004).
[5] Michel de Certeau, *L'invention du quotidien* (Paris: Gallimard, 1980).
[6] Roger Chartier, *Cultural History: between Practices and Representations* (Cambridge: Polity Press, 1988). This collection of essays was first published in English.
[7] Reinhart Koselleck, *Vergangene Zukunft* (1979: trans Keith Tribe as *Futures Past: on the Semantics of Historical Time* (Cambridge, Mass.: MIT Press, 1985), 130–55.

All the same, what follows will not be restricted to one period or one continent or even to 'history' in a narrow sense. On the contrary, I shall range from ancient to contemporary history and from Asia to the Americas. Scholars who are attached to departments of archaeology, classics, geography, literature and the history of art, philosophy and science will be included in the discussion alongside those who work in departments of history. Examples of the rising importance of the cultural history of intellectual practices will come in the main from studies published in the last fifteen years or so, together with some academic conferences that help to predict and perhaps also to shape the way in which the field is likely to develop in the near future.[8]

I

In both intellectual history and *Begriffsgeschichte*, the leading sector has been the history of political thought. By contrast, in the cultural history of intellectual practices, the lead has been taken by historians of science, especially – though not exclusively – in the USA and in Britain. An early example of the new approach is the study published by Steven Shapin in 1994 in which he discussed the connections between the practice of science, the giving of testimony and the ideal of 'civility' in seventeenth-century England, offering what the author called 'a moral history of scientific credibility'. In a study of the Scientific Revolution published two years later, Shapin devoted considerable attention to what he called 'knowledge-making practices' such as experiment.[9]

In similar fashion, Mario Biagioli has studied the relation be-

---

[8] Conferences on 'The History of the Book and Intellectual History', Princeton, 2004, organized by Robert Darnton; on 'The History of Political Thought and the History of Concepts', City University of New York, organized by Martin Burke and Mel Richter; on 'Information in der Frühen Neuzeit', Munich, 2006, organized by Arndt Brendecke and Susanne Friedrich; on 'Opening up the Archives', Radcliffe Institute for Advanced Study, Harvard, 2006, organized by Ann Blair and Jennifer Milligan; and on 'Intellectual Histories of Early Modern Asia', International Institute of Asian Studies, Leiden, 2006, organized by Sheldon Pollock.

[9] Steven Shapin, *A Social History of Truth: civility and science in seventeenth-century England* (Chicago: University of Chicago Press, 1994).

tween courtly behaviour and the everyday practice of science in seventeenth-century Italy, focusing on the years that Galileo spent at the court of the Grand Duke of Tuscany. Drawing (like Shapin) on the micro-sociology of Erving Goffman, Biagioli describes Galileo's self-fashioning and the influence of courtly codes of behaviour on the way in which he presented his discoveries in public.[10]

Studies of scientific experiments are of course a relatively traditional part of the history of science, although Shapin and others have changed the emphasis by including in their stories the 'invisible technicians'.[11] A newer trend in recent studies of scientific practices is the concern with material culture, with instruments of natural knowledge such as sundials, clocks, astrolabes, telescopes and microscopes, not to mention the increasingly complex apparatus needed for experiments from the nineteenth century onwards.

A still more distinctively recent emphasis has been on the places in which discoveries were made and analysed, 'sites of natural knowledge' such as studies, libraries, workshops, anatomy theatres, botanical gardens, laboratories, clinics and so on. Michel Foucault was one of the first people to draw attention to the importance of these 'sites', but his ideas have been refined and developed as well as followed in more recent studies on the location of knowledge, on 'centres of calculation' (as Bruno Latour calls institutions such as libraries and museums) and the problem of moving from experiments conducted in a particular milieu to conclusions supposedly valid for all places and times.[12]

---

[10] Mario Biagioli, *Galileo Courtier: the practice of science in the culture of absolutism* (Chicago: Chicago University Press, 1993): cf. Erving Goffman, *The Presentation of Self in Everyday Life* (New York: Doubleday, 1959).
[11] Shapin, *Truth*, 355–408.
[12] Michel Foucault, *Naissance de la clinique: une archéologie du regard médical* (Paris: PUF, 1963): Bruno Latour, *Science in Action: how to follow scientists and engineers through society* (Cambridge, Mass.: Harvard University Press, 1987); Adi Ophir and Steven Shapin, 'The Place of Knowledge', *Science in Context* 4 (1991), 163–90; Katharine Park and Lorraine Daston (eds.) *The Cambridge History of Science*, vol.3: *Early Modern Science* (Cambridge: Cambridge University Press, 2006), part II; Antonella Romano and Stéphane Van Damme (eds.) 'Sciences et villes-mondes, 16e-18e siècles', special issue of *Revue d'Histoire Moderne et Contemporaine* 55 (2008). On the problem of the relation between specific places and general conclusions, Jan Golinski, *Making Natural Knowledge: Constructivism and the History of Science* (Chicago: University of Chicago Press, 1998).

For example, a group of scholars based mainly in Cambridge have published a collective study of what they call 'cultures of natural history' in the West from the Renaissance to the present. In an adjacent 'field' – which he does see in spatial terms – the Harvard historian Peter Galison has made a study of what he calls the 'subcultures' of twentieth-century physics (notably theorists and experimenters), identifying what he calls 'trading zones', defined as spaces in which 'two dissimilar groups can find common ground', exchanging items of information even though they sometimes disagree about the wider significance of what is exchanged.[13]

In similar fashion to the study of cultures of science, scholars have turned to the history of religious cultures rather than the history of doctrines or theology; to political culture, or better, 'cultures' in the plural, rather than the history of political thought; and to historical cultures, rather than the traditional history of historiography.

II

In the case of religion, the new approach is particularly prominent in recent studies of the Reformation. For example Margo Todd has examined the ways in which the doctrines and values of Calvinism gradually penetrated everyday life in Scotland in the seventeenth century, while Andrew Pettegree has concentrated attention on the media – sermons, songs, plays, images and pamphlets as well as books, notably the Bible – that persuaded some people to turn Protestant.[14] There is a growing interest in the material culture of both Reformation and Counter-Reformation (or Catholic and Protestant reformations), including not only images and buildings but also church furnishings such as altars, pulpits, confession-boxes

---

[13] Nicholas Jardine, James A. Secord and Emma C. Spary (eds.) *Cultures of Natural History* (Cambridge: Cambridge University Press, 1996); Peter Galison, *Image and Logic: a material culture of microphysics* (Chicago, University of Chicago Press, 1997), 46, 803.

[14] Margo Todd, *The culture of Protestantism in early modern Scotland* (New Haven: Yale University Press, 2002); Andrew Pettegree, *Reformation and the Culture of Persuasion* (Cambridge: Cambridge University Press, 2005). The late Bob Scribner was a pioneer of this approach: see in particular R. W. Scribner, 'The Impact of the Reformation on Daily Life', in Gerhard Jarisch (ed.) *Mensch und Objekt im Mittelalter und in der frühen Neuzeit* (Vienna: Verlag der Österreichischen Akademie der Wissenschaften, 1990), 315–44.

and pews. This approach to religious history might be described as a metaphorical and on occasion a literal 'archaeology of the Reformation', since archaeologists have joined historians in the study of medieval and early modern churches.[15]

A recent attempt to write a 'new cultural history' of the Reformation takes its cue from the new history of scientific practices associated with Shapin and his colleagues. Its aim is to situate Luther in his local milieu, Wittenberg, but also to account for the spread of Luther's form of Protestantism and so to show how 'locally relevant knowledge can be turned into a more universally acknowledged truth'.[16]

In the case of the mission field, as in that of the Reformation at home, a major turn in studies of conversion has become visible. We might say that the scholars themselves have been converted from one approach to another. Whether they work on Mexico, Brazil or Japan, they have turned from an approach that emphasized doctrine to one that emphasizes practice. With this turn goes a shift from a stress on the role of missionaries in teaching what they saw as unchanging truths to one that focuses on the receivers and their active reception and 'negotiation' – not to say transformation – of the new messages, producing different forms of unconscious mixture or conscious syncretism between local traditions and newly-arrived ideas and practices.[17]

In the case of the history of political thought, we see more and more examples of a broader approach than the one associated with Pocock and Skinner: an approach that is concerned with everyone's ideas rather than those of a few major thinkers; with unspoken assumptions as well as with formal arguments, and with political practices as well as with discourses. English political thought

---

[15] David Gaimster and Roberta Gilchrist, *The Archaeology of Reformation, 1480–1580* (Leeds, Maney, 2003).
[16] Ulinka Rublack, *Reformation Europe* (Cambridge: Cambridge University Press, 2005), 16, 194–6.
[17] Serge Gruzinski, *La colonisation de l'imaginaire: sociétés indigènes et occidentalisation dans le Mexique espagnol* (Paris: Gallimard, 1988); Ronaldo Vainfas, *A heresia dos índios: catolicismo e rebeldia no Brasil colonial* (São Paulo: Companhia das Letras, 1995); Ikuo Higashibaba, *Christianity in Early Modern Japan* (Leiden: Brill, 2001).

in the middle of the seventeenth century has often been studied, but a recent book focused by contrast on what the author calls 'the political culture of the English Commonwealth'. Again, political thought and institutions have been discussed from this point of view in a collective volume on the cultural construction of 'Norden' (the Scandinavian term for Scandinavia), concerned not only, as one might have expected, with religious and national identities but also with political culture in general, including 'the culturality of the Nordic Welfare State'.[18]

The history of historiography itself offers some vivid illustrations of this change of focus, a shift from a more precise or narrow approach, especially concerned with professional historians and classic texts, to a wider approach that might be described as the cultural history of historiography. The shift is revealed by the increasing use of the phrase 'historical culture'. The pioneer in this respect was surely the French historian Bernard Guénée, who wrote about *culture historique* thirty years ago. The lack of translations of this fundamental study is a clue to its relatively cool reception, at least at first. More recently, however, Guénée's example has been followed both in Germany and in the English-speaking world, among others by the Canadian scholars Mark Phillips and Daniel Woolf.[19]

The 'cash value' of the new term, as English philosophers liked to say in the middle of the twentieth century, in other words its usefulness, is especially that it displaces attention from writers

---

[18] Sean Kelsey, *Inventing a Republic: the Political Culture of the English Commonwealth* (Cambridge, Cambridge University Press, 1997); Øystein Sørenson and Bo Stråth (eds.) *The Cultural Construction of Norden* (Oslo, Stockhol, etc, Scandinavian Universities Press, 1997).

[19] Bernard Guénée, *Histoire et culture historique dans l'occident medieval* (Paris: Aubier, 1980). For German, see Wolfgang Hardtwig, *Geschichtskultur und Wissenschaft* (Munich: Deutscher Taschenbuch Verlag, 1990); Klaus Fröhlich Heinrich Theodor Grütter and Jörn Rüsen (eds.) *Geschichtskultur* (Pfaffenweiler: Centaurus, 1992); Klaus Füßmann, Heinrich Theodor Grütter and Jörn Rüsen (eds.), *Historische Faszination. Geschichtskultur heute* (Cologne: Böhlau, 1994). Since 2000, the term has become a common one in book titles.

For English, see Mark S. Phillips, *Society and Sentiment: Genres of Historical Writing in Britain, 1740–1820* (Princeton, Princeton University Press, 2000); Daniel Woolf, *The Social Circulation of the Past: English Historical Culture 1500–1730* (Oxford, Oxford University Press, 2003).

to readers and also to people who never read history books and might not have been able to read at all, but held attitudes to the past that were derived from oral traditions or from visual images. This displacement is also visible in works that do not use the phrase 'historical culture', such as the lecture by Keith Thomas on 'the perception of the past in early modern England'.[20]

This wider approach to the study of the past is not completely new, though it has become more and more important in recent decades. To offer a personal example, I was already interested in this approach when writing, in the 1960s, a book entitled 'The Renaissance sense of the past'.[21] I borrowed that phrase from a lecture of the 1950s by Veronica Wedgwood, a well known English woman of letters of the time, about *The Sense of the Past*. Wedgwood had in turn borrowed the phrase from Henry James, whose *Sense of the Past*, an unfinished novel, was published posthumously in 1917.

In the second place, the new studies of historical culture displace attention from texts to the practices that produced them: the changing practices of historical research in archives and libraries, of source criticism and of communicating the results of research and criticism in university lectures and school textbooks as well as in works of scholarship. Thus Anthony Grafton had the unusual but fruitful idea of writing the history of footnoting as a practice of scholars, especially historians, among them Pierre Bayle and Leopold von Ranke.[22] Again, a recent study of the late nineteenth-century Belgian historian Paul Fredericq – who made considerable use of 'secretaries' (in other words, what we would call research assistants) and recorded the ways in which they accomplished or failed to accomplish the tasks he gave them – analyses their 'daily practices' such as 'reading, taking notes, corresponding, maintaining academic friendships, exchanging material, correcting proofs', noting the close links between these practices and

---

[20] Keith Thomas, *The Perception of the Past in Early Modern England* (London: University of London, 1983).
[21] Peter Burke, *The Renaissance Sense of the Past* (London: Edward Arnold, 1969); C.V. Wedgwood, *The Sense of the Past* (Cambridge, 1957).
[22] Anthony Grafton, *The Footnote: a curious history* (Cambridge, Mass.: Harvard University press, 1997).

the ideas and ideals of the new professional history.[23]

Space as well as time has been approached in this way. It is no surprise to find that one leading sector of the new cultural history should be the history of travel, studied by cultural geographers and specialists in literature as well as by the denizens of history departments and viewed as a practice and even as an art. In early modern Europe, books were written instructing their readers how to travel and what to look for in each place, advising travellers to read the inscriptions on gravestones, for instance, to view works of art and to ask questions – especially in Venice – about the nature of the local political regime.[24]

Recent studies of travel have placed particular emphasis on two practices: seeing and writing. One group of studies, following in the wake of Michel Foucault and of the well-known study of 'Orientalism' by Edward Said, focuses on the 'gaze' of travellers, described as male or female, colonial or 'picturesque', and on the way in which stereotypes and prejudices shape what the visitors see. Another group of studies is more concerned with the texts produced by travellers, whether they were written on the spot and at the time or – as was the case much more frequently – at home, and later. These studies explore the rhetoric of travelers and tourists, their claim to have left the 'beaten track' for instance, their frequent use of earlier descriptions of the same places (often without acknowledgement), as well as their own eyes, and the conventions of the travelogue as a literary genre, changing over time and shaped by the expectations of publishers and readers.[25]

---

[23] Jo Tollebeek, 'A Stormy Family. Paul Fredericq and the formation of an academic historical community in the nineteenth century', *Storia della Storiografia* 53 (2008), 58–72.

[24] Justin Stagl, *A history of curiosity: the theory of travel, 1550–1800* (London: Routledge, 1995); Joan-Paul Rubiés, 'Instructions for Travellers: teaching the eye to see', *History and Anthropology*, 1–51.

[25] Mary-Louise Pratt, *Imperial Eyes: Travel Writing and Transculturation* (London: Routledge, 1992); James Buzard, *The Beaten Track: European Tourism, Literature and the Ways to 'Culture', 1800–1918* (Oxford: Oxford University Press, 1993); James Duncan and Derek Gregory (eds.) *Writes of Passage: Reading Travel Writing* (London: Routledge, 1999); Indira Ghose, *Women Travellers in Colonial India: the Power of the Female Gaze* (Delhi: Oxford University Press, 1998).

III

One important respect in which the broad 'cultural turn' has affected intellectual history is the recent revaluation of the idea of 'tradition'. Central to 'traditional' cultural history – for example the studies of the classical tradition that have long been associated with the Warburg Institute – the notion of tradition has been relatively neglected in recent years.

Although the collective study *The Invention of Tradition* (1983) made a remarkable impact in many countries and a number of disciplines, what seems to have attracted readers was the 'invention' side of the equation rather than the 'tradition' side – as the recent spate of books with the word 'invention' in their title testifies. These books range from 'The Invention of Spain' to 'The Invention of Argentina', as well as the inventions of mythology, the people, progress, the French Revolution and even invention itself.[26] Only recently do we find attempts by historians to redress the balance, refining and redefining the notion of intellectual tradition by drawing on the ideas of Thomas Kuhn, for instance, on paradigms and 'normal science' or those of Hans-Georg Gadamer on horizons of expectation and the history of 'effects' (*Wirkungsgeschichte*).[27]

The value of the notion of tradition, like that of Pierre Bourdieu's famous notion of 'cultural reproduction', is partly that it draws attention to the effort that is always involved in passing knowledge down the generations – an effort that should not be taken for granted by historians, whether it is the work of individuals,

---

[26] Eric J. Hobsbawm and Terence Ranger (eds.) *The Invention of Tradition* (Cambridge: Cambridge University Press, 1983); Inman Fox, *La invención de España: nacionalismo liberal e identidad nacional* (Madrid: Cátedra, 1997); Nicolas Shumway, *The Invention of Argentina* (Berkeley: University of California Press, 1991); Marcel Détienne, *L'invention de la mythologie* (Paris: Gallimard, 1981); Edmund S. Morgan, *Inventing the people: the rise of popular sovereignty in England and America* (New York: Norton, 1988); Peter J. Bowler, *The invention of progress: the Victorians and the past* (Oxford: Blackwell, 1989); Gaurav Desai, 'The Invention of Invention', *Cultural Critique* 24 (1993), 119–42.

[27] Mark S. Phillips and Gordon J. Schochet (eds.) *Questions of Tradition* (Toronto: University of Toronto Press, 2004), especially the introduction.

groups or institutions such as schools and universities and whether the medium is speech, writing or print.

'Knowledge', together with 'information', is the focus of a number of recent studies on the borders of intellectual and cultural history, one of which bears the title 'Knowledge as Cultural Practice'.[28] A similar concern informs Anne Goldgar's study of the Republic of Letters which concentrates on England, France, and the Netherlands between 1680 and 1750 and differs from earlier studies primarily in its emphasis on the twin themes of conduct, including improper conduct, and community.[29] Goldgar's concern is to write a social history or, we might say, historical anthropology of the Republic, identifying the laws or at least the etiquette of a society which was clearly hierarchical, despite frequent claims to be egalitarian. Her focus – like Shapin's, as we have seen – is on the 'civility' that was expected – though not always found – in the case of scholars who claimed also to be gentlemen, since female scholars such as the Dutchwoman Anna Maria Schurman were still rare, and the Republic might be described as a male club. 'Civility', in the case of scholars, included mutual help, the exchange of information and books, and an attempt at impartiality of judgement which often conflicted with religious and political allegiances.

Giving and lending books were and remain important practices among scholarly communities, though they received little attention from historians until recently. To Goldgar's remarks we can now add a study by Natalie Davis as well as references in the work of other scholars. In the case of late imperial China, for instance, a recent study of books in the culture of the literati quotes the proverb 'To lend a book is stupid: so is to return it'. By contrast, some European humanists described their books as their property

---

[28] Hans Erich Bödeker, Peter Hanns Reill, und Jürgen Schlumbohm (eds.) *Wissenschaft als kulturelle Praxis, 1750–1900* (Göttingen : Vandenhoeck & Ruprecht, 1999). For a brief survey of an earlier period, see Peter Burke, *A Social History of Knowledge in Early Modern Europe, from Gutenberg to Diderot* (Cambridge: Polity Press, 2000).

[29] Anne Goldgar, *Impolite learning: conduct and community in the Republic of Letters, 1680–1750* (New Haven: Yale University Press, 1995).

'and that of their friends' (*et amicorum*). Some of them, including Rabelais and the French collector Jean Grolier, had the formula inscribed on the bindings of the books themselves.[30]

So far as practices are concerned, particular attention has been given to what we might describe as the 'historical anthropology' of universities, as practiced, for instance, by Françoise Waquet in France, Martin Mulsow in Germany and William Clark in the USA.[31] All three scholars are concerned in their different ways to link the history of ideas to broader cultural developments that include changes in the media of communication. They do not forget academic rituals, rites of passage such as degree ceremonies, inaugural lectures, and, of course, examinations.[32]

The concern of these three scholars with 'cultures of knowledge' and 'the everyday life of learning' (*Alltagsgeschichte der Gelehrsamkeit*, as Mulsow calls it), is linked to their emphasis on the history of cultural practices and on the material culture that supported and shaped these practices, including furniture such as blackboards and lecterns, as well as the history of the spaces in which teaching and learning took place: libraries, lecture theatres and seminar rooms as well as the laboratories, anatomy theatres and other spaces for science that were mentioned earlier in this chapter. There is room here in future studies for what might be called

---

[30] On the conventions governing gifts and loans of books, Natalie Z. Davis, 'Beyond the Market: Books as Gifts in Sixteenth-Century France', *Transactions of the Royal Historical Society* 33 (1983) 69–88; Joe P. McDermott, *A Social History of the Chinese Book: Books And Literati Culture In Late Imperial China* (Hong Kong: Hong Kong University Press, 2006); cf. Peter Burke, 'Humanism and Friendship in Sixteenth-Century Europe', in Julian Haseldine (ed.) *Friendship in Medieval Europe* (Stroud: Sutton) 1999), 262–74, drawing on an older study, G. D. Hobson, 'Et amicorum', *The Library*, 5th series 4 (1949–50), 87–99.

[31] Françoise Waquet, *Parler comme un livre: l'oralité et le savoir, 16e-20e siècle* (Paris: Albin Michel, 2003); William Clark, *Academic Charisma and the Origins of the Research University* (Chicago: University of Chicago Press, 2006); Martin Mulsow, *Die unanständige Gelehrtenrepublik: Wissen, Libertinage und Kommunikation in der Frühen Neuzeit* (Stuttgart: J. B. Metzler, 2007). On the everyday, Mulsow, 67–8.

[32] On examinations, Clark, *Academic Charisma*, 93–140; on inaugurals, Françoise Waquet, 'Academic Homage and Intellectual Genealogy: Inaugural Lectures at the Collège de France (1949–2003)', *History of Universities* 21 (2006), 202–27.

an 'archaeology of libraries', a study of spaces (reading-rooms, for instance, but also book-stacks, cafés, workshops and offices), not forgetting the heating and lighting of these spaces and their fittings (shelves, desks, chairs, comfortable or uncomfortable, and so on).[33]

The practices of teaching and learning discussed in these studies and elsewhere include ways of reading or taking notes from books or lectures.[34] We normally associate the world of learning with reading and writing, but Waquet, Mulsow and Clark all emphasize the survival of oral culture in the university in the age of print in the form of lectures, seminars and *viva voce* examinations.

Their point becomes even more persuasive if we turn from the West to studies of higher education in the Islamic world, where the traditional system of masters teaching pupils face-to-face, the students sitting cross-legged at the feet of their teacher, long remained central, as recently-studied examples from Cairo and Damascus suggest. Indeed, the resistance to print in the Islamic world until around the year 1800, according to one recent historian, was precisely because the new medium 'struck right at the heart of person to person transmission of knowledge'.[35]

On the frontier between cultural and political history, we find an increasing number of studies that are focussed on information and the state. Scholars working in this area ask what information central governments collected; how they classified it, stored it, protected it and retrieved it; and how they used this information. The crucial problem is surely whether different kinds of regime

---

[33] Peter Burke, 'Towards an Archaeology of Libraries', lecture at conference, 'Material Cultures and the Creation of Knowledge', University of Edinburgh, 23–24 July 2005, still unpublished.

[34] On note-taking, cf Ann Blair, 'Note-Taking as an Art of Transmission', *Critical Inquiry* 31 (2004).

[35] Francis Robinson, 'Islam and the Impact of Print in South Asia', in Nigel Crook (ed.) *The Transmission of Knowledge in South Asia* (Delhi: Oxford University Press 1996, 62–97); Jonathan Berkey, *The Transmission of Knowledge in Medieval Cairo* (Princeton: Princeton University Press, 1992); Michael Chamberlain, *Knowledge and Social Practice in Medieval Damascus* (Cambridge: Cambridge University Press, 1994).

gathered or employed information in different ways.³⁶
Take the case of early modern Venice, one of Europe's great centres of information at this time. It might be argued that the Venetians produced, circulated and received the information they deserved. The fact that Venice was a mercantile state rather than an agrarian one was reflected in its information services, dependent, especially in the fifteenth century, on a network of merchants. Venice welcomed immigrants (Greek, Jewish, Slavonian and so on) and these immigrants contributed to the polyglot printing for which the city was famous. The circulation of political information in and around Venice was also related to the distinctive structure of the state. Venice had an empire in the Mediterranean and a network of diplomats in Europe from whom much information came in, while a regime with a Maggior Consiglio of some two thousand members cannot keep its secrets.³⁷

One result of this interest has been the rise of studies *of* archives (as opposed to studies *in* archives), examining 'archiving' as a practice with a history, raising (as in the case of libraries and museums) problems of classification. Recent studies of archives have emphasized both the logic and the effects of the ways in which information was organized in these places, and the ways in which archives were shaped, not only by the political regimes that originally generated the documents, but also (like libraries) by the buildings that housed them. Until the nineteenth century, archives

---

³⁶ Besides contributions to the Munich conference mentioned in note 5, see Peter Burke, 'Early Modern Venice as a Center of Information and Communication', in John Martin and Dennis Romano (eds.) *Venice Reconsidered: the History and Civilization of an Italian City-State 1297–1997* (Baltimore: Johns Hopkins University Press, 2000), 389–419; Brendan Dooley and Sabrina Baron (eds.) *The Politics of Information in Early Modern Europe* (London: Routledge, 2001); Edward Higgs, *The Information State in England: the central collection of information on citizens since 1500* (Basingstoke: Palgrave, 2005); Filippo De Vivo, *Information and Communication in Early Modern Venice: rethinking early modern politics* (Oxford: Oxford University Press, 2007); and Arndt Brendecke, Markus Friedrich and Susanne Friedrich (eds.) *Information in der Frühen Neuzeit. Status, Bestände, Strategien* (Münster: Lit Verlag, 2008).
³⁷ Hans J. Kissling, 'Venezia come centro di informazione sui Turchi', in Hans-Georg Beck et al. (eds.) *Venezia Centro di mediazione tra Oriente e Occidente (secoli xv–xvi) Aspetti e problemi* (2 vols., Florence: Olschki, 1977), 97–109; Burke, 'Venice'.

were usually to be found in buildings that had been constructed for other purposes.[38]

Three of the most important of the recent studies of the political uses of knowledge concern the history of colonial India. The first argues that even apparently disinterested knowledge of India was mobilized by the British to help them control the country. The second emphasizes the importance of information for political practice and the way in which British administrators built on the work of their Mughal predecessors, while the third claims that the caste system, at least in its modern form, was not so much an expression of Indian tradition as the product of the encounter between Indian subjects and British administrators, who were much concerned with the classification of the people under their control and both adopted and adapted indigenous categories.[39]

IV

In the course of the researches discussed here, it has become apparent (or more exactly, even more apparent than before) that the simple model of ideas 'spreading' unchanged from one place to another, like the simple model of 'traditions' being handed down unchanged from one generation to another, is in serious need of revision. As the studies of religious conversion mentioned above vividly illustrate, the idea of creative 'reception', long established in literary studies, is becoming commonplace among cultural and intellectual historians as well.

---

[38] Randolph Head, 'Knowing Like a State: the transformation of political knowledge in Swiss archives 1450–1770', *Journal of Modern History* 75 (2003), 745–82; Peter Burke, *Palimpsests: Reflections on the Re-Employment of Records* (Ketelaar lecture 2004, The Hague 2005). The proceedings of the Harvard conference on archives mentioned in note 7 are now available as a special issue of *Archival Science* 7 (2007).

[39] Bernard S. Cohn, *Colonialism and its Forms of Knowledge: the British in India* (Princeton: Princeton University Press, 1996); Christopher Bayly, *Empire and Information: Intelligence Gathering and Social Communication in India, 1780–1870* (Cambridge: Cambridge University Press, 1997); Nicholas Dirks, *Castes of Mind: Colonialism and the Making of Modern India* (Princeton: Princeton University Press, 2001). Cohn and Bayly are compared and contrasted in W. R. Pinch, 'Same Difference in India and Europe', *History and Theory* 38 (1999), 389–407.

Another way to exemplify this turn from the production of ideas to their 'consumption' is to link intellectual history to the history of reading, a leading sector in the new cultural history, as the career of Roger Chartier reminds us.[40] Studies of what are now often described as 'cultures of reading' emphasize reading as a practice or a cluster of practices and especially the contrast between two kinds of reading, the 'intensive', slow and careful, and the 'extensive', in other words rapid reading, skimming or consultation.[41] Reading practices have also been linked to the history of the body, since reading has taken place standing, sitting or lying down, at desks, in armchairs, in bed and so on.

The history of reading is linked to the history of material culture, since the ways in which texts are read are shaped by the ways in which those texts are presented, as the bibliographer Don McKenzie pointed out.[42] The 'same' text may read very differently when it is offered to the reader in a large folio or a small duodecimo, with or without illustrations, prefatory letters to the reader, chapter headings, tables of contents, indexes or printed marginalia, whether they take the form of pointing fingers to emphasize arguments or brief summaries of complex expositions.

Take the case of Baldassare Castiglione's *Cortegiano*, for instance. In the ninety years following its publication, 1528–1619, there were at least 110 editions of the Courtier, sixty in the original Italian and fifty or more in the French, Spanish, Latin, English and German translations. In the course of its diffusion the meaning of the text changed. The original text was an open dialogue in which the speakers do not reach agreement about the qualities of the perfect courtier and his female counterpart. Successive editions, however, presented it – by means of tables of contexts, indexes, printed marginalia and so on – as a 'how-to-do-it' manual, a series of rules for good behaviour, apparently to appeal to men and women who

---

[40] Roger Chartier, *Lectures et lecteurs dans la France de l'Ancien Regime* (Paris: Seuil, 1987), and many of his subsequent studies.
[41] Erich Schön, *Der Verlust der Sinnlichkeit, oder, Die Verwandlungen des Lesers: Mentalitätswandel um 1800* (Stuttgart: Clett-Kotta, 1987); H. E. Bödeker (ed.) *Lesekulturen im 18 Jht* (Hamburg: Meiner, 1992);
[42] Don McKenzie, *Bibliography and the Sociology of Texts* (London: British Library, 1986).

were insecure about their status. Annotations in manuscript in particular copies of the text – since writing in books was and remains a central practice of readers – allow us to form some idea of how different individuals viewed and reacted to the same text. So do translations, since translators are particularly careful and particularly well-documented readers.[43]

Some recent studies published in English have brought together book history and the history of science, to the benefit of both.[44] Adrian Johns, for instance, has examined the relation between print and knowledge via the production and consumption of books about science, or 'natural philosophy' in a single place, early modern London, emphasizing what he calls the 'making' both of scientific knowledge and of print culture itself. Like Shapin, discussed earlier, he is concerned with what made assertions about nature credible, but he looks at the relation between credibility and print rather than civility.[45]

By contrast, James Secord focuses on the reception in Victorian Britain of a single text, the anonymous *Vestiges of the Natural History of Creation* (1844), tracking the journeys of the text to different places and the reactions of different kinds of reader. The book was mentioned in thousands of letters and diaries, denounced and praised in pulpits, discussed on railway journeys, and annotated on an Alabama river steamboat. It was discussed at dinner parties, pubs and soirées, reviewed in scores of periodicals and pamphlets, and in Britain alone sold fourteen editions and almost forty thousand copies'.[46]

For another illustration of the turn towards reception, we might examine the role of translation and the way in which key ideas change in the course of being rendered into other languages. That

---

[43] Peter Burke, *The Fortunes of the Courtier: The European Reception of Castiglione's Cortegiano* (Cambridge, Polity, 1995).
[44] For a sample of new work, see Marina Frasca-Spada and Nick Jardine (eds.) *Books and the sciences in history* (Cambridge: Cambridge University Press, 2000).
[45] Adrian Johns, *The Nature of the Book: Print and Knowledge in the Making* (Chicago, University of Chicago Press, 1998).
[46] James L. Secord, *Victorian sensation: the extraordinary publication, reception, and secret authorship of Vestiges of the natural history of creation* (Chicago, University of Chicago Press, 2000), quotation from p.3.

this can happen even in the case of similar languages, such as English and German, has been neatly demonstrated in the case of the Scottish Enlightenment thinker Adam Ferguson and his concept of 'civil society'.[47] However, the demonstration is even clearer, not to say more dramatic, in cases in which European concepts such as liberty, democracy or Christianity were translated into languages with very different structures and traditions, such as Japanese or the Wolof spoken in Senegal.[48]

In these cases, of course, the problem of translation is not so much linguistic as cultural. To choose a term or phrase in the target language with 'equivalent effect' to the original language becomes more difficult in proportion to the distance between the two cultures. In this context as in others (the study of cultural encounters, for instance), the anthropologist's metaphor of 'cultural translation' becomes an extremely useful concept, drawing attention to the effort and skill and also to the difficult decisions involved in the act of translation, walking the tightrope between infidelity to the original text and unintelligibility to its new readers.[49]

In my view, one way forward in the cultural history of intellectual practices in the near future will be to examine interlingual translation as a special case of cultural translation.[50] Take the example of Japan, recently studied by the historian Douglas Howland in a study that focuses on the way in which new concepts, borrowed from Western culture, were deployed in new contexts. After 1868, the year of the imperial restoration, the rulers of Japan set out to modernize the country by westernizing it. There was a new constitution that included a place for a parliament, although

---

[47] Fania Oz-Salzberger, *Translating the Enlightenment: Scottish Civic Discourse in 18thc Germany* (Oxford: Oxford University Press, 1995).
[48] Among the most penetrating studies are Frederick Schaffer, *Democracy in Translation: understanding politics in an unfamiliar culture* (Ithaca: Cornell University Press, 1998); Douglas Howland, *Translating the West* (Honolulu: University of Hawaii Press, 2001). The conference in New York in 2005 attempted to build on this foundation.
[49] Maria Lúcia Pallares-Burke, *Nísia Floresta, O Carapuceiro e Outros Ensaios de Tradução Cultural* (S. Paulo: Hucitec, 1996).
[50] I make this case in the introduction to Peter Burke and R. Po-chia Hsia (eds.) *Cultural Translation in Early Modern Europe* (Cambridge: Cambridge University Press, 2007).

the emperor now exercised considerable power. Scholars lent a hand in the process of modernization, translating certain books from English into Japanese.

Early choices, revealing something of the cultural climate of the time, were the books by Samuel Smiles on self-help as a means to success and by John Stuart Mill on liberty. The two books were translated by the same individual, Nakamura Keiu, and published in 1870 and 1871. The translation of the keyword or *Grundbegriff* 'liberty' makes a particularly interesting story. Some Japanese decided to borrow a foreign word, which turned into *riberuchi*, 'liberty', or *furidomo*, 'freedom'.

Other writers, including Nakamura, preferred to search for equivalents in Japanese tradition, such as the term *jiyu*. *Jiyu* had already been used in early modern times to translate the Latin *libertas* and the Dutch *vrijheid*. However, the term had become associated with selfishness. Whether for linguistic or for wider cultural reasons, *jiyu* did not completely escape from the negative idea of willfulness.[51] In short, new words imported from the West did not always fit in easily either with existing Japanese concepts or with the socio-political environment in which they were employed.

Difficulties in translating certain concepts draw attention to a well-known problem, that of deciding when a historian can reasonably assert that certain ideas are 'out of place' in a given culture, like liberalism among the slave-owning classes in nineteenth-century Brazil.[52]

The history of all these forms of translation is necessarily a comparative history, concerned with both the culture producing the ideas and the culture that consumes them. Comparisons and contrasts between cultures help both historians and their readers both to see and to explain differences in ideas and attitudes and even more important, differences in assumptions, in what is implicit or taken for granted in a given place, time and social group, as well as what is supported by local institutions.

---

[51] Douglas Howland, Translating the West, Honolulu, 2001.
[52] Roberto Schwarz, *Ao Vencedor as Batatas* (São Paulo: Livraria Duas Cidades, 1977); Elías José Palti, 'The Problem of Misplaced Ideas" Revisited: Beyond the "History of Ideas" in Latin America', *Journal of the History of Ideas* 67 (2006), 149–79.

A good example of the value of the comparative approach, taken once again from the history of science, is a recent study of the difference between organized attempts to understand the natural world in ancient Greece and in ancient China, emphasizing the long tradition of debate in the first case and that of official support for research in the second.[53] I both hope and expect that future studies in the cultural history of intellectual practices will adopt a comparative method.

V

One purpose of this article has been to name a trend in order to draw more attention to it, to make it more visible. The cultural history of intellectual practices is a trend rather than a movement. It may also be regarded as a network, with Cambridge, Chicago and Paris among the nodes, or perhaps as a cluster of networks that are not yet fully connected.

Like other recent trends, this one is not entirely new, as some of the examples cited in the footnotes reveal. Some readers may think that the cultural history of intellectual practices is little more than the social history of ideas or the sociology of knowledge under a new name, an impression fortified by the title of the book by Shapin that was cited earlier, *The Social History of Truth*. The point is partly valid in this case as it is more generally: the rise of cultural history has taken place partly as a result of invading the territory of the social. All the same, the cultural approach to ideas is distinctive in its emphasis not only on social situations but also on physical locations or 'little tools of knowledge' such as chalk or inkwells or card-indexes.[54] A number of the scholars whose work has been cited in these pages, among them Natalie Davis, Mario Biagoli and Martin Mulsow, have drawn on the work of anthropologists who have written on gift exchange and other practices.[55] More gener-

---

[53] Geoffrey Lloyd, *The Ambitions of Curiosity: Understanding the World in ancient Greece and China* (Cambridge: Cambridge University Press, 2002).
[54] Peter Becker and William Clark (eds.) *Little Tools of Knowledge: historical essays on academic and bureaucratic practices* (Ann Arbor: University of Michigan Press, 2001).
[55] Davis, 'Beyond the Market'; Biagioli, *Galileo Courtier*; Mulsow, *Gelehrtenrepublik*.

ally, one might claim that cultural historians of intellectual practices have moved closer than practitioners of intellectual history or *Begriffsgeschichte* to what has been called 'the anthropology of knowledge', with its emphasis on classification.[56]

This brief survey has allowed little opportunity for a critique. I would not have chosen this topic if I did not believe that the cultural history of intellectual practices has much to offer, that it has already delivered valuable studies and is likely to produce more in the near future. Like other approaches, it is of course vulnerable to criticism. I shall end this essay by suggesting that its weaknesses are indissociable from its strengths, in other words the reverse of the medal.

The most obvious and perhaps also the most important point to make is that the concept of culture is incorrigibly vague. This is the down side of its flexibility, which is often an asset. Traditional intellectual history is more rigorous. The history of the context and the reception of a text or idea, for instance, cannot be analyzed with the same degree of precision as the text itself. The concept of context is less precise than it may look.[57] On the other hand, the cultural history of intellectual practices reaches more widely and perhaps more deeply into past cultures and societies than alternative approaches can.

The moral that might be drawn from this combination of loss and gain, costs and benefits is that in the historiography of culture – as in the history of culture itself – a new approach should not (and usually does not) replace an old one. The normal outcome is some form of coexistence (not necessarily peaceful). This article has not argued that either traditional intellectual history or *Begriffsgeschichte* should be consigned to the waste-basket. It has simply suggested that the older approaches associated with Bal-

---

[56] Cf. Yehuda Elkana, 'A Programmatic Attempt at an Anthropology of Knowledge', in E. Mendelsohn and Yehuda Elkana (eds.), *Sciences and Cultures: anthropological and historical studies of the sciences* (Dordrecht: Reidel, 1981, 1–76; Malcolm Crick, 'Anthropology of Knowledge', *Annual Review of Anthropology* 11 (1982), 287–313; and Peter Burke, 'Classifying Knowledge', in *A Social History of Knowledge from Gutenberg to Diderot* (Cambridge; Polity Press, 2000), ch.5.

[57] Peter Burke, 'Context in Context', *Common Knowledge* 8: 1 (2002) 152–77.

timore, Bielefeld and Cambridge have recently been joined by a third. Competition is inevitable, especially in an academic environment characterized by scarce resources, but there is also space for dialogue and interaction. Indeed, such a dialogue might help to halt the inevitable diminution in the intellectual returns to new approaches as they become established in their turn and even traditional.

8: THE INVENTION OF MICRO-HISTORY

I

It is an honour, if a rather dangerous honour, to follow a series of distinguished economic historians from David Landes to Richard Goldthwaite and give a lecture in honour of a scholar who discussed some topics on which I am quite incompetent to comment, among them the history of money and prices, not to mention technology and plague. Fortunately for me, Carlo Cipolla was many other things besides an economic historian. I did not know him well, although I met him a few times and was impressed, like so many other people, by his courtesy and by the elegance of his suits as well as his sharpness of mind.

Cipolla's work fascinated me long before I met him. First of all, its breadth: demography, literacy, technology, medicine. In the second place, the grace, wit and accessibility of his clear and vivid prose, almost disguising the learning and the analytical powers of the author. In the third place, I was intrigued by Cipolla's trajectory, his turn from the global to the local, the opposite of the development one might have expected as a scholar grows older.

In the 1950s, Cipolla practised a more or less conventional economic history, working on Italy and especially on Lombardy. In the 1960s, when he was in his forties, Cipolla turned to writing small books on large subjects: *The Economic History of World Popu-*

lation (1962), *Guns and Sails* (1965), *Clocks and Culture* (1967), and *Literacy and Development in the West* (1969). I remember wondering at the time which grand topic he would choose next.

And then came the surprise. In the 1970s, now in his fifties, Cipolla turned away from grand topics. He had a research grant to study the history of public health in Italy, but wrote up his research in a series of unconventional studies. First came *Cristofano e la peste* (1973, Italian edition 1976), on an incident in Prato in 1630. Next, *Chi ruppe i rastelli a Monte Lupo?* (1977), another study of plague, set in a smaller Tuscan town and presented like a detective story («un giallo del Seicento», as the blurb on the back of the book tells the reader). And then, ending the sequence, *I pidocchi e il Granduca* (1980), once again concerned with public health but set in Florence in 1620-1 at the time of an epidemic of typhus.[1]

How does one account for this intellectual trajectory? To an outsider like myself, Cipolla's turn seems to reflect a certain disillusionment with the traditional Grand Narrative of the progress of civilization. The grand themes he explored in the 1960s, especially the history of literacy and technology, implied a vision of progress that seems to have become increasingly clouded in the seventies and eighties. A famous late work of Cipolla's, *Allegro ma non troppo* (1988) placed its emphasis on human stupidity. But *Cristofano* already begins by begging the reader's pardon for «un argomento poco allegro» - «ma non è colpa mia se le vicende umane non sono sempre né necessariamente cosa allegra».[2]

What happened in Cipolla's case, I do not know, but disillusionment with Grand Narrative is an obvious enough explanation for the collective turn that took place in the 1970s, what might be called «the invention of micro-history».[3] For *Cristofano e la peste*, first published in 1973, appeared immediately before the well-known rise of micro-history, signalled by two much-discussed and

---

[1] C.M. Cipolla, *I pidocchi e il Granduca. Crisi economica e problemi sanitari nella Firenze del'600*, Bologna, 1979.
[2] C.M. Cipolla, *Cristofano e la peste*, Bologna, 1976, p. 5, a passage absent from the English edition.
[3] Cf. G. Levi, «Microhistory», in P. Burke (ed.), *New Perspectives on Historical Writing*, Cambridge, 1991.

much-translated books, *Montaillou* (1975) by Emmanuel Le Roy Ladurie, and *Il formaggio e i vermi* (1976) by Carlo Ginzburg.

II

In the Italian case at least we can speak of a micro-historical movement, more especially of a trinity, troika or trio in which Ginzburg was associated with Edoardo Grendi and Giovanni Levi and the journal *Quaderni Storici*.[4] In 1977, Grendi published a study of the community of Cervo in Liguria as well as a now famous article on «microanalisi».[5] Levi's work on the community of Santena in Piedmont was published around the same time.[6] The trio soon became a quartet, with the addition of Carlo Poni, before expanding further, allowing Einaudi to launch their series *Microstoria* in 1981, a series that included Raul Merzario, Franco Ramella, Osvaldo Raggio, and others, eighteen volumes in all.[7]

What I should like to do here is to attempt to view this turn (after the passing of a generation) in historical perspective and offer first a bird's eye view, then a macro-history and finally a micro-history of micro-history. This account can afford to omit philology, the term *microstoria or micro-histoire*, since the history of these words have been discussed by Carlo Ginzburg with his usual learning and acuity (it might be worth adding that for some reason, «Microstoria» - in Italian - has become the name of a German pop group).[8] What I mean to do in what follows is to describe and analyse the approach, both before and after what we might call the «micro-historical moment», in the middle of the 1970s.

---

[4] H. Espada Lima, *A micro-história italiana: escalas, indícios e singularidades*, Rio de Janeiro, 2006.
[5] E. Grendi, «Microanalisi e storia sociale», *Quaderni Storici*, 35, 1977, pp. 506-20.
[6] G. Levi, *L'eredità immateriale. Carriera di un esorcista nel Piemonte del Seicento*, Torino, 1985.
[7] R. Merzario, *Il paese stretto. Strategie matrimoniali nella diocesi di Como (secoli XVI-XVIII)*, Torino, 1982; F. Ramella, *Terra e telai. Sistemi di parentela e manifattura nel Biellese dell'Ottocento*, Torino, 1984; O. Raggio, *Faide e parentela: lo stato genovese visto da Fontanabuona*, Torino, 1990.
[8] C. Ginzburg, «Microstoria: due o tre cose che so di lei», *Quaderni Storici*, 86, 1994, pp. 511-39.

The subject will be viewed from an international perspective. Micro-history is an extremely Italian theme, linked to the local loyalties sometimes described as *campanilismo*. All the same, in this analysis the international dimension is essential. For example, French historians entered the field early, including some from the group associated with *Annales*, most famously Le Roy Ladurie but also Jean-Claude Schmitt and others.[9] North American historians began later but have probably produced more micro-histories than anyone else. In Germany, as in Italy, the approach has given rise to a vigorous debate between supporters such as Hans Medick and opponents such as Hans-Ulrich Wehler and Jürgen Kocka.[10]

Defining micro-history poses problems, as the choice of books for the series *microstoria* revealed. Even the trio of Grendi, Ginzburg and Levi differ in their views, as was noted in a recent study by a Brazilian historian (curiously enough, the only book-length studies of the group known to me have both been made in South America).[11] Later Italian micro-historians, such as Gianna Pomata, differ from the earlier ones.[12] In what follows, it seems best to avoid both a wide definition (according to which all local history is micro-history) and a narrow definition that would confine the title of micro-historian to scholars like Giovanni Levi, Simona Cerutti or Maurizio Gribaudi who are suspicious of grand categories such

---

[9] E. Le Roy Ladurie, *Montaillou village Occitan*, Paris, 1975; J.C. Schmitt, *Le saint lévrier: Guinefort, guérisseur d'enfants depuis le XIIIe siècle*, Paris, 1979. Cf. G. Bois, *La mutation de l'an mil: Lournand, village mâconnais de l'antiquité au féodalisme*, Paris, 1989; A. Corbin, *Le village des cannibales*, Paris, 1990; B. Garnot, *Un crime conjugal au 18e siècle, l'affaire Boiveau*, Paris, 1993, and *Le diable au couvent: les possédées d'Auxonne*, Paris, 1995.

[10] H.U. Wehler, *Neoromantik und Pseudorealismus in der neuen «Alltagsgeschichte»: Preussen ist wieder chic*, Frankfurt, 1983; J. Kocka, *Geschichte und Aufklärung*, Göttingen, 1989; H. Medick, «Missionaries in the Row Boat? Ethnological Ways of Knowing as a Challenge to Social History», *Comparative Studies in Society and History*, 29, 1987, pp. 76–98; H. Medick (ed.), *Mikro-Historie: Neue Pfade in die Sozialgeschichte*, Frankfurt, 1994. For more sympathetic criticisms, see J.S. Amelang, «Micro-history and its Discontents: the View from Spain», in C. Barros (ed.), *Historia a Debate*, vol. 2, Santiago de Compostela, 1995.

[11] Espada Lima, *A micro-história italiana;* cf. C. Aguirre Rojas, *Contribuición a la istoria de la microhistoria italiana*, Rosario, 2003.

[12] G. Pomata, «Telling the Truth about Microhistory», *Netvaerk for historieteori og historiografi*, Working Paper No. 3, Copenhagen, 2000.

The Invention of Micro-history

as «class» and «culture» and focus on social networks and individual or family strategies.[13]

The middle-of-the road definition chosen here is to call «micro-history» any study of the local or small-scale that is undertaken in order to illuminate larger problems, problems that range from the Counter-Reformation to the Enlightenment and from family structures to the origins of the modern state.[14] The point, in the words of Hans Medick, is to view local history as general history (*Lokalgeschichte als Allgemeine Geschichte*), as in the case of what Raggio calls «the state of Genoa seen from Fontanabuona».[15]

Today, micro-history is a flourishing species that may be found in a range of varieties, of which it may be useful to distinguish three. The first and the most common variety, at least in the early days of the movement, is the study of a community: usually a village, such as Graft in the Netherlands, Laichingen in Germany, or Montaldeo, Cervo, Santena, Altopascio or Fontanabuona in Italy.[16] A few community studies focus on institutions: estates, for instance, or convents (in Italy, for instance, in France and in the Spanish Netherlands).[17]

---

[13] See their contributions to J. Revel (ed.), *Jeux d'échelle: la microanalyse à l'expérience*, Paris, 1996.
[14] On the Counter-Reformation, C. Ginzburg, *Il formaggio e i vermi: il cosmo di un mugnaio del'500*, Torino, 1976; Levi, *L'eredità immateriale*; J.C. Brown, *Immodest acts: the life of a lesbian nun in Renaissance Italy*, New York, 1986; C.E. Carline, *The Burdens of Sister Margaret*, New York, 1994. On the Enlightenment, A. Jarrick, *Mot det moderna förnuftet: Johan Hjerpe och andra småborgare i Upplysningstidens Stockholm*, Stockholm, 1992 (English trans. *Back to modern reason: Johan Hjerpe and other petit bourgeois in Stockholm in the Age of Enlightenment*, Liverpool, 1999). On the family, N.Z. Davis, *The Return of Martin Guerre*, Cambridge Mass., 1983; G. Brucker, *Giovanni and Lusanna: love and marriage in Renaissance Florence*, London, 1986. On the state, Raggio, *Faide e parentela*; G. Levi, *Centro e periferia di uno Stato assoluto. Tre saggi su Piemonte e Liguria in età moderna*, Torino, 1985.
[15] H. Medick, *Weben und Überleben in Laichingen 1650–1900: Lokalgeschichte als allgemeine Geschichte*, Göttingen, 1996; Raggio, *Faide e parentela*, 1990. Cf. M. Gray, «Micro-history as universal history», *Central European History*, 34, 2001, pp. 419-31.
[16] A.T. van Deursen, *Een dorp in de polder: Graft in de zeventiende eeuw*, Amsterdam, 1994; Medick, *Weben und Überleben*.
[17] P.O. Christiansen, *A manorial world: lord, peasants and cultural distinctions on a Danish estate, 1750–1980*, Oslo-Oxford, 1996; on convents, Brown, *Immodest acts*; Harline, *The Burdens of Sister Margaret*; Garnot, *Le diable au couvent*.

A second variety of micro-history might be called «microbiography», that is, the biography of a relatively unimportant individual, such as Ginzburg's Menocchio or Natalie Davis's Martin Guerre (although *The Return of Martin Guerre* may also be viewed as the study of a village, Artigat, situated like Montaillou in South-West France). These examples have been followed in a whole gallery of portraits. Among them are the fifteenth-century Florentine chronicler Marco Parenti; the sixteenth-century Spanish messiah Bartolomé Sánchez; the nineteenth-century American messiah Robert Matthews; the shaman Conrad Stoecklin and the burgomaster's daughter Anna Büschler, both from sixteenth-century Germany; the orphan Evert Willemsz in the seventeenth-century Dutch Republic; the businessman Joseph Sec in eighteenth-century Aix; and the «petit bourgeois» Johan Hjerpe in eighteenth-century Sweden.[18] I have the impression that as the number of new community studies has declined, the number of biographies of ordinary individuals has risen.

A third variety of micro-history is a narrative of a small-scale event which may or may not have wider repercussions. The American sociologist Robin Wagner-Pacifici studied the kidnapping of Aldo Moro, for instance, while the anthropologist-historian David Kertzer, wrote about the kidnapping of Edgardo Mortara, a Jewish boy in Rome in 1858.[19] Some micro-narratives tell the story of collective violence, of riots or lynchings, from the American South to rural France. Others tell the story of factions and feuds – the Delle Torres versus the Savorgans in Friuli, the Leverones and the Fopi-

---

[18] Davis, *The Return of Martin Guerre;* on Parenti, M.S. Phillips, *The memoir of Marco Parenti: a life in Medici Florence,* Princeton, 1987; on Stoecklin, W. Behringer, *Chonrad Stoeckhlin und die Nachtschar: eine Gescgichte aus der fruhen Neuzeit,* Munchen, 1994; on Büschler, S. Ozment, *The burgermeister's daughter: scandal in a sixteenth-century German town,* New York, 1997; on Sánchez, S.T. Nalle, *Mad for God: Bartolomé Sánchez, the secret Messiah of Cardenete,* London, 2001; on Matthews, P.E. Johnson, S. Wilentz, *The Kingdom of Mathis,* New York, 1994; on Sec, M. Vovelle, *L'irresistibile Ascension de Joseph Sec, Bourgeois d'Aix,* Aix-en-Provence, 1975; on Evert Willemsz, W. Frijhoff, *Wegen van Evert Willemsz. Een Hollands weeskind op zoek naar zichzelf,* Nijmegen, 1995; on Hjerpe, Jarrick, *Mot det moderna förnuftet.*

[19] R.E. Wagner-Pacifici, *The Moro morality play: terrorism as social drama,* Chicago, 1986; D.I. Kertzer, *The Kidnapping of Eduardo Mortara,* London, 1997.

anos in Liguria, the Riquelmes and the Sotos in Murcia, and so on.[20] An intriguingly common theme in the biographies of ordinary individuals is death.[21] There are several studies of suicides.[22] The story of formal executions has been told as well as that of informal assassinations or lynchings.[23] Accounts of murders are particularly common – the mysterious death of the cigar-seller Mary Rogers, the murder of the prostitute Helen Jewett, Maria Barbella's murder of her lover, the clergyman James Hackman's murder of the mistress of the Earl of Sandwich.[24] They include the murders of wives by husbands and of husbands by wives.[25]

The aims of the practitioners of the genre are not the same. Some are more concerned with typicality, so that Johnson and Wilentz could write about the story of their prophet that «almost every twist in the plot seemed indicative of some larger cultural trend». Others focus on individuality or indeed exceptionality (not to mention Grendi's famous *eccezionale normale*).[26] Some

---

[20] On riots, G. Vandal, *The New Orleans riot of 1866: anatomy of a tragedy*, Lafayette La., 1983; on lynchings, B. Wyatt Brown, *Southern honor: ethics and behavior in the old South*, New York, 1982, Corbin, *Le village des cannibals*; on feuds, Raggio, *Faide e parentela*; J. Contreras, *Sotos contra Riquelmes: regidores, inquisidores y criptojudios*, Madrid, 1992, E. Muir, *Mad blood stirring: vendetta & factions in Friuli during the Renaissance*, Baltimore, 1993.

[21] R. Guha, «Chandra's Death», *Subaltern Studies*, 5, 1986, pp. 135-165.

[22] D. Merwick, *Death of a notary: conquest and Change in colonial New York*, Ithaca, 1999; A. Jarrick, *Hamlets fråga: en Svenk självmordshistoria*, Stockholm, 2000.

[23] R. Telarolli, *Poder Local na República Velha*, São Paulo, 1977; Wyatt Brown, *Southern honor*; R. Bartlett, *The Hanged Man: a story of miracle, memory and colonialism in the Middle Ages*, Princeton, 2004.

[24] A.G. Srebnick, *The mysterious death of Mary Rogers: sex and culture in nineteenth-century New York*, New York, 1995; I. Pucci, *The Trials of Maria Barbella*, New York, 1996 (Italian trans. *La Signora di Sing Sing*, Florence); P.C. Cohen, *The murder of Helen Jewett: the life and death of a prostitute in nineteenth-century New York*, New York, 1998; L. Duggan, *Sapphic slashers: sex, violence, and American modernity*, Durham, N.C., 2000; P.K. Monod, *The murder of Mr. Grebell: madness and civility in an English town*, New Haven, 2003; J. Brewer, *Sentimental murder: love and madness in the eighteenth century*, London, 2004; J.R. Farr, *A Tale of Two Murders: passion and power in seventeenth-century France*, Durham, N.C., 2005.

[25] Garnot, *Un crime conjugal*; T.A. Mantecón Novellan, *La muerte de Antonia Isabel Sánchez. Tiranía y escándalo en una sociedad rural del norte español en el Antiguo Régimen*, Alcalá de Henares, 1997.

[26] Johnson Wilentz, *The Kingdom of Mathias*, p. 11; Grendi, «Microanalisi e storia sociale».

spring from the desire to understand a whole society better, others are undertaken more or less for their own sake. Some authors wish to use or to test social or cultural theories, while others do not. Some offer snapshots of a community or an individual at a moment in time, others are concerned with *la longue durée*. Some individuals studied are less unimportant than others. The Einaudi series *Microstoria* included books on Piero della Francesca and Galileo, crossing the frontier between micro-biography and normal biography.

The reasons for the success of this genre also vary. Community studies of the past appeal to nostalgia and to a concern for the survival of communities in the present, a concern illustrated by the popularity not only of *Montaillou* (a best-seller in France when it appeared in 1975) but also of Edgar Reitz's *Heimat*, a series of films about a village in the Rhineland that began to be shown in 1984 (the third and last part was shown between 2002 and 2004).

Historical narratives of small-scale events are often what journalists call «human interest stories», narrated more or less for their own sake, and combining the attraction of the past with that of a detective story or a drama (indeed, Kertzer's story of Edgardo Mortara was adapted as a play in the United States, Alfred Uhry's «Edgardo Mine»).[27] Not a few micro-histories have a strong scent of sexuality and scandal, and some have sensational titles such as «Sapphic Slashers».[28] All the same, it would be a mistake to dismiss the whole genre, or even the murder stories, as no more than sensationalism.

After all, the genre continues to attract leading historians. In the English-speaking world, for instance, two distinguished recent recruits are the medievalist Robert Bartlett and the eighteenth-century historian John Brewer, both of whom published micro-histories in the year 2004.[29] The *Journal of Microhistory* began publication in 2006 (it is produced, appropriately enough, in Iceland, edited by Sigurdur Gylfi Magnússon and Dávid Ólafsson at The Center for

---

[27] www.davidkertzer.com.
[28] Cohen, *The murder of Helen Jewett;* Ozment, *The burgermeister's daughter;* Duggan, *Sapphic slashers.*
[29] Bartlett, *The Hanged Man;* Brewer, *Sentimental murder.*

The Invention of Micro-history

Micro-historical Research). This approach to history has sustained interest and debate over more than thirty years.

One reason for the enduring popularity of the genre in academic circles is what we might call the «fit» between this approach to history and the increasing exploitation of trial records by historians over the last generation. Indeed, a number of micro-histories focus on the trials themselves.[30] Another reason is the association between the genre and other currently flourishing approaches such as the history of the everyday, women's history, «history from below» and historical anthropology.

The so-called «revival of narrative» also provides support for micro-history, especially for its third variety. Indeed, one of the main concerns of North American micro-historians in particular, is with narrative, especially «the sensational narrative». These scholars often focus on layers of narrative; the stories that victims or seducers produced about themselves, the news reports, the adaptation of the original stories as novels, and so on.[31]

Most important of all, micro-history began as and remains a critique of macro-history. The genre continues to express a distinctively post-modern loss of credibility in Grand Narrative, whether liberal or Marxist. It also implies a criticism of a more general macro-analysis of social structures, what the Germans call *Gesellschaftsgeschichte*, in the name of the history of everyday experience and history with a human face. Hence the war in Germany between Medick's group and that of Wehler and Kocka.

Looking back from the twenty-first century, the invention of micro-history, more exactly the success of the micro-historical movement in the 1970s looks like the response to a crisis and even a reaction to the events of 1968 both in Paris and in Prague, the critique of structures and the emphasis on the individual (socialism with a «human face»).

---

[30] E. Berenson, *The Trial of Mme Caillaux*, Berkeley, 1992; L. Duggan, «The Trials of Alice Mitchell», *Signs*, 18, 1993, pp. 791-814; P.C. Cohen, «Ministerial Misdeeds: The Onderdonk Trial and Sexual Harassment in the 1840s'», *Journal of Women's History*, 7, 1995, pp. 34-57; Pucci, *The Trials of Maria Barbella*.

[31] This approach is particularly visible in Srebnick, *The mysterious death of Mary Rogers*; Cohen, *The murder of Helen Jewett*; Brewer, *Sentimental murder*.

III

Of course, the story is rather more complicated than that. Like other so-called «inventions», micro-history was not a creation *ex nihilo*. Historians did not suddenly wake up in the 1970s and see the interest and the importance of the small scale. Two important examples of the history of small communities date from 1968: in Italy, there was Giorgio Doria's *Uomini e terre di un borgo collinare*, on Montaldeo (a commune controlled by the Doria family), and in Mexico a study by Luis González, *Pueblo en vila. Microhistoria de San José de Gracia*.

González makes a reference to the work of an English scholar, H.P.R. Finberg, who was one of what might be called the «Leicester school» of local historians (at that time the University of Leicester was the only English university with a Department of Local History). The most distinguished member of the Leicester group was W.G. Hoskins, whose study *The Midland Peasant* (1957) focused on a single village, Wigston Magna, over a period of about a thousand years, one of the few studies of a little community over *la longue durée*.[32]

It was Hoskins, the editor of the Leicestershire volumes of the Victoria County History, who commissioned the late J.H. Plumb, an English historian who is not normally suspected of micro-historical tendencies, but himself a Leicester man, to write a chapter entitled «Political History 1530-1885». This remarkable essay may be seen as a contribution to the history of feuds that I evoked briefly above and in addition, it raises with particular clarity recurrent and serious problems of historical explanation.

In his study of 1992, the Spanish historian Jaime Contreras explained the pursuit of *limpieza de sangre* in the small town of Lorca in the middle of the sixteenth century in terms of the conflict between two rival families, the Sotos and the Riquelmes.

Nearly forty years earlier, in 1954, and in a more ambitious fashion,

---

[32] Among the studies of the long term are W.G. Hoskins, *The Midland peasant; the economic and social history of a Leicestershire village*, London, 1957, G. Doria, *Uomini e terre di un borgo collinare. Dal XVI al XVIII secolo*, Milano, 1968, O. Hochstrasser, *Ein Haus und seine Menschen, 1549-1989: ein Versuch zum Verhältnis von Mikroforschung und Sozialgeschichte*, Tübigen, 1993, Christiansen, *A manorial world*.

Plumb had reduced the political history of Leicestershire over 350 years to the conflict between two noble families, the Greys and the Hastings, and their struggle for supremacy in the county. One family supported the Reformation, so the other opposed it. One supported Charles I, the other the Parliament. One family was Whig, the other Tory, and when the political labels changed, one was Liberal and the other Conservative. Plumb's *tour de force* demonstrates among other things the risk of cynicism that micro-historians run, especially the tendency to explain public actions by private motives.[33]

Still in the 1950s, but far from the world of Hoskins and Plumb, the Brazilian historian Gilberto Freyre published an article on what he called «microscopic history», pleading for the study of the role of minor actors, from engineers to governesses, in the drama of encounters between cultures, such as France and Brazil in the nineteenth century.[34]

It is possible to go back still further in search for precedents for micro-history. If, for instance, we compare Aby Warburg's contribution to the study of the Italian Renaissance with that of Jacob Burckhardt, the contrast between Burckhardt's macro-history and Warburg's micro-historical essays leaps to the eye.[35] Warburg's affirmation that *Der Liebe Gott steckt in Detail* has become famous. In this context, it is interesting to note that Carlo Ginzburg spent some time at the Warburg Institute in the 1960s and that he has written an essay about Warburg and his followers.[36]

It might be possible to go back even further. At one point in his *Decline and Fall of the Roman Empire*, Edward Gibbon remarked that «The simple circumstantial narrative (did such a narrative exist) of the ruin of a single town, of the misfortunes of a single family, might exhibit an interesting and instructive picture of human

---

[33] J.H. Plumb, «Political History 1530–1885», *Victoria Country History, Leicestershire*, vol. 2, London, 1954, pp. 102–34.

[34] G. Freyre, «Microscopic History: a meeting of influences», *Diogenes*, 18, 1957, pp. 1–21.

[35] P. Burke, «Aby Warburg as a Historical Anthropologist», in H. Bredekamp et al. (eds.), *Aby Warburg: Akten des internationalen Symposiums Hamburg 1990*, Weinheim, 1991, pp. 17–21.

[36] C. Ginzburg, «Da A. Warburg a E.H. Gombrich: note su un problema di metodo», *Studi Medievali*, 7, 1966, pp. 1015–65.

manners».³⁷ That was just a thought – but Justus Möser's famous history of Osnabrück, published in the 1760s, was more than a local history of the kind that had become traditional. The author claimed to be making a contribution to a «new turn» in the «history of Germany», and offered an apologia for local knowledge and «local reason».³⁸

IV

By the 1970s, other disciplines had already discovered the importance of the social microscope, among them sociology and especially social anthropology. Le Roy Ladurie himself cited as models for *Montaillou* two studies of contemporary communities, Laurence Wylie's *Village in the Vaucluse* (1957), on Provence, and Ronald Blythe's *Akenfield* (1969), describing a village in Suffolk.

Even the focus on an ordinary individual returns us to a sociological classic, *The Polish Peasant in Europe and America* (1918), since the authors, William Thomas and Floran Znaniecki, commissioned a single peasant to write his autobiography, making the point that «A social institution can be fully understood only if we […] analyze the way in which it appears in the personal experience of various members of the group and follow the influence which it has upon their lives».³⁹

Anthropology too offered models for micro-historians. Although it is not technically a micro-analysis, since it does not deal with a single event, Clifford Geertz's famous essay on the cock-fight in Bali has inspired a number of micro-histories, among them Rhys Isaac on colonial Virginia and Robert Darnton's «great cat massacre».⁴⁰

---

³⁷ E. Gibbon (1776–88), *Decline and Fall of the Roman Empire*, (ed. David Womersley, 3 vols.), Harmondsworth, vol. 3, 1995, p. 116.
³⁸ J.B. Knudsen, *Justus Möser and the German Enlightenment*, Cambridge, 1986, p. 103; F. Meinecke (1936), *Die Entstehung des Historismus* (English trans. *Historism*, London, 1972, pp. 266-7).
³⁹ W.I. Thomas, F. Znaniecki (1918), *The Polish Peasant in Europe and America*, rpr. 2 vols., New York-London, 1958, p. 1833.
⁴⁰ C. Geertz, «Deep Play», *The Interpretation of Cultures*, New York, 1973, pp. 412-53; R. Isaac, *The transformation of Virginia 1740-1790*, Chapel Hill, 1982; R. Darnton, *The Great Cat Massacre and other episodes in French cultural history*, New York, 1984.

The Invention of Micro-history

As a method, micro-history has much in common with the «extended case study» of a social situation associated with the South African anthropologist Max Gluckman and his followers, the so-called «Manchester school» of anthropology, notably Victor Turner, the originator of the concept «social drama», and Bruce Kapferer, who combined the microscopic approach with network analysis.[41] The concern with network analysis is obvious enough in micro-historians such as Levi, Merzario, and Gribaudi, while Turner's concept of «social drama» in particular has been influential in other disciplines. The sociologist Wagner-Pacifici calls her study of the kidnapping of Aldo Moro «terrorism as social drama», and a number of the micro-historical studies already mentioned might be described in similar terms.[42]

Less influential, despite its pioneering quality, is the work of a Swedish ethnologist, Börje Hanssen, whose study ofeveryday life in the village of Österlen in Skåne, in the South of Sweden, in the eighteenth century was published in 1952, three years before Hoskins on Wigston Magna. Never translated, this study is still little known outside Scandinavia.[43] Anthropologists such as Ulf Hannerz and Marshall Sahlins have also played a leading part in the debates on the relative importance of micro-analysis and macro-analysis and on the ways in which the two approaches might be usefully combined.[44]

Yet another discipline in which we can see a turn towards micro-analysis in the middle of the twentieth century is literary history,

---

[41] M. Gluckman (1940), *Analysis of a Social Situation in Modern Zululand*, rpr. Manchester, 1958; V.W. Turner, *Schism and continuity in an African society: a study of Ndembu village life*, Manchester, 1957; B. Kapferer, «Norms and the Manipulation of Social relationships in a work Context», in C. Mitchell (ed.), *Social networks in urban situations: analyses of personal relationships in Central African towns*, Manchester, 1969.
[42] Turner is cited, for instance, in P. Burke, «The Virgin of the Carmine and the Revolt of Masaniello», *Past and Present*, 99, 1983, pp. 3–21, Raggio, *Faide e parentela*.
[43] It inspired a study of the Danish estate of Giesegaard (Christiansen, *A manorial world*).
[44] U. Hannerz, «Theory in Anthropology: Small is Beautiful», *Comparative Studies in Society and History*, 28, 1986, pp. 362–7; M. Sahlins, «Structural Work: how microhistories become macrohistories and vice versa», *Anthropological Theory*, 5, 2005, pp. 5–30. Contributions by historians include J. Schlumbohm (ed.), *Mikrogeschichte, Makrogeschichte: Komplementar oder inkommensurabel?*, Göttingen, 1998, M. Peltonen, «The Micro-Macro Link in Historical research», *History and Theory*, 40, 2001, pp. 347–59.

notably Erich Auerbach's famous *Mimesis*, a study in which a textual microcosm, a paragraph or two from Cervantes, say, or Virginia Woolf, is analysed as a faithful reflection of the microcosm of the whole work.

Turning to literature itself, it might reasonably be said that the first micro-historians were novelists, notably Walter Scott and Alessandro Manzoni. In *Waverley* (1814), for instance, as Georg Lukács pointed out in his *Historical Novel* (1937), the «mediocre hero» helps the reader to understand the society being portrayed and its conflicts. A similar point may be made about *I promessi sposi* (1827). At a time when the classical idea of the «dignity of history» was still very much alive, Manzoni swam against the stream and chose humble protagonists for his novel. His friend Niccolò Tommaseo reproached him for paying too much attention to the «destino di due villanucci», asserting that peasants are the objects not the subjects of history, *pazienti* not *agenti*.[45] Manzoni, like micro-historians such as Ginzburg and Levi, appears to have believed the contrary.

Within the vast field of later historical novels, some varieties are particularly close to micro-history. One of these genres, practiced by Scott, Balzac and Fontane (among others) is concerned with «the local pocket of resistance» to invasions or revolutions. Another is the story of a family over the generations, described by one of its leading practitioners, John Galsworthy as «so clear a representation of society in miniature».[46] Recent historical novelists such as Fulvio Tomizza focus on some of the same problems as micro-historians, among them attempts to distinguish true from false

---

[44] U. Hannerz, «Theory in Anthropology: Small is Beautiful», *Comparative Studies in Society and History*, 28, 1986, pp. 362-7; M. Sahlins, «Structural Work: how microhistories become macrohistories and vice versa», *Anthropological Theory*, 5, 2005, pp. 5-30. Contributions by historians include J. Schlumbohm (ed.), *Mikrogeschichte, Makrogeschichte: Komplementar oder inkommensurabel?*, Göttingen, 1998, M. Peltonen, «The Micro-Macro Link in Historical research», *History and Theory*, 40, 2001, pp. 347-59.
[45] Quoted in U. Colombo, *Manzoni e gli Umili. Storia interna e fortuna critica*, Rome, 1972, pp. 155-6.
[46] R. Humphrey, *The Historical Novel as Philosophy of History: three German contributions: Alexis, Fontane, Döblin*, London, 1986, p. 94; J. Galsworthy, *The Forsyte Saga I: The Man of Property*, London, 1906, 1.

saints (Anne Schutte's introduction to the translation of Tomizza's *Heavenly Supper* links the contemporary historical novel to micro-history).[47]

V

It is time to conclude by returning to the work of Carlo Cipolla. Curiously enough, Cipolla did not refer to Manzoni in *Cristofano and the Plague*, although he described his story – in the preface to the English edition, which was published three years before the Italian one – as one of reactions to crisis, revealing «initiative, courage, civic sense, humanity» on the part of some, but «pettiness and avarice» on the part of others.[48] This description is reminiscent, perhaps deliberately so, of Manzoni's reference – in a letter that he wrote to Claude Fauriel on 29 May 1822, describing the progress of his novel – to «une peste qui a donné de l'exercice à la scélératesse la plus consommée [...] aux préjugés les plus absurdes, et aux vertus les plus touchantes».[49] Indeed, it might be asked whether one aim of Cipolla's micro-historical trilogy was not precisely to rewrite Manzoni, presenting the history of the plague from a viewpoint less sympathetic to the clergy.

This theme for a «Lettura Cipolla» was chosen in order to insert Carlo Cipolla into the story of the rise of micro-history in the 1970s. Having emphasized variety, it may be useful to end by attempting to locate his work on the map of micro-history. Unlike some contributors to the genre, Cipolla was not a post-modernist. Unlike the *Quaderni Storici* group, he seems to have taken little interest in anthropology or network analysis. All the same, he seems to have shared the basic aims of Ginzburg, Levi and Grendi.

In the first place, Cipolla was concerned to use the microscope in order to reach larger conclusions. *Cristofano* is presented as a case-

---

[47] F. Tomizza, *La finzione di Maria*, Milan, 1981 (English trans. *Heavenly Supper: the story of Maria Janis*, Chicago, 1991); Brown, *Immodest acts*.
[48] C.M. Cipolla, *Cristofano and the Plague. A Study in the History of Public Health in the age of Galileo*, London, 1973, preface: this section does not appear in the Italian edition.
[49] C. Arieti (ed.), *Tutte le lettere/Alessandro Manzoni*, Milano, 1986.

study, «Un caso di storia del sistema sanitario». *Chi ruppe i rastelli* begins by saying that the story it tells will illuminate the dialectics of «Chiesa e Stato, Fede e Ragione».[50]

In the second place, Cipolla's three micro-historical studies tell stories, adopting a different literary strategy from his other books, not only the more technical works on money and prices but also the general studies of guns and clocks.

In the third place, despite his interest in major economic trends over the long term, Cipolla clearly believed, like Ginzburg and Levi, that individuals make a difference, including ordinary people such as the health officials Cristofano Ceffini and Michelangiolo Coveri, or indeed friars such as Giovanni Dragoni. Whether they acted for better or worse, these individuals are presented, to invert the words of Tommaseo, as *agenti* not *pazienti*. As Cipolla wrote of his hero Cristofano, «Occorrevano mente lucida, calore umano e giudizio equilibrato. E queste rare qualità bisognava saperle mettere in atto in un agghiacciante clima di morte, di miseria e di terrore».[51]

For these reasons, Carlo Cipolla has his place in the history of micro-history.

---

[50] Cipolla, *Cristofano e la peste*, title-page; C.M. Cipolla, *Chi ruppe i rastelli a Monte Lupo?*, Bologna, 1977, p. 6.
[51] Cipolla, *Cristofano e la peste*, p. 52.

Chapter 9

9: A Short History of Distance

"Communication is always a matter of overcoming distance – physical distance first and then social distance" (Robert Park).[1]

The central theme of this chapter, like the conference that generated it, is historical distance, together with its complementary opposite, nearness or proximity. An increasing number of historians think that, to quote the first sentence in L. P. Hartley's *The Go-Between* – now cited by many people who have not read the novel – 'The past is a foreign country: they do things differently there'.[2]

Most historians also believe it to be their task to bring that past closer to the present, at least in imagination. In other words, they concern themselves not only with the relatively passive perception of historical distance or proximity but also with active techniques of familiarization or, shall we say, 'approximation' (on the model

---

[1] Park quoted in Rolf Lindner, *The Reportage of Urban Culture: Robert Park and the Chicago School* (Cambridge, 1990), 107.
[2] Leslie P. Hartley, *The Go-Between* (London: Hamish Hamilton, 1953); cf. David Lowenthal, *The Past is a Foreign Country* (Cambridge: Cambridge University Press, 1985).

of *rapprochement*), of which an extreme case is that of re-enactment, discussed in section five below.

A few historians have also been concerned with techniques of distanciation, looking through the wrong end of the binoculars and so making what is close or familiar appear to be distant. In deciding between distanciation and approximation on different occasions, students of the past may have something to learn from the example of translators, for whom the relative advantages and disadvantages of the two approaches, domestication and "foreignizing" have long been a matter of debate. Domestication makes the text translated more immediately intelligible to its new readers, while foreignizing makes it clear that the text comes from another, more or less distant culture.[3]

It is probably still too soon to write a global history of historical distance. We know all too little, for instance, at least in the West, about changes in the Chinese sense of the past.[4] Even the ancient Greek and Roman historians, who have been studied so intensively, have rarely been approached from this point of view. In the case of Tacitus, for instance, one might speak of "moral distanciation", in which the author separates himself and his readers from the crimes and follies that he narrates. However, the great example of distanciation in classical antiquity is surely the satirist Lucian. In his guide to historical writing, Lucian recommended the point of view of the outsider or foreigner (*xenos*), while in his satires he adopted what we might call an "Olympian" viewpoint, high above the world, to look down on human follies. The strategy is a recurrent one. Physical distance – what the geographer Jay Appleton calls "prospect" – both expresses and encourages moral distance.[5]

The short history that follows will be confined to Europe in the

---

[3] Lawrence Venuti, *The Translator's Invisibility* (London: Routledge, 1995).

[4] Craig Clunas, *Superfluous Things: material culture and social status in early modern China* (Cambridge: Polity Press, 1991); Benjamin A. Elman, *From Philosophy to Philology: Intellectual and Social Aspects of Change in Late Imperial China* (1984; revised edn, Los Angeles: UCLA, 2001); On-cho Ng, "A Tension in Ch'ing Thought: 'Historicism' in Seventeenth-and Eighteenth-Century Chinese Thought", *Journal of the History of Ideas* 54: 561–83.

[5] Jay Appleton, *The Experience of Landscape* (1975: 2nd edn, New York: Wiley, 1996), 63ff.

last six centuries or so, from the Renaissance to the present. Focusing on historical distance and attempting to place it among other kinds of cultural or social distance, it will distinguish four major "moments" – rather long moments – when the sense of distance became particularly acute, around the years 1400, 1800, 1920 and 1970.

I

In the Middle Ages, according to the French scholar Gaston Paris, writing in the 1880s, people thought that the world had always been the way they saw it.[6] It is this sense of continuity that underlies what is sometimes called "exemplary history"; that is, accounts of the past presented as a storehouse of good examples for readers to imitate and bad ones for them to avoid. The conclusions reached by Paris were reinforced by some later scholars. For example, an essay on the Anglo-Saxon sense of the past emphasized the lack of any sense of anachronism at that time, while a study of the ninth-century monk-historian Notker suggested that "to a large extent", his chronicle "lacks any sense of chronological development or historical time".[7]

It is not difficult to illustrate these conclusions from medieval art and literature. Images of Roman soldiers arresting Christ or sleeping at the sepulchre during the Resurrection regularly showed them wearing the armour of the artist's own time. For example, an illustration in a manuscript of about 1025 from Gembloux or Liège shows the soldiers in eleventh-century coats of mail, reminiscent of the warriors on the Bayeux tapestry.[8] In the twelfth century, the French poet Chrétien de Troyes described the Greeks and Romans in his romances as fighting in tournaments like medieval knights. Whether we regard the phenomenon as a naïf assumption of con-

---

[6] Gaston Paris, *La littérature français au Moyen Age* (Paris: Hachette, 1888), 30.
[7] Michael Hunter, "The Sense of the Past in Anglo-Saxon England", in *Anglo-Saxon England* 3 (1973): 29–50; Matthew Innes, "Memory, Orality and Literacy in an Early Medieval Society", *Past & Present* 158 (1998): 3–36.
[8] Hanns Swarzenki, *Monuments of Romanesque Art* (1954: second edn., London: Faber, 1974), plate 79.

tinuity or as the "suppression" of distance by "an act of intellectual will", these examples illustrate a sense of proximity to the past.[9]

All the same, it is misleading to make a simple, dramatic contrast between a Middle Ages in which a sense of historical distance was absent, and later periods in which it was and is present. It is more illuminating to make distinctions between different groups of people and different centuries, to introduce nuances, to speak of a more or less acute consciousness rather than of presence versus absence.[10] It has been suggested, for instance, that some eighth-century scholars expressed a sense of "radical discontinuity" between their own world and that of ancient Rome.[11] It is possible that people had a sharper sense of distance from the past at both the beginning and the end of what we call the Middle Ages than they did in between.[12] If this was the case, major events such as the barbarian invasions or the move of the popes to Avignon surely lie behind these perceptions.

In the fourteenth and fifteenth centuries, in particular, attitudes to the past can be seen to change, at least the attitudes of some scholars and artists. From Petrarch onwards, the scholars whom we now call "humanists" began to perceive what they described as the "Middle" or even the "Dark Ages" as distant, barbarous or "Gothic", although they liked to imagine classical antiquity as close to them.[13]

Another group of scholars with a sense of discontinuity or even estrangement from the past were the reformers of the Church who

---

[9] Jean Dunbabin, "Discovering a Past for the French Aristocracy", in *The Perception of the Past in Twelfth-Century Europe*, ed. Paul Magdalino (London: Hambledon Press, 1993), 1–14, at 13; Gabrielle Spiegel, *Romancing the Past: the Rise of Vernacular Prose Historiography in Thirteenth-Century France* (Berkeley: University of California Press, 1993), 104.

[10] For the simple view, Peter Burke, *The Renaissance Sense of the Past* (London: Edward Arnold, 1969); for the nuances, *id.*, "The Sense of Anachronism from Petrarch to Poussin", in *Time in the Medieval World*, ed. Chris Humphrey and W. M. Ormrod (Woodbridge: York Medieval Press, 2001), 157–73.

[11] Matthew Innes, "The Carolingians and the Germanic Past", in *The Uses of the Past in the Early Middle Ages*, ed. Yitzhak Hen and Matthew Innes (Cambridge: Cambridge University Press, 2000): 227–49, at 235.

[12] My thanks to Matthew Innes for this suggestion.

[13] Lucie Varga, *Das Schlagwort vom Finsteren Mittelalter* (Baden: Rohrer, 1932).

A Short History of Distance

contrasted the ecclesiastical corruption of their own day with a golden age in the past, the "primitive church" (*ecclesia primitiva*), as they called it. Churchmen with attitudes of this kind can already be found in the twelfth century, but the movement for reform became stronger in the fourteenth and fifteenth centuries, in the age of John Wyclif and Jan Hus.[14]

Wyclif and Hus were condemned as heretics but the orthodox Jean Gerson expressed a similar sense of contrast between the primitive and the later Church, as well as a general sense of the *varietas temporum*, in other words an awareness that what is appropriate in one epoch may not be necessarily so in another.[15] At a time when the popes were living in Avignon, discontinuity was of course unusually visible.

This general awareness of different pasts as more or less remote is surely linked to the more precise sense of anachronism that was shown by scholars such as Valla and Erasmus and artists such as Mantegna. Valla and Erasmus were extremely aware of changes in Latin over the centuries, while Mantegna studied ancient sculpture in order to represent Roman soldiers in the armour of their day.[16]

It was in this context that Lucian's technique of distanciation was imitated and adapted to contemporary situations by humanists such as Erasmus, Ulrich von Hutten and Alfonso de Valdés. Luther and Calvin, followed by Protestant historians such as the "Centuriators" of Magdeburg, went still further than the humanists in condemning the Middle Ages as a time of corruption and superstition.[17] On the other hand, the smashing of images, the burning of manuscripts and the demolition of monasteries during the Reformation provoked a nostalgia for the Middle Ages in some scholars, who reacted by salvaging as many fragments

---

[14] Giovanni Miccoli, "Ecclesiae primitivae forma", *Studi medievali* 1 (1960): 470–98; Anthony Kemp, *The Estrangement of the Past* (New York: Oxford University Press, 1991): 67–75.
[15] L. B. Pascoe (1974) "Gerson and the Donation of Constantine", *Viator* 5: 469–85.
[16] Burke, "Sense of Anachronism".
[17] John M. Headley, *Luther's View of Church History* (New Haven: Yale University Press, 1963); A. Geoffrey Dickens and John Tonkin, *The Reformation in Historical Thought* (Cambridge, MA: Harvard University Press, 1985).

of the past as they could. Not for the last time, the destruction of many traces of the past encouraged a more acute sense of history.[18]

The consciousness of the past as different from the present itself developed over time. The very attempt to assimilate antiquity – to make the distant close – led on occasion to a sense, at least on occasion, that the task was impossible. The humanist lawyer François Hotman, for instance, argued in his *Anti-Tribonian* (1567) for the irrelevance of Roman law to the France of his time.[19] Despite this development of the sense of development, another major moment of change in consciousness did not occur for centuries.

II

A second moment of awareness of distance from the past may be discerned in the late eighteenth century. As in the case of the Renaissance, the self-conscious movement of 'enlightenment' implied a contrast with an earlier age of darkness, and Voltaire in particular made effective use of techniques of distanciation, notably in *Candide* and in *Micromegas* (1752), in which he imagines the earth as observed from the star Sirius. In his histories of Britain, David Hume was much concerned with what has been called "the control of historical distance", including proximity as well as detachment.[20]

A similar point might be made about Gibbon, who often kept the past, as C. V. Wedgwood remarked, 'at a safe distance both from himself and from the reader', so aloof that he 'gives the impres-

[18] R. W. Southern, "The Sense of the Past", *Transactions of the Royal Historical Society* 23 (1973); Margaret Aston, 'English Ruins and English History', *Journal of the Warburg and Courtauld Institutes* 36 (1973), 231–55.
[19] J.G.A. Pocock, *The Ancient Constitution and the Feudal Law: a Study of English Historical Thought in the Seventeenth Century* (1957: second edn., Cambridge: Cambridge University Press, 1987), 11–15; cf. D. Kelley, *Foundations of Modern Historical Scholarship* (New York: Columbia University Press, 1970).
[20] Mark Phillips, *Society and Sentiment: Genres of Historical Writing in Britain, 1740–1820* (Princeton: Princeton University Press, 2000), 60–78, at 61; id., "Distance and Historical Representation", *History Workshop Journal* 57, 123–41.

A Short History of Distance

sion sometimes almost of inhumanity'.[21] Self-consciously remote from what he regarded as the opposite errors of 'enthusiasm' and 'superstition', Gibbon wrote of 'swarms' of fanatical monks, thus distancing himself from them by reducing them to insects. On the other hand, he wrote about the emperor Diocletian, for instance, as if he were an eighteenth-century ruler, approximating himself and his readers to the third century.

If eighteenth-century historians such as Hume and Gibbon aimed at a balance between detachment and proximity, it was the latter that triumphed in the next generation or two. Literary scholars have often spoken of the Romantic sense of the past, especially but not exclusively the medieval past, present in the novels of Walter Scott, Alessandro Manzoni and others and also in the many historical paintings of the time. All the same, it is worth noting that in their famous descriptions of popular riots in eighteenth-century Edinburgh and seventeenth-century Milan respectively, Scott (in *The Heart of Midlothian*, 1818) and Manzoni (in *The Betrothed*, 1827), moved back and forth between distance and proximity. They dehumanized the crowd by comparing it to a storm but at the same time they allowed their readers to hear the voices of individual rioters.

Intellectual historians, especially the German Friedrich Meinecke, have spoken of the rise of "historicism" or *Historismus* at this time, defining it in terms of the concern with both individuality and development.[22] Meinecke's Dutch contemporary Johan Huizinga added the point that the new attitude to the past included "a longing for distance and for foreign things".[23] Again, in the history of translation, the years around 1800 were the moment of

---

[21] C. V. Wedgwood, *The Sense of the Past* (Cambridge: Cambridge University Press, 1957), 16.

[22] Friedrich Meinecke, *Die Entstehung der Historismus* (2 vols., Munich: Oldenbourg, 1936), 5. Cf. Peter H. Reill, *The German Enlightenment and the Rise of Historicism* (Berkeley: University of California Press, 1975); Georg G. Iggers, "Historicism", *Journal of the History of Ideas* 56 (1995), 129-52; on Germany, Ernst Wolfgang Becker, *Zeit der Revolution! - Revolution der Zeit?: Zeiterfahrungen in Deutschland in der Ära der Revolutionen 1789-1848/49* (Göttingen: Vandenhoeck und Ruprecht, 1999).

[23] Quoted in Pim den Boer, *History as a Profession: the study of history in France, 1818-1914*, (English trans. Princeton: Princeton University Press, 1998), 124.

the rise of the theory and practice of "foreignizing", translating in such a way as to retain the cultural distance between the text translated and its new readers.[24] German writers and scholars played a central role in these changes, as Italians had done in the case of the Renaissance sense of the past.

In the nineteenth century, "empathy" or *Einfühlung* became the slogan of historians who tried to make remote periods seem near (although these historians sometimes distanced themselves from their eighteenth-century predecessors, including Hume, precisely by accusing them of lack of empathy). This concern with approximation encouraged scholars to publish a number of intimate first-person testimonies from the past. These 'ego-documents' included autobiographies, diaries and letters that have become famous by individuals such as Benvenuto Cellini in Italy, John Evelyn, Samuel Pepys and Dorothy Osborne in England, Jan Chrysostom Pasek in Poland, Archpriest Avvakum in Russia and others.[25]

An interplay between distanciation and approximation dominates the ruminative essay by Thomas Carlyle, *Past and Present* (1843), who evokes the Middle Ages through the chronicle of Jocelin of Brakelond, a monk of Bury St Edmunds. Carlyle described the chronicle as 'an extremely foreign book', stressing 'how remote it is from us; exotic, extraneous; in all ways, coming from far abroad'. At the same time Carlyle is concerned 'to get across the chasm of Seven Centuries', and to do this he makes use of opposite techniques. On occasion he identifies with the monks, using the first person plural to declare that 'in our convent here we are a peculiar people'. Elsewhere the writer perpetrates deliberate anachronisms, describing Jocelin as 'a kind of born Boswell' and the Danish invaders as 'Heathen Physical-Force Ultra-Chartists'.[26] Carlyle also makes an example of historians who use the historic present as a form of approximation.

---

[24] Antoine Berman, *L'épreuve de l'étranger: culture et traduction dans l'Allemagne romantique* (Paris: Gallimard, 1984).

[25] Phillips, *Society and Sentiment*, 296.

[26] Thomas Carlyle, *Past and Present* (1843: new edn, Berkely 2005), 44–5, 52, 57, 70. On the use of anachronism for approximation, Peter Burke, 'Triumphs and Poverties of Anachronism', *Scientia Poetica* 10 (2006), 291–8.

A Short History of Distance

Nationalist historians in particular perceived the national past as close and tried to bring it closer by employing different techniques of approximation. Jules Michelet offers an extreme instance of "introjection" or identification with the past, especially the French past. He fell ill when he wrote about the Terror. Attempting to achieve a similar effect by opposite means, Whig historians projected the present onto the past. Thomas Macaulay, for instance, once presented himself to his Edinburgh constituency as the member of the party which according to him had resisted monopolies in the age of Queen Elizabeth. Macaulay's descendant G. M. Trevelyan often employed a revealing "we" when he wrote about English history: "our writers", "our ancestors", "our civil storms", "our troops" and so on.[27]

On the other hand, the rise of positivism and the prestigious model of the natural sciences encouraged the growing body of professional historians to aim at detachment or distance as a sign of their objectivity. One nineteenth-century historian who employed the distant viewpoint was Fustel de Coulanges, who formulated what has been called "le principe de distance" and wrote about the "radical and essential differences' between ancient and modern societies.[28] Another was Hippolyte Taine, who viewed the French Revolution in pathological terms and described seventeenth-century sentiments as "so different from our own that we understand them with difficulty". When he had to deal with a recent traumatic event, the defeat of France by Prussia in 1870-1, he claimed to have written "comme si j'avais eu pour sujet les revolutions de Florence ou d'Athènes".[29] Yet another was Gaston Paris, whose view of the Middle Ages (distant from the nineteenth century precisely because it viewed the past as close) has already been quoted. Lucien Febvre's famous discussion of "primitive" ideas in the age of

---

[27] Arthur Mitzman, *Michelet, historian: rebirth and romanticism in nineteenth-century France* (New Haven: Yale University Press, 1990); G. M. Trevelyan, *England under the Stuarts* (1904: 17th edn, London: Longmans, 1938), 7, 29-30, 237, 508.

[28] On Fustel, André Burguière, *L'école des annales: une histoire intellectuelle* (Paris: Odile Jacob, 2006), 47, 65; cf. Jonathan Dewald, *Lost Worlds: the emergence of French social history, 1815-1970* (University Park: Pennsylvania State University Press, 2006), 106.

[29] The first quotation from Taine is in Dewald, *Lost Worlds*, 105; the second from *Origines de la France contemporaine*, 6 vols., Paris: Hachette, 1876-94, preface to vol.1.

Rabelais continued and refined the tradition, while his colleague Marc Bloch's *Strange Defeat* was a remarkably detached, dispassionate attempt to understand the French collapse in 1939 from the point of view of a historian.[30]

All the same, we might say that in the nineteenth century, empathy or attempts at empathy were dominant, especially if we include representations on the past in novels or plays or in the many historical paintings of the time, many of which aimed at pathos: the life and death of Mary Queen of Scots was a favourite subject, on the Continent as well as in Britain.

In this second moment, the obvious explanations for the increase in sensitivity to change and to the otherness of the past are the modernization of society following the Industrial Revolution and the sense of the acceleration of history following the French Revolution and the rise of Napoleon, expressed with particular clarity by Chateaubriand.[31] Both the Industrial and the French Revolutions made people who lived through them conscious of their increasing distance from the old political and social regimes, what a later generation would call "the world we had lost".[32] The idea of "estrangement" seems to be even more applicable to this second moment than it is to the first.

However, it is surely significant that it was around 1800, in the course of the second moment of distancing, that philosophers and historians became aware of the Renaissance sense of distance from the past. Like other forms of consciousness, historical consciousness fascinated Hegel, who discussed it in his *Philosophy of History* (1837).[33] There were doubtless good reasons for the rise of this consciousness of consciousness in the nineteenth century, especially in the German-speaking world.

---

[30] Lucien Febvre, *Le problème de l'incroyance au XVIe siècle: la religion de Rabelais* (Paris: Albin Michel, 1942), 473, 480; Marc Bloch, *L'étrange défaite* (1957: new edn, Paris: Gallimard, 1990). Bloch wrote this essay in 1940.

[31] Chateaubriand, quoted in François Hartog, *Régimes d'historicité: présentisme et expériences du temps* (Paris: Seuil, 2003).

[32] Georg Lukács, *The Historical Novel* (1937: English translation, London: Merlin books, 1962).

[33] Georg W. F. Hegel, *Vorlesungen über die Philosophie der Geschichte* (1837: rpr Stuttgart: Reclam, 1975).

A Short History of Distance

The cultural historian Karl Lamprecht, for example, emphasised the lack of a sense of historical distance in the Middle Ages and its discovery in the age of Columbus, writing about a simultaneous expansion of horizons in space and time ("Ausdehnung des raümlichen Horizonts" and "Ausdehnung des zeitlichen Horizonts").[34] The literary historian Erich Auerbach also contrasted the earlier medieval references to "chivalry" or "vassals" in Biblical times with the rise of a sense of distance in the age of humanism.[35]

However, the idea of anachronism was studied with most precision by German historians of art, notably by Aby Warburg before 1914 and by his followers Fritz Saxl and Erwin Panofsky after the First World War. Warburg, who believed that the conscious creation of distance between the self and the outside world was fundamental to civilization, noted Botticelli's concern with correct period costume – *eine gewisse archäologische Treue des Kostüms*.[36] For his part Saxl focussed on the historical interests of Mantegna, noted above, and his friendship with the antiquarian Fra Feliciano of Verona.[37] Perhaps the most famous discussion of the topic is Panofsky's comparison between the sense of historical perspective and the pictorial perspective of the Renaissance.[38]

As later essays in this volume will show, there are obvious visual analogies to literary distanciation and approximation, as the visual metaphors of "perspective", "foreshortening", and above all, "point of view", remind us. Artists and photographers can pay more or less attention to foreground or background. The cinema offers a long series of examples as well as a vocabulary for discussing them, "close-ups" versus "long shots".

---

[34] Karl Lamprecht, *Deutsche Geschichte* part 2, vol. 2 (Freiburg: Heyfelder, 1904), 3–56.
[35] Erich Auerbach, *Mimesis* (1946: English trans, New York: Doubleday, 1950), 140.
[36] Aby Warburg, "Sandro Botticellis 'Geburt der Venus' und 'Frühling'" (1893: rpr *Die Erneuereung der Heidnischer Antike*, 2 vols., Leipzig und Berlin: Teubner, 1932, vol. 1, 3–58). Cf. Ernst Gombrich, *Aby Warburg* (London: Warburg Institute, 1970), 288.
[37] Fritz Saxl, "Jacopo Bellini and Mantegna as Antiquarians" (1935: rpr his *A Heritage of Images*, Harmondsworth: Penguin Books, 1970, 57–70).
[38] Erwin Panofsky, "The First Page of Vasari's *Libro*", (1930: English trans. in his *Meaning in the Visual Arts*, New York: Doubleday, 1957, 169–225).

III

A third moment in the history of the perception of historical distance occurred in Europe at around the end of the First World War. It was at this time that the technique of distanciation was named by the Russian Formalist critic Viktor Shklovsky (as *ostranenie*), while the dramatist Bertolt Brecht wrote of the "*V-Effekt*", in other words the effect of alienation (*Verfremdung*).[39] What was new at this time was the increasingly sharp sense of distance from a past that was relatively recent.

As in the case of Scott and Manzoni in the second period, some of the most eloquent witnesses to this third moment are novelists, among them Josef Roth, author of *Radetzkymarsch*, a novel about three generations of a single family the Trotta, through whose eyes we watch the decline and fall of the Habsburg Empire.[40] What is particularly remarkable about this novel is precisely its sharp sense of the gulf between the present and the past, despite the fact that the year in which it was published, 1932, was less than two decades away from 1914, the date marking the end of the world Roth presents as lost.

Radetzkymarsch illustrates the use of explicit comparison as a means to distanciation. "In those days before the Great War", Roth wrote, "when the events narrated in this book took place, it had not yet become a matter of indifference whether a man lived or died". Or again: "in the crises that were calamitous to them and which would in the times we are living in be dismissed with a quick joke, these brave old gentlemen maintained a heroic calm". "Nowadays the notions of honour – personal, family and professional – by which Herr von Trotta lived, are the nearest relics of childish, superstitious legends".[41] The recent past, one might say, had rapidly become a foreign country to the author and doubtless to his early readers as well.

---

[39] On Shklovsky, Carlo Ginzburg, *Occhiacci di legno: nove riflessioni sulla distanza* (Milan: Feltrinelli, 1998) 15–17.
[40] Josef Roth, *Radetzkymarsch* (1932: English trans. Michel Hofmann, London: Granta, 2003).
[41] Roth, *Radetzkymarsch*.

That metaphor reminds us that L. P. Hartley, who was cited at the beginning of this essay, was in a similar situation to Roth, doubly so in fact. Nineteen years old in 1914, Hartley remembered the pre-war years very well and chose them as the setting for his country-house novel. However, he wrote *The Go-Between* after the Second World War, recreating the world of his childhood from which he was doubly estranged as a result of the two great wars. Major events have often had the effect of distancing people, sometimes traumatically, from their own pasts.

IV

All the same, the last of the four moments to be discussed here, around 1970, is not marked by a traumatic event, but rather by the acceleration of social and cultural change, which has made people's early lives appear in retrospect to be as obsolete as the gadgets that were once part of it, from gramophones with needles to telephones with dials.

A generation earlier, the Olympian mode appeared to dominate, at least in France. In the mid-twentieth century, Fernand Braudel's desire "voir grand", as he put it, to think about vast spaces and *la longue durée*, kept him far away from the hopes and fears of individuals such as King Philip II of Spain, on whom he seemed to look down from a great height (though Braudel allowed himself to express his sense of proximity to a region, the Mediterranean).[42] It is tempting to juxtapose Braudel, who was writing in the 1930s, with his contemporary the anthropologist Marcel Griaule, an ex-aviator who, unlike the majority of anthropologists, was "particularly conscious of the advantages of overview". Griaule made use of aeroplanes in his fieldwork in Africa, writing that "Seen from high in the air, a district holds few secrets".[43] One is reminded of the rise of archaeology from the air, a method inspired by the read-

---

[42] On Fustel, André Burguière, *L'école des annales: une histoire intellectuelle* (Paris, 2006), 47, 65.
[43] James Clifford, "Power and Dialogue: Marcel Griaule", in George W. Stocking (ed.) *Observers Observed: essays on ethnographic fieldwork* (Madison, Wis: University of Wisconsin Press, 1983), 121–56, at 133.

ing of aerial photographs during the Second World War.

In Germany, Golo Mann's Kafkaesque decision to refer to Hitler as "H." throughout his history of modern Germany produces a strange sense of remoteness.[44] So does Elias Canetti's use of images of fire and water to describe crowds in his *Crowds and Power* (1960), although such images are traditional and were employed by Scott and Manzoni. Historians writing about crowds or "mobs" were also prone to describe such groups – consciously or unconsciously – via distancing images taken from nature. E. P. Thompson memorably denounced what he called the "spasmodic school" of historians of riot for using metaphors that denied the rioters human agency.[45]

Quantitative history with its graphs and tables had similar effects, even if its practitioners were not consciously concerned with distanciation. In both France and the USA, the world leaders in the writing of history at this time, the concern with quantitative methods and also with what the historical sociologist Charles Tilly liked to call "big structures" was dominant in the 1950s and 1960s. The rise of global history has encouraged the distant view. In his *Millennium* (1995), reworking Voltaire, Felipe Fernandez Armesto has imagined how earthly history would be viewed by the "galactic museum keepers" of the future.

However, from the 1970s we have witnessed a widespread reaction against these approaches, a reaction associated with an interest in "microhistory", in other words with local events and minor figures who only become visible when the observer moves close to them.[46] It was also at this time that the "question of the Other", with a capital O (or more exactly a capital A, since it is in French and German that so many discussions of *l'Autre* or *Alterität* have taken place) became a major theme for students of philosophy,

---

[44] Golo Mann, *Deutsche Geschichte des neunzehnten und zwanzigsten Jahrhunderts* (Frankfurt: Suhrkampf, 1958).
[45] Edward P. Thompson, "The Moral Economy of the English Crowd", *Past and Present* 50 (1971), 76–136.
[46] For a brief survey, see Karl Appuhn, "Microhistory", in Peter Stearns (ed.) *Encyclopaedia of European Social History* vol. 1 (New York: Scribners, 2001), 105–12; for a personal comment, Carlo Ginzburg, 'Microhistory: two or three things that I know about it", *Critical Inquiry* 20 (1993–4) 10–35.

literature and history alike. One thinks for instance of the work of critics such as Hans-Robert Jauss, for instance, Edward Said or Tristan Todorov, all three of them concerned with the problems of understanding people who are distant from us in space or time.[47]

Sociologists have become interested in the problem of distanciation, witness the essay by Norbert Elias known in English as *Involvement and Detachment* and in German as *Engagement und Distanzierung* (1983). Anthropologists have long taken a professional interest in "other cultures", the title of a once famous introduction to the subject.[48] Professing a kind of cultural relativism, they have sometimes used techniques of both distanciation and approximation in order to combat the possible ethnocentrism of their readers. A famous case of distanciation is that of a mock-ethnography of the tribe of the "Nacirema", who turn out of course to be the Americans spelled backwards.[49]

Another technique, as effective as it is unobtrusive, is to write as if a belief or practice from which most readers have distanced themselves were true or efficacious. The French anthropologist Marc Augé has written of his witnessing devils coming to the West African village in which he was working in order to confess their crimes, commenting pages later that he deliberately left out the inverted commas around "devils" in order to give readers an impression equivalent to his own, as an observer who had suddenly to accept everyday references to devils as normal [*la suppression des guillemets au début de ce texte voulait donner au lecteur une impression équivalente à celle de l'observateur qui doit tout soudainement tenir pour habituelle et normale la reference quotidienne aux "diables"*].[50]

It was at this time that what had been the relatively small and esoteric subject of anthropology began to grow and to interest

---

[47] Hans-Robert Jauss, *Alterität und Modernität der mittelalterlichen Literatur* (Munich: Fink, 1977); Edward Said, *Orientalism* (London: Routledge, 1978); Tristan Todorov, *La conquête de l'Amérique: la question de l'autre* (Paris: Seuil, 1982).

[48] John Beattie, *Other cultures; aims, methods and achievements in social anthropology* (London: Cohen and West, 1964).

[49] Horace Miner, "Body Ritual among the Nacirema", *American Anthropologist* 58 (1956), 503–537.

[50] Marc Augé, *Théorie des pouvoirs et idéologie: etude de cas en Côte d'Ivoire* (Paris, 1975).

scholars in other disciplines. A movement for 'historical anthropology' goes back to the 1970s in Britain (with Keith Thomas), France (Jacques Le Goff), the USA (Natalie Davis) and Italy (Carlo Ginzburg), while the phrase "literary anthropology" became a current one in the 1980s, at least in the USA and Germany, from R. Howard Bloch to Helmut Pfotenhauer.[51] As a litmus paper making change visible we might take the reception of the phrase, "the past is a foreign country'", coined by a novelist in a book first published in 1953 but taken up by historians from the 1970s onwards. A few historical archaeologists moved in a similar direction some decades later, attempting to show, for instance, that the recent past is less familiar than it looks.[52]

V

Meanwhile, outside the academic world for the most part, we have seen a rise of collective attempts to re-enact episodes from the past. The idea that one major historical event is effectively the re-enactment of another is not new. The French Revolution was experienced by some contemporaries as a re-enactment of ancient Roman history, as the driving out of a new Tarquin. The French revolutions of 1830, 1848 and 1871 were viewed in their turn as re-enactments of 1789. In similar fashion, the Bolshevik Revolution of 1917 was experienced (by Trotsky, among others) as a replay of the French Revolution, while the Spanish Civil War was viewed by some participants – on both sides – as a re-enactment of the Revolution of the Bolsheviks.

Self-conscious, planned re-enactments of historical events have often taken place in the context of anniversaries and especially of centenaries, which began to be celebrated regularly from the late eighteenth century onwards. Early examples include the Shake-

---

[51] R. Howard Bloch, *Etymologies and genealogies: a literary anthropology of the French Middle Ages* (Chicago: University of Chicago Press, 1983); Helmut Pfotenhauer, *Literarische Anthropologie: Selbstbiographien und ihre Geschichte – am Leitfaden des Leibes* (Stuttgart: Metzler, 1987).
[52] Sarah Tarlow and Susie West (eds.) *The Familiar Past? Archaeologies of Later Historical Britain* (London: Routledge, 1999).

speare Jubilee (1769), two hundred years after the birth of the dramatist; the centenary of the "Glorious Revolution" (1788); and the tercentenary of the landing of Columbus in the New World (1792). In the first half of the twentieth century, the interest in re-enactment seems to have been strongest in the USA, as in the case of the Battle of Chancellorsville (1863), re-enacted on the site in 1935, or the pageant in Marietta, Ohio in 1938, re-enacting the trek of the first settlers, or Washington's journey from Mount Vernon to Manhattan, re-enacted in 1939.[53] The interest in re-enactment seems to have been linked with that in "living history", as exemplified by colonial Williamsburg, rebuilt from 1926 onwards.

In the second half of the twentieth century, the practice spread much more widely and became much more frequent than before, often organized by societies founded for the purpose such as the Sealed Knot (1968) dedicated to the English Civil War, or the History Re-enactment Workshop (1985). The love of dressing up (as legionaries, Vikings, medieval knights and so on) obviously plays its part, but other reasons, such as national or regional pride, underlie the many re-enactments of episodes from the American Civil War. The Battle of Gettysburg now takes place every year, and it is likely that some of the participants keep on hoping that the southern general Robert E. Lee will win this time.

VI

It would be too mechanistic to write the historiography of distanciation and approximation in terms of the swing of a pendulum, but there do seem to be reactions (including reactions against reactions). It might also be useful to distinguish two kinds of historian, respectively attracted by what is distant (both in space and in time) and by what is close.

It might be unwise to assume that distance is either a simple help or hindrance to the historian, and more plausible to suggest that distance and distanciation carry both advantages and disadvan-

---

[53] John Bodnar, *Remaking America: public memory, commemoration, and patriotism in the twentieth century* (Princeton: Princeton University Press, 1992), 129.

tages. Take the case of the masterpiece of one of the great cultural historians of the twentieth century, Johan Huizinga. In my view at least, the religious chapters of his *Autumn of the Middle Ages* (1919) are weakened by fact that the author (the son of a Protestant pastor) was so distant from beliefs and practices that, taking over the language of Erasmus and the Protestant reformers, he called "mechanical". On the other hand, the fact that Huizinga had begun his scholarly career as an Indologist, studying Sanskrit literature, and then switched to the study of Europe, enriched his study of the Middle Ages by distancing him from his predecessors in his second field and making it easier for him to ask new questions about the past. For example, he described the transition from Middle Ages to Renaissance as the succession of two different mentalities or "forms of thought" (*denkvormen*), the symbolic and the causal, a transition that could be studied at the level of everyday life as well as that of philosophy.[54]

We might speak of both "positive" and "negative" distance. On one side, what Nietzsche called "Pathos der Distanz", the sense of loss or estrangement that has inspired important novels, as we have seen, as well as historical studies. Guicciardini's history of Italy expresses nostalgia for the world before 1494, when the French invaded and the Italian tragedy began. Turning to twentieth-century examples, the Brazilian Gilberto Freyre's *Casa Grande e Senzala* (1933) has often been described, with partial truth, as fuelled by nostalgia for Brazil's colonial past, especially for the "Big House" and the patriarchal family of the Northeast. Similar emotions underlie its French equivalent, *L'enfance et la vie familiale sous l'ancien régime* (1960) by Philippe Ariès.[55]

On the other side, there is what we might call "condescending distance", remembering E. P. Thompson's famous phrase about "the enormous condescension of posterity". If condescending dis-

---

[54] Johan Huizinga, *The Autumn of the Middle Ages* (1919: English trans. Chicago: University of Chicago Press, 1996).
[55] On Freyre, Peter Burke and Maria Lúcia Pallares-Burke, *Gilberto Freyre: Social Theory in the Tropics* (Oxford: Peter Lang, 2008); on Ariès, Patrick Hutton, *Philippe Ariès and the politics of French cultural history* (Amherst, Mass.: University of Massachusetts Press, 2004).

tance is to be rejected, together with pure nostalgia, there is surely still a place in historical studies for attempts at other kinds of detachment, alongside its opposite, empathy. We need somehow to combine local knowledge with the big picture; the advantages of hindsight with a sense of how events appeared to the people who experienced them; and awareness of the manifold ways in which people in the past were different from us with a concern with their common humanity. In other words, historians might aim for an alternation of historical close-ups and long shots, a deliberate multiplication of points of view.

10: Involvement and Detachment in Historical Writing

In a fascinating book with a curious title, *From Anxiety to Method in the Behavioral Sciences*, a psychoanalyst, the Hungarian turned Frenchman Georges Devereux once investigated the reasons or motives for which social scientists were drawn to particular subjects of study.[1] It would be equally fascinating to examine historians from this point of view, asking not only why they choose to spend their lives studying history but also why they choose the problems and periods on which they come to specialize. Whether different psychological types write different kinds of history is probably a question best left to psychologists, but social and political explanations are less remote from a historian's normal expertise. Accident plays a part: it was for an example an exhibition of fifteenth-century paintings from the Netherlands, held in Bruges in 1902, that inspired the Dutch historian Johan Huizinga to write his famous book on 'the Autumn of the Middle Ages', published seventeen years later.

Are there more general explanations? A good place to begin might be a famous study by a sociologist, the German turned Eng-

---

[1] George Devereux, *From Anxiety to Method in the Behavioral Sciences* (The Hague: Mouton, 1967).

lishman Norbert Elias, on what he called 'problems of involvement and detachment'.[2] Elias was concerned in this study with method in the social sciences. More recently, the historian Mark Phillips, a South African turned Canadian, has studied what he prefers to call 'historical distance', from two points of view.[3] In the first place, distance is 'historically given', 'a reflection of external events', in the sense that some historians, especially historians in certain places and periods, such as Europe in the nineteenth century, view the past as remote, as a 'foreign country', while other historians, such as medieval European chroniclers, assume that the past is close to them.[4] In the second place, distance may be 'a textual construction designed to shape the reader's response'. Some historians, including the eighteenth-century Scottish philosopher David Hume made deliberate attempts either to distance their readers from the period or the events they are writing about, or on the contrary, to quote Thomas Macaulay, 'to make the past present, to bring the distant near'.[5] There is an obvious parallel between these forms of writing and the techniques of the cinema, notably the 'long shot' on the one hand, and the 'close-up' on the other.

My starting-point, then, will be a division into two kinds of historian, between those who prefer themes close to their own experience and those who prefer the remote and exotic. We might describe the two groups as insiders and outsiders and their intellectual styles as respectively involved and detached.

On one side, then, the historians who keep relatively close to their own experience, writing on the fairly recent past of their own region or at least their own country. For example, such a high proportion of Italian historians spend their lives working on their native region that it would only be useful to mention the few, Carlo

---

[2] Norbert Elias, 'Problems of Involvement and Detachment', *British Journal of Sociology* 7 (1956), 226–252.
[3] Mark S. Phillips, *On Historical Distance* (New Haven: Yale University Press, 2013); Mark S. Phillips, Barbara Caine and Julia A. Thomas (eds.) *Rethinking Historical Distance* (Basingstoke, Palgrave Macmillan, 2013).
[4] The phrase was coined by the English writer L. P. Hartley, who used it in the first sentence of his novel *The Go-Between* (1953).
[5] Phillips, *Distance*, 1 (quoting Macaulay) and 88–9.

Ginzburg and the late Marino Berengo for example, who do not do so. It may be significant that both Ginzburg and Berengo are Jewish and that Ginzburg's father was Russian.

The identification of historians of this kind with their subjects is so obvious that it is rarely studied, with the major exception of the classic and almost pathological case of Michelet, who became ill when he was writing about the French Revolution, and mentioned his own birth (in 1798) in his history. Michelet may have projected his own feelings onto the past, as many of us do, but he also seems to have 'introjected' the past, which is rather more unusual.[6]

For a milder case of identification, we might turn to a leading English historian from the first half of the twentieth century, George Macaulay Trevelyan (the historian Thomas Macaulay was an ancestor of his, hence his middle name). It is revealing to note the frequent use of the term 'we' in Trevelyan's histories of England, since it indicates the extent of the author's identification with the upper class from the seventeenth century onward, if not before, as well as with the Whig party.[7] It is common knowledge (at least among Cambridge historians) that Herbert Butterfield's critique of the 'Whig interpretation of history' was aimed in particular at Trevelyan, his Cambridge colleague.[8]

On the other side, there are the historians who are fascinated by more remote places and the more distant past. Although the British are often regarded as insular and inward-looking, British historians are more likely to write about other countries than are (say) the French or the Germans.[9] Among the recent historians who have discussed the 'otherness' of the past are Robert Darnton and Carlo Ginzburg, while David Lowenthal has devoted a book

---

[6] Lionel Gossman (1989) 'Michelet and the French Revolution', in *The Transformation of Political Culture*, ed. François Furet and Mona Ozouf, Oxford, 639–64; *id.*, 'Jules Michelet: histoire nationale, biographie, autobiographie' in *Littérature* 102 (1996), 29–54.

[7] For an introduction to his thought, see David Cannadine, *G. M. Trevelyan: a life in history* (London: HarperCollins, 1992).

[8] Herbert Butterfield, *The Whig Interpretation of History* (London: Bell, 1931).

[9] Richard J. Evans, *Cosmopolitan islanders: British historians and the European continent* (Cambridge: Cambridge University Press, 2009).

to visions of the past as a 'foreign country'.[10] This desire to capture and to understand 'otherness' lies behind the anthropological turn of a number of living historians, Darnton, Ginzburg and myself included.

It is tempting to use the word 'romanticism' to describe if not to explain the attraction of the unfamiliar. In Europe, northern historians have been drawn to the south much more than the reverse. The Swiss Jacob Burckhardt was drawn to Italy; the Lorrainer Braudel to the Mediterranean; the Norman Emmanuel Le Roy Ladurie to Languedoc. There are far more Anglophone historians studying Italy, France or Spain than there are Italian, French or Spanish historians studying Britain.

For another form of distance – and in some cases at least, of romanticization – we may turn to the history of rebels, criminals and social 'deviants'. Eric Hobsbawm, for example, wrote two books about the people whom he described as 'primitive rebels' and 'social bandits'. He observed in his introduction to *Primitive Rebels* that 'historians, being educated and townsmen, have until recently simply not made sufficient effort to understand people who are unlike themselves'.[11] On the surface, Hobsbawm seemed to personify detachment. He liked to be, or to appear, 'cool'. All the same, we are entitled to suspect that there was a rebel inside this virtually lifelong member of the Communist Party, who was also the author of a brilliant study of jazz written under a pseudonym borrowed from a Black Communist trumpeter, Francis Newton.[12]

Turning to the other great English Marxist historian, Edward Thompson (who was actually middle-class himself, the son of the writer Edward John Thompson, in other words 'patrician' not 'plebeian'), it may be suggested that he romanticized the working

---

[10] Robert Darnton, *The Great Cat Massacre* (New York: Basic Books, 1984), 4ff. Carlo Ginzburg, *Occhiacci di legno*, 1998, English translation *Wooden Eyes: nine reflections on distance* (London: Verso, 2002); David Lowenthal, *The Past is a Foreign Country* (Cambridge: Cambridge University Press, 1985; revised edn forthcoming, 2014).
[11] Eric J. Hobsbawm, *Primitive Rebels* (Manchester: Manchester University Press, 1959).
[12] 'Francis Newton', *The Jazz Scene* (London: MacGibbon and Kee, 1959).

class. So did Raphael Samuel, founder of History Workshop, who was middle-class and Jewish and so once again remote from the working class, the 'quarry roughs', for instance, whom he studied sympathetically and brought back to life. In the eyes of Thompson and Samuel, the history of the working class had an epic quality.

A special case of interest in the 'other' which deserves closer analysis, not to say psychoanalysis, is that of historians who are drawn to the study of groups or individuals that they dislike or even hate. Take the case of the Oxford historian Hugh Trevor-Roper, later Lord Dacre. Dacre began his career with a biography of archbishop Laud that makes no attempt to hide the author's dislike of his subject. He made his reputation with a book on Hitler that may be described as Tacitean in its controlled savagery (Trevor-Roper was trained as a classical scholar). He continued to be attracted to the study of groups he disliked, notably the Scots (or the 'Scotch', as he liked to call them), taking delight in demonstrating that the famous Scottish kilt was invented by an eighteenth-century Quaker businessman.[13]

In other cases, a historian undertakes the study of an apparently distant subject because it reminds him or her of something much nearer home. For example, one of the outstanding articles published by the outstanding historian Natalie Zemon Davis deals with the religious wars in sixteenth-century France and the way in which, thanks to the ritualization of violence, Catholics and Protestants each dehumanized the other. As Davis later confessed, as a Jewish woman who was a teenager at the time of the Holocaust, awareness of the dehumanization of the Jews in Auschwitz and elsewhere underlay her involvement with Catholics lynching Protestants and vice versa.[14] It is likely that a number of other historical studies, such as Norman Cohn on messianic revolutionaries of the Middle Ages, and David Nirenberg on the persecution of minori-

---

[13] Hugh R. Trevor-Roper, *Archbishop Laud, 1573–1645* (London: Macmillan, 1940); id., *The Last Days of Hitler* (London: Macmillan, 1947); id., *The Invention of Scotland: myth and history* (New Haven: Yale University Press, 2009).

[14] Natalie Z. Davis, 'The Rites of Violence: religious riot in sixteenth-century France', *Past and Present* 59 (1973), 51–91; id., *A Passion for History* (Kirksville, MO: Truman State University Press, 2010), 63.

ties, again in the Middle Ages, represent indirect confrontations with the horrors of the Holocaust.[15]

On occasion, historians may be unaware of the similarities between the topic they chose to study and their own experiences or memories. In other cases, they might be described as 'hyperaware', and as intending their readers to see the analogies between the event they are writing about and another one, usually much closer in time. I should like to describe the second case as one of writing history as allegory.[16]

Allegory is an obvious method, though not free from danger, of evading censorship in authoritarian regimes, as the following three examples suggest. Towards the end of the reign of Queen Elizabeth I, Sir John Hayward was imprisoned in the Tower of London after publishing a history of the reign of Henry IV of England. Henry had come to the throne after deposing his predecessor, Richard II. The Queen believed that she was being identified with Richard and that Hayward's book encouraged attempts to depose her.[17] In China, a major stir was caused by Wu Han's historical play, *Hai Rui Dismissed from Office* (1960) depicting a virtuous official of the Ming dynasty who was dismissed by the tyrannical emperor Zhu Yuanzhang. Wu Han was a historian. In 1949 he had published a biography of the first Ming emperor, Zhu Yuanzhang, and discussed it with Mao Zedong. In 1959, Mao suggested that Wu Han write about Hai Rui. However, Mao later criticized Wu Han for using Hai Rui to stand for Peng Dehuai, a minister whom Mao himself dismissed in 1959. During the Cultural Revolution, Mao's wife Jiang Qing criticized Wu Han for having dared to represent Mao Zedong as a tyrant and he was sent to prison, where he died.[18]

---

[15] Norman Cohn, *The Pursuit of the Millennium* (London: Secker and Warburg, 1957); David Nirenberg, *Communities of Violence* (Princeton: Princeton University Press, 1996).
[16] Peter Burke, 'History as Allegory', *Inti* 45 (1997), 337–51.
[17] David J. Womersley, 'Sir John Hayward's Tacitism', *Renaissance Studies* 6 (1992), 46–59.
[18] Clive Ansley, *The Heresy of Wu Han: his play Hai Jui's Dismissal and its Role in China's Cultural Revolution* (Toronto: University of Toronto Press, 1971). Cf. Mary G. Mazur, *Wu Han Historian: Son of China's Times* (Lanham MD: Lexington Books, 2009), 345, 407, 416, 422.

Involvement and Detachment in Historical Writing

A third example, again from the Communist world, is that of the philosopher Leszek Kołakowski. In 1965 Kołakowski published *Christians without a Church*, a study of some dissident intellectuals at the time of of the Reformation who looked forward to what we might call the 'withering away of the Church'. The relevance of this book to political debates in Poland was obvious enough. In any case, Kołakowski made his views explicit a year later, on the tenth anniversary of the Gomułka regime, before he went into exile in the USA and later, in Britain.[19]

Dividing historians into two lists, teams or parties, as I have done so far, is a useful corrective to any idea that there is one basic motive for studying the past, or indeed only one kind of past. All the same, this binary opposition is obviously too simple. To complicate it, let us consider the need to consider the other as a second or substitute self.

The British historian Richard Cobb described his attitude to the France he studied all his adult life as a 'second identity'.[20] Burckhardt's early identification with Italy is revealed by his signing his name 'Giacomo Burcardo'.[21] His successor in Renaissance studies, Aby Warburg, described himself as *d'anima fiorentino* ('Florentine in spirit' – his use of Italian is part of the message).[22] As in the case of other kinds of attraction, attraction to a research topic is a mysterious cocktail of similarities, differences and complementarities. A story is told about a student going to see Burckhardt and asking him to suggest a topic for research. Burckhardt's reaction was to say, 'You might as well ask me to find you a wife!'

It is not difficult to find instances of an attraction to the history of an apparent 'other' which turns out (for the historian concerned) to be something like the self in disguise. Renaissance Florence had

---

[19] Leszek Kołakowski, *Chrétiens sans Eglise* (1965: French translation, Paris: Gallimard, 1969).
[20] Richard Cobb, *A Second Identity: essays on France and French history* (London: Oxford UniversityPress, 1969).
[21] Werner Kaegi, *Jacob Burckhardt: eine Biographie* (vol.1, Basel: Schwab, 1947).
[22] Ernst H. Gombrich, *Aby Warburg: an intellectual biography* (London: Warburg Institute, 1970).

something in common with the Basel in which Burckhardt grew up (his family being patricians who had ruled the city in the seventeenth century) or with the Hamburg of Aby Warburg (whose banking family suggests a parallel with the Medici).

For more cases of the other as a new self, we might turn to three immigrants to England from Central and Eastern Europe. The Oxford medievalist Paul Vinogradoff was a Russian liberal, a disappointed liberal, who resigned from his chair at the University of Moscow in 1901 because the government would not free the universities from state control. He was appointed a Professor at Oxford two years later. Vinogradoff was a life-long admirer of England. In the year of the Bolshevik Revolution, Vinogradoff published an essay on Magna Carta. It is not difficult to see the connexion between his medieval studies and his reforming ideals. Indeed, in the preface to his *Villainage in England* (1892) he explained that he was attracted to the topic of medieval serfdom because in his own country, the emancipation of the serfs had happened only a generation earlier: 'We in Russia', he wrote, 'are still living in surroundings created by the social revolution of the peasant emancipation'. He hoped to 'learn from Western history what is to be particularly avoided' in this situation, and 'what is to be aimed at'.[23] Conversely, as his friend F. W. Maitland suggested, Vinogradoff's experience of Russian village communities helped him to understand medieval England. Richard Cobb's phrase fits Vinogradoff like a glove: England was for him 'a second identity'.[24]

An example of an outsider trying to become an insider is that of the Cambridge historian Geoffrey Elton. Elton (born in Germany and originally known as Gerhard Rudolf Ehrenberg) began his history of *The English* (1992) with the confession that when he arrived in England in 1939, at the age of seventeen, 'within a few months it dawned on me that I had arrived in the country in which I ought to have been born'. In his inaugural lecture as Regius Professor of History, he told students that they should study

---

[23] Paul G. Vinogradoff, *Villainage in England* (Oxford: Clarendon Press, 1892), preface. This book was published in Russian in 1887.
[24] Herbert A. L. Fisher, *Paul Vinogradoff* (Oxford: Clarendon Press, 1927).

Involvement and Detachment in Historical Writing

'our' history, in other words English history.[25]

A third example, perhaps the most interesting, since it combined involvement with detachment, is that of Lewis Namier. Namier came from Russian Poland and was originally known as Ludwik Bernsztajn Niemirowski. Born in 1888, Namier came to England in 1907 and studied at Balliol College Oxford. He became a British subject – and changed his name to 'Namier'- in 1913, and he was a Professor of History at Manchester from 1931 to 1953.

Namier's identity is not easy to define. An outsider in England because he was a Polish immigrant, he was also an outsider in Poland because he was Jewish and an outsider among the Jews because he was the son of a landowner. He came to identify with England and his work on English history, especially the history of Parliament expressed this identification. On the other hand, he did not become a purely empiricist historian like the majority of his English colleagues. He read Freud, for instance, and Pareto, and made use of their ideas in his books.

It might also be said that his distance from British culture allowed Namier to take a fresh look at English history, indeed to demystify it, notably by criticizing the idea that eighteenth-century Whigs and Tories behaved like members of modern political parties. He may have identified with the England of his own day but he saw eighteenth-century England as a foreign country.[26] The result of this combination with identification and distance was one of the most brilliant works of history published in twentieth-century Britain.[27]

---

[25] Geoffrey R. Elton, *The History of England* (Cambridge: Cambridge University Press, 1984).
[26] Linda Colley, *Namier* (London: Weidenfeld and Nicolson, 1989).
[27] Lewis Namier, *The Structure of Politics at the Accession of George III* (London: Macmillan, 1929).

11: Exemplarity and Anti-Exemplarity in Early Modern Europe

The principal aim of this essay is to discuss the relation between historical thought in the Renaissance and François Hartog's three regimes of historicity, thinking with and occasionally against his central concept. To anticipate the conclusion, the essay will argue that historical thought and writing in early modern times (more or less 1350–1750) had distinctive characteristics of its own. It was a kind of regime within Hartog's spacious first regime, extending from Homer to Chateaubriand or from the *Achsenzeit* to the *Sattelzeit*.

One of the major features of this first regime is the idea of history as a storehouse of *exempla* offering a guide to life: *historia magistra vitae*, as Cicero wrote in his treatise *De oratore*. Like the late Reinhard Koselleck, Hartog argues that early modern European readers and writers believed in what he calls 'the authority of the past'. Like their classical and medieval predecessors, these readers and writers believed in a usable past, claiming or assuming that history offered a repertoire of *exempla*. The assumption was abandoned after (and in part thanks to) the events of 1789, which offered the prospect of a future so different from the past that earlier models became irrelevant. Hence Koselleck speaks of the 'dissolution' (*Auflösung*) of the ciceronian *topos* in the course of what he called the *Sattelzeit* of the late eighteenth century, the frontier zone between traditional and modern culture.¹

For this reason the following essay will focus on *exempla*, contrasting two views that coexisted in the early modern period. The majority of writers and readers – so far as the views of readers can be recovered – continued to recognize the value of examples from the past as guides to conduct in the present, thus supporting the narrative offered by Koselleck and Hartog. However, there was also a minority view – shared by some distinguished writers and thinkers – that denied or criticized the applicability to the Renaissance and post-Renaissance of ancient *exempla* or even the relevance of *exempla* in general. The cases for exemplarity and anti-exemplarity will therefore be discussed in turn.

Exemplarity

The first point to make is that the notion of 'exemplum' is not as clear or simple as it may look. In the early modern period, the term had a range of meanings, ranging from 'example' in the modern sense, adduced to support a generalization, to the better-known and more common moral meaning of an action worthy of imitation, whether for moral or for political reasons.

The second point is that the motives for reading and writing about the past cannot be reduced to the search for moral and political models. In his well-known survey of humanist historiography, Eric Cochrane notes that chronicles and histories might also be written for entertainment, or to praise the author's family or city, or to escape from the problems of the present.²

However, there can be little doubt that the Ciceronian phrase *historia magistra vitae* was a Renaissance *topos*, quoted again and again.³

---

[1] Reinhart Koselleck, 'Historia Magistra Vitae' (1967) rpr Futures Past (1979: English translation Cambridge, Mass., MIT Press, 1985, 21–38; François Hartog, Régimes d'historicité: présentisme et expériences du temps (Paris: Seuil, 2003).

[2] Eric Cochrane (1981) *Historians and Historiography in the Italian Renaissance* (Chicago: University of Chicago Press) (1981) 13–17.

[3] Rüdiger Landfester, *Historia Magistra Vitae: Untersuchungen zur humanistischen Geschichtstheorie des* 14. bis 16 Jahrhunderts (Geneva: Droz, 1972).

In Italy, for instance, the great historian Francesco Guicciardini copied out the famous passage from Cicero about the value of history and placed it at the beginning of the manuscript of his *Storia d'Italia*. In England, the title-page of Sir Walter Raleigh's *History of the World* (1614) showed the figure of History (labelled with the ciceronian phrase), holding up the world and treading down Death and Oblivion.

Magistra vitae was also a faithful summary of what Renaissance humanists in particular believed to be one of the main reasons for writing and reading history. History, like poetry, was viewed as a kind of applied ethics, offering both positive examples for readers to imitate and negative ones for them to avoid. The advantage of the concrete example was that it appealed to the emotions and so acted as a greater stimulus to virtuous action than a general precept. Petrarch, for example, wrote to his friend Giovanni Colonna that 'Nothing is more moving than the examples of famous men' [*Nihil est quod moveat quantum exempla clarorum hominum*].[4]

Again, the Florentine humanist Coluccio Salutati, for instance, presented history as a stimulus to virtue, or at any rate to the more ambiguous *virtus*: 'For we are incited by an *exemplum* and virtually impelled to virtue by its stimulus' [*incitamur enim exemplo et quodam quasi stimulo ad virtutem impellimur*]. For his part, Salutati's friend Leonardo Bruni suggested that reading history taught prudence, allowing the reader to learn at the expense of others, *ex alienis periculis*.[5]

Given these views, it is scarcely surprising to find that Plutarch's collection of biographies of Greek and Roman heroes should have been received with such enthusiasm during the Renaissance. It was studied in schools, in the famous school of the humanist Vittorino da Feltre in Mantua, for instance, in the leading Calvinist school in Geneva, the Academy, and in the schools of the Jesuits. It was translated into Italian, French, Spanish, English and German.[6]

---

[4] Hartog, this volume, 'Les humanistes et le passé antique'; Karlheinz Stierle, 'Three Moments in the Crisis of Exemplarity: Petrarch, Montaigne and Cervantes', *Journal of the History of Ideas* 59 (1998), 581–96, at 583.

[5] Landfester (1972) 58, 139.

The life of Alexander by Quintus Curtius was translated into Italian, Spanish, French and English, and it seems to have been an inspiration to a number of rulers and commanders of the period.[7]

Again, the collection of memorable deeds and sayings compiled by Valerius Maximus was one of the classical texts most frequently printed and translated at the Renaissance. At least eight editions in Latin were produced in the 1470s alone, followed by translations into French (1485, 1548), German (1489, 1533), Spanish (1495) and Italian (1504, 1539).[8]

The translations of Valerius Maximus were accompanied by imitations that often copied his arrangement of examples by virtues such as *fortitudo* and the distinction between classes of example (in his case between Roman and non-Roman). In his *Exempla* (1507) Marcantonio Sabellico, for instance, historian to the Venetian Republic, separated 'pagan examples' (*ethnica exempla*) from Jewish and Christian ones, while the Venetian priest Giambattista Egnazio, in *De exemplis* (1554) separated Venetian examples from the rest, presenting doge Lorenzo Loredan, for instance, as an example of *fortitudo* and doge Francesco Foscari as an example of *patientia*. The interest in *exempla* seems to have been unusually strong among the Venetian ruling class, but it can be found virtually everywhere in Renaissance Europe.[9]

One might compare the function of books of this kind to that of narrative paintings (known in the Renaissance as *historiae*), representing and re-presenting famous *exempla* such as the clemency of Alexander, the continence of Scipio, the chastity of Lucretia, the bravery of Mucius Scaevola in placing his hand in the fire and so on.[10] Titian's Lucretia and the Alexanders by Veronese and Leb-

---

[6] Robert R. Bolgar, *The Classical Heritage and its Beneficiaries* (Cambridge: Cambridge University Press, 1954), 333, 354, 359, 520–3; François Hartog, *Anciens, modernes, sauvages* (Paris: Galaade, 2005), 99–147.

[7] Bolgar (1954), 528–9.

[8] Bolgar (1954), 536–7; cf. Peter Burke, 'The Popularity of Ancient Historians 1450–1700', *History and Theory* 5 (1966), 135–52.

[9] Dorit Raines (2006) *L'invention du mythe aristocratique: l'image de soi du patriciat vénitien au temps de la Sérénissime* (2 vols., Venice: Istituto Veneto, 2006), 199–208.

[10] Olaf Reumann, 'L'exemplum humaniste comme moyen de légitimation dans la galerie François I', in Thomas W. Gaehtgens and Nicole Hochner (eds.) *L'image du roi de François I à Louis XIV* (Paris: Maisons des Sciences de l'Homme, 2006), 131–48.

run are only the most famous of many paintings of this kind. Such images were sometimes displayed in public places, for example, Beccafumi's frescoes in the Palazzo Pubblico in Siena, or the various 'halls of illustrious men' in Italian cities, decorated with their portraits. Fiction too was often intended to be exemplary, with the advantage that in contrast to historical writing, the plot was tailor-made for the author's moral.

The historical practice of the early modern period suggests that the exemplary function of historical writing was taken seriously. Petrarch himself produced a collection of the biographies of famous Romans, *De viris illustribus*. Two Italian humanists, Antonio Beccadelli ('Panormita') and Galeotto Marzio, produced biographies of rulers, Alfonso of Aragon and Matthias Corvinus, that were structured on the *dicta-facta* model of Valerius Maximus. Moral and political generalizations, known as maxims or aphorisms, regularly recurred in these texts.

Humanist histories also devoted considerable space to what were known as 'characters', in other words moral portraits describing the virtues and vices of leading figures in the story. Francesco Guicciardini's characters of Alexander VI, Clement VII and Lodovico Sforza of Milan offer a famous example of a general trend, like Lord Clarendon's gallery of portraits of leading figures in the English Civil War, from Charles I to Oliver Cromwell via the Duke of Buckingham, the Earl of Strafford and John Hampden.

Biography, which also flourished in this period, was sometimes justified in terms of exemplarity (a point that undermines Jacob Burckhardt's famous presentation of Renaissance biographies as a manifestation of 'individualism'). The Spanish bishop Antonio de Guevara's *Reloj de Principes*, a largely fictional biography of the Roman emperor Marcus Aurelius (first published in Valladolid in 1528 and often reprinted), advised Charles to take Marcus as a guide, master, friend, example and rival. Guevara must have known what appealed to his contemporaries, for his book was a great success, with French, Italian, English and Latin translations as well as numerous Spanish editions for the rest of the century.

Again, the French historian-magistrate Florimond de Raemond dedicated his edition of the memoirs of the soldier Blaise de Monluc to the nobility of Gascony with the remark 'ils vous y serviront de modele, de mirouer et d'exemplere'. The title of the memoirs was the *Commentaires*, suggesting that Monluc in his turn had taken Julius Caesar as his model.

Looking at history from the reader's side, we find a good deal of evidence of the search for *exempla*. One of the authors of the popular genre of books on how to read history, Pierre Droit de Gaillard, in his *Methode en la lecture de l'histoire* (1579), called history 'vray miroir et exemplaire de nostre vie'.

Whether Montaigne should be regarded as a humanist is a matter of controversy. What we can say with confidence is that like the humanists, the early Montaigne, at least, believed that history should be read above all for its moral lessons (1. 26). He loved Plutarch's book and he venerated some of the ancients, especially two Greeks, Epaminondas and Socrates. His interest in exemplarity is suggested by the fact that his *Essays* used the term *exemple* 165 times in the singular and 132 times in the plural. Indeed, Montaigne's early essays have been described as little more than chains of *exempla*.[11]

Anthologies of aphorisms taken from different historians and indexes of the aphorisms to be found in particular histories offer evidence of the interest that printers expected readers to take in a literary form that made explicit the lessons of exemplarity. An index of maxims or *gnomologia* was added to some editions and translations of the histories of Dionysius of Halicarnassus, Procopius, Curtius, Herodian and Zosimus, and, among moderns, Guicciardini.

It might be useful to distinguish three modes of reading at the Renaissance: rhetorical, moral and political. The rhetorical mode concentrated on the eloquence of the speeches delivered by leading figures in the story but invented by the historian, often anthologized and sometimes arranged according to rhetorical categories such as praise and blame, suasion and dissuasion. Here too *exempla* had a place. Writing on rhetoric in his *De copia*, Erasmus pointed out

---

[11] Karlheinz Stierle, 'L'histoire comme exemple, l'exemple comme histoire', *Poétique* 10 (1972), 176–98, at 195.

that quoting *exempla* was one mode of the amplification of a text.[12]
By contrast, both the moral and political modes of reading focused on maxims and the *exempla* that illustrated them. As the translator pointed out in the dedication to Guicciardini's *Hypomneses politicae* (1597), history teaches 'not by means of naked and cold precepts, but by famous and living examples' [*non nudis ac frigidis praeceptis, sed illustribus et vivis exemplis*]. However, precepts were not despised either. One seventeenth-century English gentleman, Sir William Drake, whose voluminous notes on his historical reading have survived, may be described as a collector of maxims.[13]

The past was taken seriously as a guide to public affairs, offering concrete instances of prudence or imprudence. Machiavelli, discussing the relevance to his own time of the *exempla* discussed by Livy, went so far as to claim in the proem to his *Discorsi* (1532) that history repeated itself, that 'the world has always been the same' [*giudico il mondo sempre essere stato ad un medesimo modo*] and that successful political action followed general rules 'which rarely or never fail'. Guicciardini included many maxims in his history, maxims that were published separately after his death and also translated into Latin. No wonder then that Richelieu, Olivares and other statesmen owned so many history books.[14]

We can also follow the political uses of history through the records of speeches in assemblies. In the Polish parliament or Sejm of 1582, according to the papal nuncio, Livy was quoted as if he were scripture. In the House of Commons debates in 1621, which were recorded in particular detail, there were references to ancient Sparta (Lycurgus), the Roman empire (Tiberius), the Norman Conquest and Richard II, suggesting that members knew

---

[12] Peter van Moos, *Geschichte als Topik: das rhetorische Exemplum von der Antike zur Neuzeit und die 'historiae' im Policraticus Johanns von Salisbury* (Hildesheim: Olms, 1988). Cf John D. Lyons, *Exemplum. The Rhetoric of Example in Early Modern France and Italy* (Princeton: Princeton University Press, 1990); Michael Jeanneret (1998) 'The Vagaries of Exemplarity', *Journal of the History of Ideas* 59 (1998), 565–80, at 569;
[13] Kevin Sharpe, *Reading Revolutions: the Politics of Reading in Early Modern England* (New Haven: Yale University Press, 2000) 201.
[14] John H. Elliott, *Richelieu and Olivares* (Cambridge: Cambridge University Press, 1984), 24.

their Plutarch and their Tacitus as well as their English history.[15]

No wonder then that books on modern history was not infrequently seen, by official eyes at least, as too dangerous to publish. Take the case of Niccolò Contarini, for instance. Contarini was a patrician who became an official historian of Venice and ended his career as doge. After his death, the Council of Ten had to decide whether to publish his history. They consulted two advisers who reported that the history should not be published because 'It contains maxims revealing the secret principles on which the regime operates, and we really do not know whether it is a good idea to make these maxims public [*Contiene massime molto intime del governo, che per verità non sappiamo se stia bene divulgarle*].[16] The history was not published until 1982.

Hence it was only prudent for Renaissance writers on prudence to confine their examples to ancient history. Hundreds of commentaries on the work of the master of prudence, Tacitus were published in this period. These commentaries attempted to distil his wisdom into a few general statements and to use figures such as Tiberius or Sejanus as negative *exempla*.[17]

One of the humanists most concerned with the study of Tacitus was the Netherlander Justus Lipsius, who believed that the study of the late Roman Empire was particularly relevant in the 1570s because Europe's political history was going through a similar phase. When Lipsius read Tacitus on the emperor Tiberius, for example, he was reminded of the Duke of Alba and the cruel way in which he governed the Netherlands for Philip II. He was also the author of a famous textbook on politics, (1589) which was sometimes published under the title *Monita et exempla politica*. It was effectively a collection of commonplaces or generalizations about political behaviour.

---

[15] Walter Notestein (ed.) *House of Commons Debates, 1621* (New Haven: Yale University Press, 1935).
[16] Gaetano Cozzi, *Il Doge Niccolò Contarini* (Venice: Istituto per la collaborazione culturale, 1958), 200.
[17] Peter Burke, 'Tacitism', in T. A. Dorey (ed.) *Tacitus* (London: Routledge, 1969), pp.149–71; T. J. Luce and A. J. Woodman (eds.) *Tacitus and the Tacitean Tradition* (Princeton: Princeton University Press, 1993); Jacob Soll, 'Amelot de la Houssaie annotates Tacitus', *Journal of the History of Ideas* 61 (2000), 167–88.

It seems, then, that we may speak of the belief in exemplarity as one of the main features of the first regime of historicity. It characterized what we might call the 'mentality' – a mixture of conscious beliefs and unconscious assumptions – of readers and writers over the *longue durée*, from classical antiquity itself to the Renaissance and beyond – it was, after all, in the eighteenth century that Lord Bolingbroke wrote his much-quoted sentence in his *Letters on the Study and Use of History* (1752) that 'history is philosophy teaching by example'.

Long after Bolingbroke, however, *exempla* were collected for the edification of children. In nineteenth-century French schools, history was expected to teach virtue as well as patriotism.[18] In the English-speaking world, the best-selling early twentieth-century *Children's Encyclopaedia* included 'the child's book of golden deeds'. These deeds offered what modern psychologists call role models – implying that even today, exemplarity has not completely lost its relevance.[19]

These examples add some nuances to the Hartog-Koselleck thesis according to which a new regime of historicity began in the late eighteenth century. As in so many cultural domains, we need to take account of *décalage*, 'cultural lag', or what Ernst Bloch and others have called 'the contemporaneity of the non-contemporary'. The theory of regimes needs to find a place for both continuities between regimes and for variation within them. The long second regime was not completely monolithic.

The first regime was not monolithic either. Attitudes to the past were not the same in classical, medieval and Renaissance culture. Medieval sermons, for instance, may have been full of *exempla*, but the examples that the faithful were exhorted to follow were religious ones, generally taken from lives of the saints. Renaissance *exempla*, in contrast, were generally secular.

However, the aspect of the Renaissance – or more generally, the early modern period, 1350–1750 – on which I should like to insist here is the fact that exemplarity could no longer be taken for grant-

---
[18] Pim den Boer, *History as a Profession: the study of history in France, 1818–1914* (English translation, Princeton: Princeton University Press, 1998), 165.
[19] Cf. Børge Bakker, *The Exemplary Society* (Oxford: Oxford University Press, 2000).

ed. In the course of the period it became the subject of a vigorous debate.

Anti-Exemplarity

The humanists not only encouraged exemplarity, they also undermined it. As the American critic Timothy Hampton has claimed in a perceptive essay on this topic, 'Humanism needs and promotes exemplarity even as it subverts it'.[20] It might be more exact to say that one group of humanists, more philosophical in their interests, promoted exemplarity, while another group, more philological, subverted it, but certain individuals, as we shall see, were ambivalent.

The important point is that in the culture of the Renaissance what we might call the 'sense of exemplarity' co-existed with its opposite, the sense of anachronism. In other words, a view of the past as more or less homogeneous, so that ancient exempla and precedents were relevant to the present coexisted with the opposite view, that the past was culturally distinct and also distant from the present. The first view was probably the one held by the majority of the writers and readers of history, but the second, which I have described elsewhere as 'the Renaissance sense of the past' was not only more distinctive but also becoming more important in that period.[21]

Like many other groups in history, the humanists constructed a collective identity by contrasting themselves with the 'other', especially European culture in the centuries between antiquity and their own day. They invented the term 'Middle Ages' [*medium tempus, medium aevum*], just as they invented the terms 'Dark Ages', 'Gothic', and 'schoolmen' [*scholastici*], all labels which remained influential for centuries.

---

[20] Timothy Hampton, *Writing from History: the rhetoric of exemplarity in Renaissance Literature* (Ithaca: Cornell University Press, 1990), 16.
[21] Peter Burke, *The Renaissance Sense of the Past* (London: Edward Arnold, 1969); id., 'The Sense of Anachronism from Petrarch to Poussin', in Chris Humphrey and W. M. Ormrod (eds.) *Time in the Medieval World* (York: York Medieval Press, 2001), 157–73.

However, the sense of historical distance included, or more exactly came to include, ancient Greece and Rome. The story of the encounter of the humanists with the classical past is an ironic one. Ancient history was originally studied with enthusiasm in order to imitate the example of the Greeks and Romans. All the same, the more the humanists studied that ancient past, the more aware they became of the differences, discontinuities or as we might say, the cultural distance between their own time and earlier periods, not only the 'barbarous' or 'dark' Middle Ages, but antiquity as well.

In the case of their attitudes to antiquity one might speak of 'nostalgic distance', an awareness of difference joined with admiration and a desire to annihilate that difference. In the case of Renaissance attitudes to the Middle Ages it might be better to speak of 'ironic distance'. In practice, however the range of attitudes to the Middle Ages expressed by sixteenth-century Italians runs from the affectionate irony with which Ariosto rewrote the medieval romance in his *Orlando Furioso* to the contempt with which Vasari (at times, at least), dismissed Byzantine and Gothic art (which he described as the *maniera greca* and *maniera tedesca* respectively).

The humanist project of resurrecting the ancient world (like Augustus's attempt at *restitutio*) inevitably proved to be a failure. Indeed, it was essentially self-destructive. Some humanist students of Roman law, for instance, (notably François Hotman in his *Anti-Tribonian* of 1567), came to reject it as irrelevant to their own time because institutions had changed so much over the previous thousand years.[22]

Language in particular was the domain in which humanists such as Lorenzo Valla, for whom philology was so important, discovered the remoteness of the past. It was, for instance, its linguistic anachronisms that allowed Valla to expose the so-called 'Donation of Constantine' as a later forgery.[23]

This discovery was at the same time a problem for humanists. Historians who wrote about the post-classical world faced a di-

---

[22] John G. A. Pocock, *The Ancient Constitution and the Feudal Law* (1957: 2nd edn Cambridge: Cambridge University Press, 1987), 11–13.

[23] Franco Gaeta, *Lorenzo Valla: filologia e storia nell'umanesimo italiano* (Naples: Istituto italiano per gli studi storici, 1955).

lemma, either to use post-classical words like *mahometani*, which they generally regarded as 'barbarisms', or to find classical equivalents which were not altogether appropriate. The problem was discussed explicitly in the *Ciceronianus* (1528), a dialogue by Erasmus in which one of the characters remarks that if Cicero returned to earth today he would not write in the same way as he did in Roman times. The point was that the world had changed, thanks above all to the coming of Christ.

The question was not a purely linguistic one and it was not seen as such. The fundamental problems were twofold: whether it is appropriate for people in one culture to imitate another and whether it is possible to formulate general precepts about human behaviour. Some leading humanists wrestled with these problems, pulled first one way and then the other.

Erasmus, for instance, was an enthusiast for Plutarch.[24] He made his reputation by publishing a collection of maxims taken from ancient writers, the *Adagia*. However, when he came to write a book of advice for Charles V, the *Institutio Principis Christiani*, Erasmus expressed his doubts about the propriety of Christians following examples from pagan antiquity. Where others cheerfully juxtaposed Biblical and classical *exempla*, Erasmus distinguished them.[25] Another difficulty raised by Erasmus was that of polysemy: a given exemplum, such as the death of Socrates, does not come with a single meaning or moral attached, but can be interpreted in a number of different ways.[26]

Guicciardini revealed a similar ambivalence, coining maxims but also undermining generalizations, especially in two texts that were not published in his own day, his *Ricordi* ('Reflections') and his *Considerazioni* ('Considerations' on the *Discourses* of his friend Machiavelli). In a now famous passage of the *Ricordi*, Guicciardini noted 'how mistaken are those who quote the Romans at every step', since 'one would have to have a city with exactly the same conditions as theirs' for their example to be relevant. Elsewhere he asserted that 'judging by examples [concrete examples rather than

---
[24] Hartog (2005), 115–6.
[25] Hartog (this volume) 'Le christianisme et l'Eglise'.
[26] Hampton (1990) 48–62; Jeanneret (1998), 571.

exempla] is extremely fallacious' [*E fallacissimo il giudicare per gli essempii*], because 'every tiny difference in the example can be the cause of a very great variation in the effect' [*ogni minima varietà nel caso può essere causa di grandissima variazione nel effetto*].

Again, Guicciardini's *Considerazioni* criticized Machiavelli's generalizations on the grounds that they were 'put forward too absolutely' (*posto troppo assolutamente*). Guicciardini wished to make distinctions, 'because cases are different' (*perché i casi sono vari*), and human affairs 'differ according to the times and the other events' (*si varia secondo la condizione de' tempi ed altre occorrenzie che girano*).[27] Incidentally, Koselleck did mention Guicciardini – as he did Montaigne – in his famous essay on *historia magistra vitae*, but still (in my view) continued to overemphasize the belief in the constancy of human nature and to underestimate the interest in circumstances during the Renaissance.[28]

Guicciardini himself was praised by some contemporary readers, such as the French soldier François de La Noue, in his *Discours Politiques et Militaires* (1587), precisely because he was careful to note the circumstances of events, in other words the differences in place, time and protagonist (*les circonstances des temps, lieux et personnes*). As La Noue remarked elsewhere, adapting a commonplace to his own purposes, a particular course of action does not suit all countries any more than a slipper fits all feet (*comme un soulier ne convient pas à tous pieds, aussi un fait ne se peut approprier a tous pais*).[29]

Again, the Spanish political commentator Baltasar Alamos de Barrientos, in his *Tacito español* (1614), insisted that politics was an art not a science, and that the maxims of Tacitus had to be modified according to the situation or occasion. In his pamphlet *Of Reformation* (1641), Milton criticized the commentators who 'cut Tacitus into slivers and steaks', extracting maxims and applying them without regard for differences in circumstances.

---

[27] Francesco Guicciardini, *Considerazioni intorno ai Discorsi del Machiavelli*, ed. Roberto Palamarocchi (Bari: Laterza, 1933) 8, 19, 41.
[28] Koselleck (1967) 13, 23, 26.
[29] François La Noue, *Discours politiques et militaires* (1587: ed. Frank E. Sutcliffe, Geneva: Droz, 1967), 121n, 111.

The Renaissance critique of exemplarity was worked out most fully in two texts that have become literary classics, Montaigne's *Essais* and *Don Quixote*. Although he was closer to philosophical than to philological humanism, the later Montaigne – unlike his younger self, discussed above – may be regarded, as a recent critic has suggested, as 'the exemplary figure of problematized exemplarity'.[30] In his essay 'on the education of children' (Book 1, ch.26), while continuing to regard the study of Plutarch's *Lives* as necessary, Montaigne advised students to judge models rather than follow them, leading another critic to refer to his 'attempt to work out a type of posthumanist notion of exemplarity'.[31] The great problem was that *exempla* belong to a static world, while Montaigne saw the world as in constant motion.[32]

The later Montaigne agreed with Erasmus about the polysemy of *exempla* and with Guicciardini about the importance of circumstances (the *Essais* make 45 references to *circonstances*). For instance, in his final essay 'on experience' (Book 3, ch. 13), he argued that 'La vie de César n'a point plus d'exemples que la nôtre pour nous'. More generally, he claimed that no two men judge the same thing in the same way, that 'every *exemplum* limps'[*tout exemple cloche*] and that it 'simply foolish to chase after foreign exempla' [*c'est pure sottise qui nous fait courir après les exemples étrangers*].

Like Montaigne, Cervantes seems to have been somewhat ambivalent about exemplarity, making him an example of what has been called 'the co-presence of exemplarity and its crisis'. He published a collection of stories under the title *Novelas ejemplares* (1613), with a prologue explaining that each story offered 'some useful *exemplum*' [*algún ejemplo provechoso*].[33] On the other hand, Don Quixote's failed attempt to lead his life on the model of the heroes of his favourite romances of chivalry implies the weakness

---

[30] Stierle (1998), 585n. Stierle (1972) had already complained that Koselleck marginalized Montaigne.
[31] Hampton (1990) 134–9, at 139; cf Stierle (1998).
[32] Jean Starobinski, *Montaigne in Motion* (1982: English translation, Chicago: Chicago University Press, 1986); cf Hartog (2005), 119.
[33] Stierle (1998), 589.

Exemplarity and Anti-Exemplarity in Early Modern Europe

of any attempt to base life on literature.³⁴ The second part of the novel has been interpreted as a story about 'the impossibility of exemplarity', especially the chapter in which Don Quixote expresses his awareness of 'the exemplar's alterity', notably the difference between himself and the great saints and knights of the past. What he does is 'to confront the limitations of humanist discourse and to narrate the failure of exemplarity, to underscore both exemplarity's value and its impossibility, to leave his reader caught between the nostalgic desire for a heroic model and the poignant awareness that such desire is madness'³⁵

Descartes' critique of attempts to follow historical exemplars is analogous to, and may even deliberately echo that of Cervantes. At the beginning of his *Discours sur la méthode* (1638) Descartes argued that the study of history was not only futile but dangerous as well. His main attack was levelled at the humanist principle of the dignity of history. His point was that writing history according to this principle involved leaving out trivial circumstances [*les plus basses et moins illustres circonstances*]. It therefore encouraged readers 'to fall into the extravagances of the paladins of our romances' and to conceive plans that it was beyond their power to execute.³⁶

To conclude. In the case of exemplarity during what we might call the 'long Renaissance', it seems useful to distinguish a strong argument with weak support from a weaker or more moderate argument with stronger support. The strong argument concerns the coming of what has been described as the 'crisis of exemplarity'.³⁷ It comes from literary historians, skilled at close reading and

---

³⁴ Hampton (1990) 237–96.
³⁵ Hampton (1990) 282–3, 296; cf. Stierle (1998).
³⁶ René Descartes, *Oeuvres Philosophiques*, ed. Ferdinand Alquié (Paris: Garnier, 1963), 574.
³⁷ Hampton (1990) x, 30, 240; François Rigolot, 'The Renaissance Crisis of Exemplarity', *Journal of the History of Ideas* 59 (1998), 557–64; cf. Stierle (1998), and François Rigolot (2004) 'Problematizing Renaissance Exemplarity', in Dorothea Heitz and Jean-François Vallée (eds.) *Printed Voices* (Toronto: University of Toronto Press), 3–24. Hartog himself (2005, 119–23) now accepts this notion, at least for the last quarter of the sixteenth century. He argues that the crisis was overcome after 1600, but it returned in a new form at the time of the famous *querelle* between ancients and moderns.

199

sensitive to the complexities of texts, but concerned only with a few outstanding writers, notably Petrarch, Erasmus, Machiavelli, Montaigne, Tasso, Shakespeare and Cervantes.

Looking at a wider range of texts, as a cultural historian must, we find less evidence of crisis and more evidence of continuity. Indeed, we find that a majority of readers and writers still accepted the value of exemplarity. For this reason it might be advisable to avoid the dramatic word 'crisis' and to speak only of a critique of exemplarity, a critique that co-existed with its broad acceptance in early modern culture and even within individuals such as Guicciardini and Montaigne.[38]

However, the existence of the minority of critics is surely sufficient to make the period (1530–1750 though not 1400–1530) a distinctive one. It inspires a more general question: how much variety in attitudes to the past is compatible with Hartog's concept of 'regime'?

---

[38] The notion of crisis is also rejected by Moos (1988) and Jeanneret (1998), 578–9.

12: Historical Discourse in Renaissance Italy

This chapter is concerned with the writing of history in Renaissance Italy and in particular with the representation in printed texts of the spoken word, especially formal speeches (*orazioni or discorsi*), which may be regarded as a kind of 'ritual (or ritualized) language', communications which follow a recurrent sequence.[1] In other words, I am offering you a discourse on discourse, a kind of pun but one that leads to conclusions that I hope readers will find illuminating. So far as rupture and transformation, central themes in this volume, are concerned, this essay will discuss both continuities and discontinuities between historical writing in the Renaissance, more or less the period 1400–1600, and the periods before and after it. It is arranged like a series of Chinese boxes, moving from historical discourse to Renaissance examples, Italian examples and finally to the speeches in Francesco Guicciardini's *Storia d'Italia*.

I

Given the variety of meanings of the term 'discourse', in English as in other languages, it may be useful to begin by saying something about it. A number of scholars have opted for a broad, inclu-

---
[1] James J. Fox (ed.) *To Speak in Pairs: Essays on the Ritual Languages of Eastern Indonesia* (Cambridge: Cambridge University Press, 1988); *Ritual Language Behaviour*, ed. by Marcel Bax, special issue of *Journal of Historical Pragmatics*, 4 (2003).

sive definition that emphasizes 'interpretative frameworks'. Other scholars, including myself, tend to work with a narrower concept of discourse. The concept, used widely in the humanities – not to say in the discourse of the humanities – in the last generation, has been shaped by different theorists from different disciplines. Among them are specialists in literature such as Mikhail Bakhtin (whose term was *slovo*) and Roland Barthes (discussed below); philosophers, notably Michel Foucault; and linguists, especially socio-linguists such as John Gumperz and Deborah Tannen. These scholars have worked in different contexts and with different purposes.[2]

It is clear that distinctions between discourses are in order. Distinctions between disciplinary discourses, for instance – legal, medical and so on – despite Foucault (who showed very clearly what different disciplinary discourses had in common in a given period).[3] It is also useful to make distinctions such as official, revolutionary, colonial, anti-colonial and so on. A discourse is often recognizable by a tendency to jargon, but it reveals something more important that might be described in terms of attitudes, values or mentalities.

Besides the problem of ambiguities, we need to confront the problem of controversies. A common objection to discourse analysis (DA for short) in its various forms is its displacement of emphasis away from the author, or in its extreme form the denial of authorship. Another objection concerns the rejection of context by some students of discourse, notoriously by Roland Barthes in a once notorious controversy over Racine with Raymond Picard.[4]

As a result, in intellectual history, for instance, Quentin Skinner is – or at any rate was – an enemy of the concept for this reason. On the other hand, his older colleague John Pocock has described the history of discourse as 'the best terminology so far found' to

---

[2] Mikhail Bakhtin, 'Discourse in the Novel' (1975: English trans. in his *The Dialogic Imagination* (Austin: University of Texas Press, 1981), pp.259–422; Roland Barthes, 'Le discours de l'histoire' (1967), English trans. in Structuralism, ed. Michael Lane (New York: Basic Books, 1970), pp.145–55; Michel Foucault, *L'ordre du discours* (Paris: Gallimard, 1971); John Gumperz, *Discourse Strategies* (Cambridge: Cambridge University Press, 1982.

[3] Michel Foucault, *Les mots et les choses* (Paris: Gallimard, 1966).

[4] Roland Barthes, *Sur Racine* (Paris: Seuil, 1963).

describe a major shift in intellectual history a description that fits Pocock's concern with the 'languages' of political thought).[5]

Let us see whether it is possible to work with the concept of discours while retaining a sense of context and some place for individual authors.

II

Let use take the case of historical discourse.[6] So far as theory is concerned, I shall focus on Roland Barthes, the first to write about this topic in an essay on 'Le discourse de l'histoire' first published in 1967, with examples ranging from Herodotus and Joinville to Machiavelli and Michelet. Faithful to the model of linguistics in general and the linguistics of Louis Hjelmslev in particular, as in the case of his analyses of meals, fashion, and so on, Barthes emphasized unchanging structures and rules of substitution and transformation, listing subjects such as dynasties, princes, generals, soldiers and peoples and verbs such as 'dévaster, asservir, allier, faire une expedition, régner, user d'un stratagème, consulter l'oracle etc.'.

Reading this essay soon after its publication, at a time when I was working on the history of historical writing in the Renaissance, I found this focus on 'invariants' to be an opening of new doors, a challenge to the historiographical assumptions on which I had been trained. All the same, the essay on historical discourse was not completely satisfying.

In this chapter I shall try to think both with and against Barthes, comparing and contrasting his invariants with what the French classicist François Hartog describes as different 'regimes of historicity'.[7] In this way it may be possible to encourage a kind of dialogue between Renaissance texts and twentieth-century literary theories.

---

[5] J. G. A. Pocock, 'Languages and Their Implications: the Transformation of the Study of Political Thought', in his *Politics, Language and Time* (London: Methuen, 1971), pp.3–41.

[6] Besides Barthes, see *Geschichtsdiskurs*, ed. Wolfgang Küttler and others (Frankfurt: Fischer, 1997.

[7] François Hartog, *Régimes d'historicité* (Paris, Seuil, 2003).

My strategy is to juxtapose and counterpose Barthes's concept of *discours* to the Renaissance idea of *discorsi*, best known from Machiavelli's famous discourses on Livy, but a common term at the time, used for instance in the title of the sixteenth-century translation of Montaigne's *Essais* into Italian. 'Discourses' were reflections, presented in a conversational rather than an academic way, and usually written in the vernacular rather than in the language of the university, Latin.

The term *discorsi* was also used of speeches, which at some periods have been considered a legitimate and even a necessary part of historical discourse while at other times they have been either neglected (as in the Middle Ages) or rejected (as they were in the nineteenth century). Barthes missed this point, despite his discussion of Machiavelli, so that an analysis of speeches offers some useful counter-examples to his theory. In what follows I shall focus on the speeches that formed an important part of humanist historical writing as of the ancient historians whom the humanists imitated and emulated.

From the mid-nineteenth century to the mid-twentieth, speeches in works of history were an embarrassment to scholars. The ancient historian Jacqueline Romilly and the historian of humanism Nancy Struever were unusual in taking this topic seriously in 1956 and 1970 respectively.[8] Today, however, when historians, like their colleagues in both literature and the social sciences, have become more interested in the fluid boundaries between fact and fiction, they are coming to give the topic more attention, in the case of the Renaissance as in that of classical antiquity.[9]

Discorsi are examples of the representation of speech and more

---

[8] Jacqueline Romilly, *Histoire et raison chez Thucydide* (Paris: Les belles lettres, 1956), pp. 180–239; Nancy S. Struever, *The Language of History in the Renaissance* (Princeton: Princeton University Press, 1970).

[9] Marc Cogan, *The Human Thing: the speeches and principles of Thucydides' history* (Chicago: University of Chicago Press, 1981); Charles W. Fornara, *The Nature of History in Ancient Greece and Rome* (Berkeley: University of California Press, 1983), pp.142–68; Anthony Grafton, *What was History? The Art of History in Early Modern Europe* (Cambridge: Cambridge University Press, 2007); Sverre Bagge, 'Actors and Structures in Machiavelli's Istorie Fiorentine', *Quaderni d'Italianistica*, 28 (2007), 45–88, especially 54, 60–2.

especially of speeches. Since they may well seem alien to many readers, it may be useful to bring a sociolinguist, Deborah Tannen, and her book on conversation analysis into the discussion. Tannen describes 'reported speech' in conversation as 'constructed speech', in other words as creative, interpretative and transformative.[10] The invented speeches to be found in the texts that we are about to examine may therefore be regarded as elaborated written versions or transformations of an everyday oral practice.

The main questions with which this essay is concerned are the following. Why were speeches introduced into histories? What were their functions in the text and their uses for readers? On what grounds were they criticized at the time? Why were they eventually abandoned?

III

In the ancient world, composing speeches formed an important part of education, just as delivering speeches formed an important part of political life, in ancient Athens and Rome in particular. This was the case for obvious political reasons, but we should also remember that speech-making was only one part of a lively oral culture that also included, for instance, the reading aloud of works of poetry and prose, by their authors, to an invited audience. A belief in the persuasive power of spoken words was commonplace, made explicit in treatises on the art of rhetoric.

The speeches to be found in ancient historians should be replaced in this context. Thucydides, for instance, included in his account of the Peloponnesian war not only the famous funeral speech of Pericles but also a number of 'antilogies' or pairs of opposed speeches. These pairs made a major contribution to historical analysis because they allowed readers to weigh the arguments for and against particular decisions. Indeed, as has been noted recently, the 'multiple perspective' of these speeches makes readers aware of 'diverse points of view'.[11]

---
[10] Deborah Tannen, *Talking Voices* (Cambridge: Cambridge University Press, 1989).
[11] Romilly, pp. 180-239, esp. pp.180, 222; on perspective, James V. Morrison, *Reading Thucydides* (Columbus, Ohio: University of Ohio Press, 2006), pp. 29-39.

Turning to Rome, one thinks in particular of Livy, Sallust (who included some dramatic antilogies, like the debate between Caesar and Cato in his *Conspiracy of Catiline*) and of Quintus Curtius, whose life of Alexander the Great may be almost forgotten now but was much appreciated in the Renaissance and even later.[12] It is worth noting the importance in a number of ancient historians of one particular type of speech, the address (*allocution*) to the troops made by a military leader on the eve of battle.

Speeches might be criticized (as Polybius criticized the ones in the history written by Timaeus) because they did not represent the gist of what was actually said.[13] All the same, it was virtually taken for granted in the ancient world that there should be speeches in a written history and also that the exact words would have to be invented by the historian.

By contrast, the representation of formal speeches is much rarer in medieval chronicles or histories. There are of course exceptions to this rule such as Henry of Huntingdon, whose chronicle gives a speech to the bishop of Orkney before the Battle of the Standard, and Geoffrey of Monmouth, who gives speeches to King Arthur, King Hoel and others.[14] William of Poitiers adapted a speech of Catiline to William the Conqueror's speech to his troops before Hastings. However, William of Malmesbury in his *Life of Dunstan* objected that such speeches could not be genuine.

In late medieval historians such as Giovanni Villani, Geoffroi de Villehardouin, Jean Froissart or the Portuguese chronicler Fernão Lopes, what the reader is likely to find is direct speech of a relatively informal kind.[15] For example, there are fifteen short passages in direct speech in Villehardouin's chronicle, including some by himself and others by the Doge of Venice, Enrico Dandolo.[16] Dino

---

[12] N. P. Miller, 'Dramatic Speech in the Roman Historians', *Greece and Rome*, 22 (1975), 45–57.
[13] Fornara, p. 157.
[14] Beryl Smalley, *Historians in the Middle Ages* (London: Thames and Hudson, 1974).
[15] Joan Argenter, 'Responsibility in Discourse', *Language in Society*, 35 (2006), 1–26.
[16] Jean Frappier (1946) 'Les discours dans la chronique de Villehardouin' (1946: rpr in his *Histoire, Mythes et Symboles: études de litterature française* (Geneva: Ambilly-Annemasse, 1976), pp.55–71.

Compagni's chronicle also contains vivid but short passages in direct speech.[17]
Froissart too includes some lively passages of direct discourse, some of them put into the mouth of King Edward III. As in the case of Villehardouin, these passages are not set speeches, but relatively short and informal. Unusually, he includes passages in what has been called 'collective direct speech'.[18] As for Fernão Lopes, he occasionally writes an oration that lasts for a couple of paragraphs, but his normal practice, like that of the other chroniclers mentioned here, is to produce short passages of direct speech.[19]

For us, at least, the informality gives more of the effect or illusion of reality, although informal conversations may actually be as much inventions as formal speeches. The passages of direct speech add to the reality effect, but unlike the orations that appear in classical and Renaissance historians, they do not do very much explanatory work. To employ the useful distinction drawn by Mark Phillips, in the Middle Ages speeches were used as a means of 'representation', but in antiquity and in the Renaissance as a means of 'argument'.[20]

IV

It is time to turn to a case-study of Renaissance humanism, emphasizing two moments of discontinuity, change or 'rupture', c.1400 and c.1600. At the first moment, the moment of a 'rhetorical turn' in the age of the Florentine humanist Leonardo Bruni, for-

---

[17] For example, Dino Compagni, *Cronica*, ed. by Gino Luzzatto (Torino: Einaudi, 1968), 22, 35, 37, 63, 67.
[18] Jean Froissart, *Chroniques*, ed. by G. T. Diller (3 vols, Geneva: Droz, 1991-2), vol.1, pp.175-6; vol. 2, pp. 201, 305-6; vol.3, pp.225-8. Cf. Stephen G. Nichols Jr, 'Discourse in Froissart's *Chroniques*', *Speculum*, 39 (1964), 279-87, and on collective speech, Peter F. Ainsworth, *Jean Froissart and the fabric of history: truth, myth and fiction in the Chroniques* (Oxford: Clarendon Press, 1990), pp.270-1.
[19] Fernão Lopes, *Crónica de El-Rei D. João I*, ed. by José H. Saraiva (Lisboa, 1977), 137-8 (a longer speech), 130, 132, 134, 149, 150-1, etc
[20] Mark Phillips, 'Representation and Argument in Renaissance Historiography', *Storia della storiografia/Histoire de l'historiographie*, 10 (1986), 48-63.

mal speeches were introduced into written histories. At the second moment, the moment of an anti-rhetorical turn, the age of Paolo Sarpi, speeches were generally abandoned. In other words, for two centuries they formed a normal though not a universal element of historical writing, or historical discourse. It may not be coincidence that the Renaissance was a time when the drama flourished, including historical drama. Shakespeare's history plays, for instance, are full of speeches, including antilogies in the ancient manner. Indeed, *Richard II* begins with a series of paired speeches, a debate between Henry Bolingbroke and Thomas Mowbray.

Focussing on Italy, note the importance of speeches in a series of humanist historians: notably Bruni, Poggio Bracciolini, Lorenzo Valla, Paolo Giovio, and of course Machiavelli and Guicciardini. Bruni, for instance, gives paired speeches to Guelfs and Ghibellines and to Perugians and Florentines. He does not claim to transcribe the actual words, but uses formulae such as 'it is said that he spoke in this way' (*in hunc modum traditur allocutus*).[21]

Whose discourse, who speaks? Speeches in written histories were employed for the purposes of the historian, not the original speaker – although historians sometimes comment on their efficacy at the moment that they were delivered. 'The speech affected the attitudes of the listeners' (*Movit oratio mentes*), Bruni commented on the appeal for help by the envoys from Arezzo to Florence.[22]

The humanist pope Pius II went further in his *Commentaries*, citing his own speech to the Diet of Regensburg, on a mission from the emperor to argue in favour of war with the Turks. 'He spoke for almost two hours' [like Julius Caesar, Pius wrote of himself in the third person], 'and was heard with such absorbed attention that not once did anyone clear his throat or take his eyes from the face of the speaker'.[23]

Speeches by generals before battles, known by ancient Romans as *allocutiones*, were often described as reviving the morale of the

---

[21] Struever, pp. 127–32 (on Bruni) and pp.173–7 (on Poggio).
[22] Leonardo Bruni, *History of the Florentine People*, ed. and trans. by James Hankins, 3 vols (Cambridge: Harvard University Press, 2001–7), vol. 1. p.318.
[23] Pius II, *Commentaries*, ed. and trans by Florence A. Gragg and Leona C. Gabel (Northampton, Mass.: Smith College, 1937), p.72.

soldiers (in this way resembling the 'pep talk' that football coaches still give their players before the match). In early modern times they were sometimes represented in art, most famously by Giulio Romano in his 'Speech of Constantine' in the Vatican, by Titian in his 'Speech of Alfonso d'Avalos' (represented quelling a mutiny in 1532), and by Rubens in his 'Speech of Decius Mus'.[24] These 'speech acts' may be regarded as performatives that helped rulers, assemblies or councils take decisions as well as encouraging soldiers to fight.

Lorenzo Valla defended invented speeches in his history of the ruler of Naples, *Ferdinandus*, on the grounds that they teach both eloquence and wisdom. In similar vein the insertion of speeches was generally recommended in the treatises on the art of history that began to be written around the year 1500 and proliferated in the later sixteenth century. The Neapolitan humanist Giovanni Pontano saw them as an adornment, provided they fitted the place and time. The Italians Viperano, Foglietta and Sardi, the Spaniard Fox-Morcillo and the Frenchman La Popelinière agreed.[25] Indeed, the Spanish scholar Antonio Agustín criticized the history written by his fellow-countryman Jerónimo Zurita precisely because Zurita's text lacked speeches.[26]

The speeches usually run to a general pattern, so that we might say that they represent collective rather than individual discourse. Some of these speeches were stolen from earlier historians. For example, the speech that Henry of Huntingdon gave to the bishop of Orkney echoed Sallust. Again, the Spanish Jesuit Juan de Mariana, author of a well-known history of his own country, lifted an entire speech from Livy, transferring it from ancient Rome to fifteenth-century Spain with only the slightest of alterations.[27] This is an extreme case of a more general phenomenon: the generic similarity of speeches that are represented as delivered in recurrent situations: before a battle, to a ruler, at a council, and so on.

---

[24] Erwin Panofsky, *Problems in Titian, Mostly Iconographic* (London: Phaidon, 1969), pp.74–7.
[25] Quoted in Grafton, pp.36–8, 41–5.
[26] Grafton, p.232.
[27] G. Cirot, *Juan de Mariana historien* (Bordeaux and Paris: Feret et Fils, 1905), pp.346ff.

What is History Really About? A Historian Reflects on Theory and Practice

The function of the speeches in the stories in which they occurred was partly ornamental, ornament being an important part of rhetoric. However, as in the case of Thucydides and other ancient historians, speeches also carried part of the burden of explanation, especially the paired speeches or antilogies, offering arguments pro and contra, or, in the case of pre-battle speeches, suggesting in turn that each side was in the right. As Struever suggests, 'The core of the antilogic method is to consider the same events from different points of view'.[28] These paired speeches gave written histories a dialogic element. We might also speak of a dialogue between the speech-writers (that is, the historians), and with their models, especially classical models. The reader needs to be aware of quotations and allusions, as well as of simple plagiarism.

As in the case of ancient Athens and Rome, the interest in speeches should be linked to the place of oratory in Renaissance culture and to assumptions about the power of words. The Florentine *ringhiera* was constructed in 1323 as a place for 'harangues': that is how it received its name.[29] Making speeches was a kind of ritual, and they were composed in a special form of discourse, a formal or ritualized language (as was noted earlier), with a pre-existing structure or sequence, rather like a series of boxes into which, on each occasion, some specific information could be placed.[30]

Speeches were also virtuoso displays of rhetoric that might reasonably be compared to a later Italian enthusiasm, arias in an opera. They took the same general form, but there were also opportunities for individual historians to show off their rhetorical skills and gain the applause of connoisseurs. The Bolognese humanist Achille Bocchi praised Guicciardini in this respect, while Agustín praised both Guicciardini and Giovio.

On a few occasions there were serious divergences from the model. The most famous comes from Machiavelli's *History of Florence*, in which an important speech is given to a man of low status,

---

[28] Struever, pp.129–30.
[29] Stephen Milner, 'Citing the *Ringhiera*: The Politics of Place and Public Address in Trecento Florence', *Italian Studies*, 55 (2000), 53–82.
[30] *Political Language and Oratory in Traditional Society*, ed. by Maurice Bloch (New York: Academic Press, 1975.

a participant in the fourteenth-century revolt of the Ciompi, the unskilled workers in the Florentine woollen cloth industry.[31] A rare example of an imitator of Machiavelli in this respect is the seventeenth-century historian and rhetorician Agostino Mascardi, who was criticized for giving an important speech to a 'base person' in his account of the Fieschi conspiracy.

V

It is time to focus more sharply on Guicciardini: a case-study within the case-study, considering the function of speeches within his historical discourse. The existence of these speeches has often been noted, but they have rarely been discussed in any detail.[32] Unlike many ancient historians, Guicciardini has no particular liking for speeches on the eve of battle: in the cases of Fornovo, Cerignola and Agnadello, the arguments on both sides are summarized in indirect speech (Book 2, chapter 8; Book 5, chapter 15; Book 8, chapter 3). However, the French leader Gaston de Foix is allowed to make a speech at the battle of Ravenna (Book 10, chapter13).

The *Storia d'Italia* includes twenty-four speeches, including six pairs (there is also a space left blank in the manuscript for another one in Book 18, chapter 10). One famous pair is represented in the debate on the Florentine constitution and attributed to Paoloantonio Soderini (in favour of *governo popolare*) and Guidantonio Vespucci, 'in contrario', for the rule of a few (Book 2, chapter 2), offering a classic example of arguments *pro* and *contra*. Again, in the Venetian senate in 1523, Andrea Gritti is represented speaking in favour of the alliance with France, while Giorgio Cornaro supports a new alliance with the emperor (Book 15, chapter 2). Yet

---

[31] Nicolò Machiavelli, *Istorie Fiorentine*, ed. by Eugenio Garin (Florence: Le Monnier, 1990), Book 3, chapter 13.
[32] Felix Gilbert, *Machiavelli and Guicciardini* (Princeton: Princeton University Press, 1965), p. 274; Mark S. Phillips, *Francesco Guicciardini: the historian's craft* (Manchester: Manchester University Press, p.180; Eric Cochrane, *Historians and Historiography in the Italian Renaissance* (Chicago: University of Chicago Press, 1981), p.304; Robert Finlay, 'The Myth of Venice in Guicciardini's *History of Italy:* Senate Orations on Princes and the Republic', in *Medieval and Renaissance Venice*, ed. by E. Kittell and T. Madden (Urbana, Ill.: University of Illinois Press), pp. 294–326.

again, the bishop of Osma and the duke of Alba, in the presence of the emperor, offer conflicting advice on what should be done with the King of France after his capture at the battle of Pavia (Book 16, chapter 5). The speeches allow readers to participate in the hopes, fears and dilemmas of the protagonists of the *History*.

Guicciardini admitted that he invented speeches, which are generally introduced with a formula warning his audience that they are not going to hear or read the actual words of the speakers: 'parlò, secondo si dice, in questa sentenza' (Book 1, chapter 4); 'Queste cose, dette in sostanza dal cardinale' (Book 1, chapter 9); 'parlò, secondo si dice, così' (Book 2, chapter 2).[33] The language of these speeches is much like Guicciardini's own historical discourse, full of maxims and references to interest as well as honour. All the same, the speeches are not pure ventriloquism. Guicciardini does make some effort to imitate playwrights and suit the speech to the speaker. The bishop of Osuna, for instance, uses arguments that might be expected from a churchman.

Like Mariana later, Guicciardini sometimes stole from Livy. The speech of the Venetian ambassador Antonio Giustinian to the emperor Maximilian, suing for peace after the Venetian defeat at the battle of Agnadello, was – as some contemporaries were not slow to point out – suspiciously similar to Hannibal's speech to Scipio before the battle of Zama, repeating phrases such as 'perhaps we are worthy to assess our own reparations'. On the other hand, Guicciardini did follow a manuscript source, so one cannot dismiss the possibility that the thief was Giustinian himself rather than the historian.[34]

VI

As evidence of the Renaissance reader's attitude to this aspect of historical discourse, it is worth noting that the one-volume epitome of Guicciardini's long history, edited by Francesco Sansovino and

---

[33] Francesco Guicciardini, *Storia d'Italia*, ed. by Silvana Seidel Menchi, 3 vols (Torino: Einaudi, 1971). Given the number of editions of this text, as in the case of ancient historians, references will be given to books and chapters, not to pages.
[34] Guicciardini, Book 8, ch. 6, cf. Livy, Book 30, ch. 30; the similarity was noted by Dirk (Theodore) Graswinckel, *Libertas Veneta* (Leiden: Commelin, 1634), p.366.

still being reprinted in the 1630s, contains almost all the speeches. A Spanish manuscript in the Bibliothèque Nationale transcribes the speeches, perhaps for publication in translation.[35]

Anthologies of speeches from ancient and modern historians may also be cited. For example, the German professor Nicolas Frischlin compiled his *Selectae orationes* (1588) for his students at Braunschweig. Two volumes of speeches from historians ancient and modern appeared in Italian in 1557 and 1561, edited by the Dominican Remigio Nannini, who was active as a translator. An amplified version of Nannini appeared in one volume in French in 1572, edited by another prolific writer, François de Belleforest.

The organization of these anthologies gives some idea of how they were used by their readers, or at least how the printers expected them to be used. Nannini and Belleforest each produced a separate section of military speeches, while Nannini also edited a volume of 'civil and criminal' orations. The arrangement of one anthology followed traditional rhetorical categories such as praise versus blame and persuasion versus dissuasion.[36]

Speeches by characters in histories did not please all readers. There had already been critics of the practice in the ancient world such as Polybius and Trogus. In the Renaissance, Francesco Patrizzi criticized speeches in his ten dialogues on history, published in 1560.[37] In his *Methodus ad facilem historiarum cognitionem* (1566), Jean Bodin was critical of Giovio for inventing speeches 'in the manner of a scholastic disputation' (*conciones vel potius declamationes scholasticorum in modum finxit*). Bodin also quoted Jacques Gohorry's comparison of Giovio's history to the romance of *Amadis de Gaule*.[38]

In the case of Guicciardini, the Venetians objected to speeches that they considered 'no less false than full of hatred and poison'.

---

[35] Vincent Luciani, *Francesco Guicciardini and his European reputation* (New York: Karl Otto, 1936), p.306.
[36] *Orationi militari*, ed. by Remigio Nannini (Venice: Giolito, 1557); *Orationi in materia ciuile, e criminale*, ed. by Remigio Nannini (Venice: Giolito, 1561); *Harengues militaires et concions de princes, capitaines, embassadeurs et autres, maniant tant la guerre que les affaires d'estat*, ed. by François de Belleforest (Paris: N. Chesneau, 1573).
[37] Quoted in Grafton, p.39.
[38] Jean Bodin, *Method for the easy comprehension of history*, trans. by Beatrice Reynolds (New York: Columbia University Press, 1945), pp.60-1; cf Grafton, p.46.

Paolo Paruta, a Venetian historian, described one speech of Guicciardini's as not only false but not even 'plausible' [*verosimile*].[39]

However, the reaction against speeches went further at the time of the anti-rhetorical turn of a group of historians working in the early seventeenth century, among them the Venetian Paolo Sarpi, the Frenchman Jacques-Auguste de Thou, or Thuanus, and the Englishman William Camden.[40] 'I have thrust in no orations', wrote Camden, in the preface to his *Annals* of the reign of Queen Elizabeth, 'but such as were truly spoken; or those reduced to fewer words; much less have I feigned any'.[41]

In similar fashion Paolo Sarpi excluded orations from his *History of the Council of Trent* – a decision all the more remarkable given that speech-making was, after all, one of the major activities of the Council. He summarized the speeches in *oratio obliqua*, rather than attempting to reproduce or represent them in *oratio recta*. One might think that this was a move away from historical realism, but it was a move prompted at once by Sarpi's awareness of the problems of evidence of what was actually spoken and by his desire to have nothing to do with what have been described as 'Clio's cosmetics'.[42] Like Camden and Thuanus, Sarpi preferred to insert documents rather than speeches into his narrative. One might view these documents, recording voices other than that of the historian, as transformations of the speech.

The attitude of these three 'pragmatic' historians, as one might call them, who wrote to be useful rather than to display their rhetorical skills, was not shared by all their colleagues. Agostino Mascardi, for instance, who was a professor of rhetoric as well as a historian, continued the Renaissance tradition of the oration in his book on the conspiracy of the Fieschi, and so did the Cardinal de

---

[39] Luciani.
[40] Peter Burke, 'The Rhetoric and Anti-Rhetoric of History in the Early Seventeenth Century', in *Anamorphosen der Rhetorik: Die Wahrheitspiel der Renaissance*, ed. by Gerhard Schröder and others (Munich, 1997), pp.71–9.
[41] William Camden, *Annals*, trans. by Robert Norton (3rd edn, London: Benjamin Fisher, 1635), preface.
[42] Timothy P. Wiseman, *Clio's Cosmetics: three studies in Greco-Roman literature* (Leicester: Leicester University Press, 1979).

Retz in his adaptation of Mascardi's book.[43] At the end of the seventeenth century, the Dutch scholar Gerard Jan Vos still advocated the insertion of speeches into histories.[44]

It was only gradually that the tide turned. Leopold von Ranke was not breaking new ground when he criticized the practice, taking Guicciardini as his example of what not to do in his famous *Kritik Neuerer Geschichtschreiber* (1824). A few years later Thomas Macaulay – no mean speech-maker himself – declared the invention of speeches by Machiavelli, Guicciardini and others to be an 'absurd practice'. Even at this time, however, some readers still appreciated the speeches, among them the English essayist William Hazlitt, who declared that 'I should like to read the speeches in Thucydides, and Guicciardini's *History of Florence* ... in the original'.[45]

VI

The example of the place of speeches in historical discourse illustrates very clearly the zigzag rather than linear development of historiography. It was not sufficient to criticize speeches because they were invented, while pretending to come from the protagonists. Historians who rejected this generic convention needed and still need to find a functional equivalent for speeches.

Macaulay, for instance, recommended what he called the 'declamatory disquisition' as a substitute for orations, and his *History of England* abounds with examples of reported speech.[46] In chapter

---

[43] Agostino Mascardi, *La congiura del conte Gio. Lvigi de' Fieschi* (Milan: Lantoni, 1629); Jean François Paul de Gondi, Cardinal de Retz, *La conjuration du comte Jean-Louis de Fiesque* (Paris: Claude Barbin, 1665).
[44] Gerardus Johannes Vossius, *Ars historica* (Leiden: Maire, 1623). Cf. Nicholas Wickenden, *G. J. Vossius and the Humanist Concept of History* (Assen: Van Gorcum, 1993), pp.211–12..
[45] Leopold von Ranke, 'About Guicciardini's Speeches', in id., *The Secret of World History,* ed. and trans. by Roger Wines (New York: Fordham University Press, 1981), pp.73–98; William Hazlitt, 'On Reading Old Books', in his *Plain Speaker* (1826) ed. by Duncan Wu (London: Pickering and Chatto, 1998), pp.206–14, at p. 214.
[46] Macaulay's unpublished diary, 10 December 1850, quoted in George O. Trevelyan, *The Life and Letters of Lord Macaulay* (2 vols, London: Longmans, 1877), vol.2, p.21.

9, for instance, William of Orange bade farewell to the States of Holland. 'He thanked them ... he entreated them' and so on. In chapter 18, it is James II who 'had in vain insisted ... had in vain addressed', etc. The free indirect style may be regarded as a substitute, practised more or less self-consciously from Guicciardini (in the case of battles, as we have seen) to our own day.[47] A number of historians are taking an increasing interest in the representation of multiple viewpoints within their narratives, and so, returning to the example of Thucydides, we might suggest that an equivalent for his speeches was never so much needed as it is today.[48]

In this essay I have tried to work with some structuralist ideas and attempted to reconcile the opposite insights of Bakhtin and Jakobson. Bakhtin memorably described language as a collective creation in which individuals simply appropriate, re-employ or quote words that have often been heard in the mouths of others. As Julia Kristeva, paraphrasing Bakhtin, put it, 'any text is constructed as a mosaic of quotations'. Jakobson made the complementary yet opposite point in an essay on quotation, suggesting that whenever we quote, for our own purposes and in our own situation, we necessarily make the quoted words our own.[49] It would be good to see a 'dialogic' history of historical writing that presented historians as interacting with their predecessors, whether following them or diverging from them.

---

[47] Frappier, p.70; cf Nichols, passim.
[48] Peter Burke, 'History of Events and the Revival of Narrative', in *New Perspectives on Historical Writing*, ed. by Peter Burke (Cambridge: Polity Press, 1991), pp. 233-48.
[49] Bakhtin; Roman Jakobson, 'Language in Operation', *Lingua*, 21 (1964), 269-81.

www.ingramcontent.com/pod-product-compliance
Lightning Source LLC
Chambersburg PA
CBHW060951230426
43665CB00015B/2146